Practical
MEDIA

A GUIDE TO
PRODUCTION
TECHNIQUES

D0736244

Nick Dimbleby   Richard Dimbleby   Ken Whittington

Hodder & Stoughton

A MEMBER OF THE HODDER HEADLINE GROUP

British Library Cataloguing in Publication Data

A catalogue for this title is available from the British Library

ISBN 0 340 595 48 5

First published 1994
Impression number   10 9 8 7 6 5 4 3 2 1
Year   1999 1998 1997 1996 1995 1994

Typeset by Wearset, Boldon, Tyne and Wear.
Printed in Great Britain for Hodder & Stoughton Educational, a division of Hodder Headline
Plc, 338 Euston Road, London NW1 3BH by The Bath Press, Lower Bristol Road, Bath.

Acknowledgements

Our grateful thanks to all who made this book possible. But especially we should like to thank: All at France 3 Nancy, Lucy Aitken, Francesca Baglione, Khamis Ali Bakari, Robin Beveridge, BBC Bristol, David Bowyer, Ann Brown, Paul Brunsch, Graeme Burton, John Chard, Harry Chuma, Nicola Coe, Matthew Coombs, Corinna Corden, Claire Crawford, Caroline and Gill Dimbleby, Yousif Gadalla, Lee Gooding, Yvonne Guildford, Heather Hancock, Sarah Hinsley, Hans-Gerd Hojak, Barry Hulett, HTV (West), Ilford Photographic, Wajuai Kamau, Alan Lindfield, Jason Lee, Jessop Photocentre Taunton, Margherita Marvasi, Denise Murphy, Anya Paul, Peter Palmer, Bob Phillips, Becky Reid, David Ross, Kristy Siegfried, Farne Sinclair, The University of Sussex, Raoul Thomas, Richard Thorneycroft, Virginie Vieville, John Ward (Television Buyer), Vicki Wright.

A special thanks to all those who have appeared in or particpated in our videos, photographs, audio cassettes, and DTP projects over the years, and also to the people who have taught us in various ways – without you much of this book would not have been possible!

Without our editors at Hodder and Stoughton this book would neither have been started nor completed, so our thanks to Justine Davis, Rowena Gaunt, Lesley Riddle, Julian Thomas and Elisabeth Tribe.

The authors and publishers would also like to thank the following for permission to use material in this book:

Bronica: Figure 2.9; Canon UK: Figures 2.3, 2.6, 2.10, 2.24; Matthew Coombs: Figure 2.45; Nick Dimbleby: Figures 2.1, 2.4, 2.12, 2.13, 2.14, 2.15, 2.16, 2.18, 2.22, 2.27, 2.28, 2.32, 2.34, 2.35, 2.38, 2.39, 2.40, 2.43, 2.49, 2.51, 2.52, 2.53, 2.54, 2.55; Durst UK: Figure 2.50; Fuji Photographic: Figure 2.33, Hans-Gerd Hojak: Figure 2.36; Jessop of Leicester: Figures 2.24, 2.31, 2.47; Lastolite Limited: Figures 2.30, 2.46; Lowel Lighting: Figures 2.41, 2.42; Manfrotto: Fig 2.25; Metz: Figure 2.19; Nikon UK: Figures 2.5, 2.29; Panasonic UK: Figure 2.45: Pentax UK: Figures 2.2, 2.4, 2.7, 2.8; Photax Group: Figure 2.26; Sigma UK: Figure 2.11; Alan Lindfield: Fig 3.15; Canford Audio: Figures 3.6, 3.7, 3.14; Raper and Wayman: Figures 3.8, 3.10, 3.11, 3.12, 3.13; Imatronic Audio Visual: Figure 4.1; Elf: Fig 4.2; Autocue Limited: Figure 5.17; Bryant Broadcast: Figure 5.49; Nick Dimbleby: Figures 5.12, 5.15, 5.16, 5.18, 5.21, 5.22, 5.23, 5.24, 5.25, 5.26, 5.27, 5.41, 5.45, 5.48; Fuji Film: Figures 5.50, 5.51, 5.54; Lee Gooding: Figure 5.40; JVC UK: Figures 5.35, 5.44; Maxell UK: Figures 5.52, 5.53; Optex Limited: Figure 5.32; Panasonic UK: Figures 5.3, 5.36; Sony UK: Figures 5.1, 5.2, 5.7, 5.34, 5.37, 5.38, 5.39; Strand Lighting: Figures 5.10, 5.31; University of Sussex Media Service Unit: Figure 5.20; Vinten: Figure 5.6; John Ward (Television Buyer): Figure 5.47; Yorkshire Television: Figures 5.8, 5.14, 5.33; Aldus Europe: Figures 6.6, 6.8, 6.9, 6.35; Apple Computers: Figures 6.2, 6.3, 6.4; Dynamic Graphics: Figures 6.31, 6.32; QSS: 6.7, 6.16.

Contents

Preface

In many homes, and certainly in every school, college and university, people now have access to a range of media technologies – still cameras, video cameras, video players and editors, slide projectors, computers with various software packages, sound systems and so on.

If you have access to such equipment and want to make your own successful productions, then this book is designed for you.

You may be a student of the media or you may be a professional working in audio visual media. Whether you are using audio-visual equipment for fun, for study or for employment, we aim to give you useful knowledge and skill to help you to create professional productions.

Here you will find in one volume an introduction to using a range of audio-visual media.

We stress the need for planning and preparation, the need for imagination and team work, and the need for some technical and practical know-how to create productions that obtain the desired effects.

This is a practical, hands-on book with plenty of hints on how to do it and clear explanations of technical and professional jargon. Chapter 1 also deals briefly with some aspects of media theory and types of productions as well as suggesting some ways of approaching the production of creative work in whatever medium.

We have written it with a student in college or university in mind. We do not assume previous knowledge of media technologies or of production techniques. We have sought to write in a clear, easy-to-read style with lots of illustrations, examples, case studies and practical activities.

We also think this book will be of use to teachers and 'general readers' who want to develop their knowledge and skills in using cameras, planning productions, and editing and presenting material for different purposes and different audiences.

The glossaries in several chapters provide brief explanations of technical jargon. The Resources lists suggest further sources of more detailed information for you to follow up.

We hope that this collection of material will give you the confidence to be ambitious and imaginative in your own media work.

Richard Dimbleby
Nick Dimbleby
Ken Whittington

1 Creating Audio-visual Productions

Pictures and sound take on a life of their own on the screen. The viewer judges them for what they are, not for where they came from. It doesn't matter if they reach the screen via a transmitter or cable or are replayed on a videocassette recorder. It doesn't even matter if they were shot on tape or film. What does matter is that they should have impact and tell the story the producer intends.

(*On Camera: how to produce film and video* by Harris Watts)

Imagination and Technique

There is no easy formula to guarantee successful productions, but there are processes of thinking and methods of working used by experienced audio-visual producers which are likely to ensure more successes than failures.

Whatever media you are using – still photography, audio tape, video tape or film, or a combination of these – there are general principles and conventions that can assist you to realise your aims and visions. In this book we shall be introducing you to some of these principles and conventions to enable you to use audio-visual equipment with confidence to gain the results you intend. This is not a technical manual, but rather a guide to help you to be effective and creative in your own productions.

However sophisticated the technical equipment and processes, it is the person, or rather the team of people, using the equipment who create the finished product. It is the quality of their thinking, their imagination, their planning, and their know-how that determines the quality of the final production. We aim to share some of our thinking and know-how with you.

Traditions of published and broadcast media have created professional techniques that make the received products look 'natural' or easy to create. Anyone who has picked up a camera, still or video, with the aim of recreating professional looking pictures and sound is likely to feel disappointed with the results. What looks 'natural', just the way it is, in a magazine or on screen is the result of careful planning and preparation and highly developed techniques and practised skills.

There are accepted conventions of production that the reader or viewer is unlikely to know or recognise – until they are broken. Indeed, these conventions can be seen as a system of 'grammar' that rules audio-visual productions in the same way that each verbal language has its own grammar that rules the way we use the language. The 'conventions', 'rules', and 'hints and tips' described in Desmond Davis's seminal book, *The Grammar of Television Production*, which was first published in 1960, have largely become instinctive to professional production.

Of course, as with all grammar rules, creative users of a language challenge the rules and accepted practices for deliberate effect. State-of-the-art video, using computer systems for previously undreamt-of effects, enables producers to challenge and break those traditional rules quite consciously. Almost any video made for promoting a particular pop song or artist will seek to create startling visual effects, and by doing so, break the conventional grammar of television production. Desmond Davis never intended that his description of the grammar of TV production should become prescriptive. For example, with regard to rules he commented: 'These may be regarded as binding and should only be broken in exceptional circumstances, to achieve some special surprising, comic or bizarre effect'. Some production genres seem to demand bizarre effects to be effective.

Different types of productions made for different audiences are inevitably judged by different standards. We shall say more about various types, or genres, of productions later in this chapter (see 'Types of Production', p. 11.)

Similarly, you may be in a position to select one or more audio-visual media according to your purposes, intended audience, available equipment or budget. The range of media to be discussed in this book includes photography, sound tapes, synchronised slide/tape, video tapes, and desktop publishing – in other words, visual images, sound and typescript in various combinations including still and moving images.

It is tempting to consider that video is now the most powerful of these. However, a collection of well-composed photos effectively displayed can make a visual statement, create an atmosphere and lead people to see people, places, things, machines, landscapes, environments, and relationships in quite new ways.

Alternatively, the attention to sound without pictures via a sound tape or radio broadcast can enable a listener to concentrate on the words or music or ambient sounds in a way that is not possible when the sound source is the only one element of a mixed-media experience. Sound can be presented as a personal intimate style – for instance, through headphones – or can be loudly amplified for a mass audience. The way in which any production is received and the environment in which it is received (from bedroom to auditorium) affects the style of production.

A slide/tape sequence using arresting still images and striking complementary sound (voices, dialogue, commentary, music, effects) can have a particular impact, especially in a darkened room, that video cannot achieve. In particular, easily updatable multi-screen or multi-projector presentations can be used for dramatic and large-scale effects. Slide/tape productions can be used in large-scale presentations; they can also be used in a personal way, with single tape and projector within a single machine for individual viewing.

There is no magic short-cut to creating successful productions in whatever medium. But there are practical tips and approaches that can help to avoid some of the pitfalls. Some people have a 'natural' eye for detail and a more developed imagination for the right shot or sound. We aim to help you to develop the natural eye, which has often been learned from practice and development of technique.

As an example, to explore successful techniques in photography, we suggest you spend some time analysing holiday photographs. Review a collection of holiday snapshots. They may be considered poor photos in terms of lighting, of composition, and of capturing effective images of people and places. However, as a record of moments for recalling later they may fulfil their aim quite successfully. At the same time, review the photographs in a few package holiday brochures. Since these are the products of professional photographers, you will expect to see eye-catching and persuasive images of people and places. Analyse three or four images that seem to be particularly eye-catching and list the features that make them successful images, e.g. colour, lighting, composition, angle, point of view.

Audio-visual Media as a Means of Communication

All audio-visual productions are made in order to communicate something to somebody. Can you think of any example for which this blanket statement is untrue?

We shall base our ideas here on this statement. There seems to be no point in creating any sort of production unless there is an intention to share it with at least one other person. (Of course, we might create something and then decide that it is not suitable or worthy of showing to any one else. We also might want to create something purely for our own record or own use.) As a piece of communication, audio-visual productions have certain specific qualities which we believe it is useful to recognise and to exploit. Some of these qualities which seem significant to us include the following.

Sequential time-based presentation
It is necessary to visualise a sequence of images and/or sounds. Although a sequence can be 'freezed' on a single image and indeed replayed over and over again, it cannot be viewed and scanned in the same way as a montage of images or as a newspaper page can be. Nor can it be reviewed and scanned as a page of print such as this, or held in the eye as a display of photographic images.

Audio presentation
It is important to use sound, including voice, music and effects, as a central element in the total production – not as an afterthought which is considered subsidiary to vision. It is common to think of film and video as primarily visual media, but sound should always complement, support and enhance the visual dimension. Of course, 'talking heads' alone do not make for interesting audio-visual presentation, since viewers expect something to view and need visual variety.

Visual presentation

Visual impact and variety are essential to an effective production. Images are not there for decoration, as they are in an illuminated manuscript, but are there as a prime channel of content.

For example, in a news presentation you are seeking images that encapsulate the key issues or sum up the message. Students of mass media will immediately think of the debates around the nature of news: ideas around 'the manufacture of news', the selection of extreme images that are visually arresting but may be unrepresentative of events, the inevitable filtering that results from the camera person's position and point of view (both a physical and mental perspective), and the whole issue of whether it is possible to achieve an unbiased or objective account of any event or issue.

Visual media, particularly with regard to factual rather than fictional presentations, are often criticised for being 'superficial'. They are contrasted with print media that for the past few hundred years have been the prime vehicle for the expression and argument of ideas. Newspaper editors would argue that for the presentation of complex ideas paragraphs of print are more effective and that sound and vision, which demand the rapid presentation of issues, have given rise to the 'sound bite' of 'the two minute culture' of broadcasting. This may be so if the aim of the production team is to present easily understood popular programmes at the level of intellectual and emotional demand of, say, the British tabloid press.

However, audio-visual productions are not necessarily superficial. We shall say more about this when we consider different types of productions. An example of audio-visual presentation that is intellectually demanding and in every respect educational would be the programmes broadcast for the British Open University. We suggest that you view some of these from different academic disciplines so that you see both familiar and unfamiliar ideas. At their best, these productions use the qualities of audio-visual presentation to the full. These capabilities include analysis of images, access to visual information, graphic presentation of data and its manipulation on screen, concise explanation through the spoken word and printed summaries, and visually presented practical demonstrations that can be seen in close up. These are of course made for a committed and motivated audience who are prepared to concentrate on viewing as fully as they would concentrate on reading.

With the use of computer graphics and miniaturised cameras, and the positioning of cameras where the human eye cannot reach, visual presentation can achieve messages that are not available in any other media.

Created out of ideas

As mentioned above, there is a view that audio-visual productions are, by their nature, not driven by ideas and intellectual activity, but are rooted in images and emotional appeal. Such an opinion is based on far too narrow a view of the use and potential of these media. In the past a similarly narrow view has been taken of 'comics'; but, in recent years, with the publication of graphic novels or comic book Shakespeare, we recognise that as a medium of communication.

In the next section of this chapter we shall stress the importance of clarifying the aims of any production and of being as precise as possible about the audiences for whom it is designed and their needs. Basic concepts and principles of human communication apply as much to producing a video presentation, as they do to holding a conversation with a friend. We shall say more about this in the section of this chapter on theories and issues. However, the fundamental advice that any communicator should 'have something to say, say it well, and make it interesting to those who'll receive it' certainly applies to sound and picture production.

A composition of choices by the production team

The finished product is never inevitable or pre-determined. It is the result of a series of decisions and choices made by all involved. The director or producer is the person who has the final decision, but sometimes that may well be influenced (or dictated) by the person or organisation who commissions and pays for the production.

Whilst at each stage of a production – from initial ideas, through planning and scripting, to recording and editing – it is individual personal choices that are being made, the final result is the product of a team. The actual relationships and processes of that team are significant in the final production.

A sharing of meaning between 'producer' and 'receiver'

One of the strong traditions of mass media study is a study of audiences – how they view productions, how they respond to them and how they are affected by them. The quotation at the head of this chapter points to the way in which a production takes on a life of its own. The intended message of the producer may not be the same as the message interpreted by the receiver.

Channel 4, in the UK, broadcast a series of programmes that sought to analyse how audiences 'view' television and also published a book, both with the title *Open the Box*. One of the main themes of their approach was that TV viewers are not 'television zombies'. During the 1980s there was extensive research carried out on how people actually use television, leading to a 'new perspective':

This new perspective suggests that how we understand a programme depends on who we are. It sees viewers with social lives and domestic habits, likes and dislikes. They gain a gender and a sexual preference, a class, a race and even, perhaps, imagination and a sense of irony; attributes unimaginable in the slumped, passive hoards. . . .Findings of this kind involve a dramatic shift away from the ideas of the effects theorists. For them, television programmes were simple, easily transmitted messages, which meant exactly the same to everyone who watched them. For writers like Brunsdon, Morley and Lewis, the meaning of a programme depends on who the viewer is and which 'method' of watching they are using. This does not mean, however, that viewers have complete freedom to make just ANY interpretation of the programme at will.

(*Open the Box* by Jane Root)

For a more academic treatment of these issues we refer you to *Television Culture* by John Fiske, particularly Chapter 5, 'Active Audiences', and Chapter 6, 'Activated Texts'.

Any production can be seen as an end in itself, but we wish to emphasise here that it is rather a means of communicating ideas, feelings, opinions and so on from one person (or group or organisation) to another person or group. The nature of the audience and how it will use the programme is important. A production broadcast to millions worldwide requires quite a different approach to communication from a production made for a precisely defined group – for example, a promotional video made to encourage students to apply for a college or university.

We have used the phrase 'a sharing of meaning' quite deliberately. We might have said 'sending a message' but this implies a one-way flow from active producer to passive receiver, and also that the message is self-evident. Even if one of the aims of a production is to explain something in an easily understandable way, it demands an active interpretation by the person receiving it. The receiver has to reach their own understanding of it. Hence we prefer to use the term 'meaning', which indicates a sort of negotiation or interaction between the receiver, the producer, the production and whatever the production is referring to (its content). The meaning or several meanings exist inside the heads of the producer and receiver and are coded or decoded through sound and image through reference to their own perceptions, values, beliefs and knowledge.

It is beyond the scope of this book to seek to define the nature of meaning: many different approaches have been made in defining this concept which is at the heart of any communication process. At the end of this chapter you will find a resource list that provides you with some further information on this; in particular, John Fiske's *Introduction to Communication Studies* deals with these issues. For our purposes, we want to stress that as producers of communication artefacts, we should try to be clear about what meanings we wish to share with potential viewers and to treat those viewers not as passive receivers of a sequence of sounds and images. The meanings that our audiences derive from our productions will be the product of the interaction between them and our production. We will explore that interaction later in this chapter.

Processes of Production

In this section we are taking a general view of the processes of production that you are likely to find useful regardless of the particular medium you are using. We shall approach it in five stages: preparation, planning, making, viewing and reviewing.

It is tempting to see the making element as the whole production process but we suggest that the key to successful creation of communication artefacts lies in the careful and imaginative planning and evaluating of what you do, as well as the ability and technical know-how to use cameras, microphones, lights, edit suite and other equipment – from the first germ of an idea to the finished product.

We believe that it is important to keep asking yourself – why am I doing this and how can I best achieve what I want?

Preparation

As we indicated in the section 'Audio-visual Media as a Means of Communication', page 3, ideas and how to communicate them are fundamental. All productions begin with a reason for doing them and some idea of whom they are intended for and what effects are sought.

Equipment, materials and time are expensive, so time spent preparing and planning is likely prove economical in the long term. An analogy could be decorating a room: having decided the finished result, you do not immediately pick up a paintbrush, but rather have to spend time on preparing the room and the materials.

So, where do you begin with producing a piece of audio-visual communication?

Ask four basic questions: Why? What? How? For whom?

Why?

The more precise you can be about the aims and intended effects of the finished product, the better. These may be clear in the minds of whoever is commissioning the product, but they may also be comparatively unfocused at the start. Before beginning detailed planning and scripting, it is important to settle some basics, such as whether you are expected to entertain, or inform, or educate, or persuade, or teach, or provoke, or sell, or . . .

As we suggested above, the message of a production may not be self-evident to viewers, who will bring their own interpretations and opinions and decode their own meanings. But a producer and her/his team do need to be clear about the ideas, information, feelings or attitudes they want to convey and share through their particular selection of sounds and images.

What?

You cannot start unless you have some idea of the intended content or message. This may, of course, develop and unfold differently as you proceed with the making of the programme, and you may be exploring ideas or information that you do not fully understand at the start. If by the end you and the team are still not clear, then the chances of your audience understanding it are remote.

How?

The way you are going to treat the 'story' needs to be outlined. Since an audio-visual production is time-based, it will tend to be perceived as a story. How you will enable the viewer to follow it is important. What sort of techniques are appropriate? At this stage you may want to commit your ideas for content and how it will be presented to paper for your own benefit, or to explain it to others. This is often called a 'treatment' which will give some idea of sequence and of sound and image elements.

One form of presentation for this is as a 'storyboard' (see Figure 1.1 overleaf). This gives very simple line drawings for each shot, and beneath these indicates the sound and any other effects to be included. **7**

Storyboards can help to visualise the 'what' and 'how'. For example, the drawings will show if the visual line consists solely of talking heads or long shots of the same scene, which will indicate that some variety of treatment and presentation is needed. In a short sequence every visual may be shown, but in a longer sequence just the principal sequences may be shown. Thus, in an interview sequence it is not necessary to keep indicating visuals of heads, but if you wanted to cut away and show a diagram or a different visual during the interview you would indicate that.

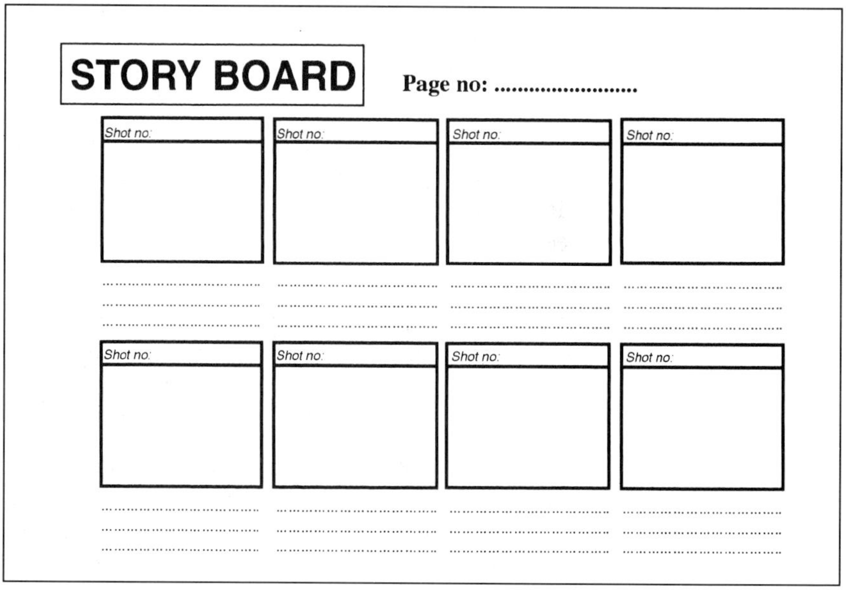

Figure 1.1
A storyboard

| STORY BOARD | Page no: .... |

Shot no:	Shot no:	Shot no:	Shot no:

Shot no:	Shot no:	Shot no:	Shot no:

Storyboards are helpful in the pre-production planning stage as a way of seeing your intended treatment. They are also helpful during production to remind you and the team what you had planned. Additionally, a storyboard can be a useful way of selling your planning ideas to a client. Thus a storyboard may be a very rough personal *aide-mémoire*, or it may be part of a formal presentation, even using photos instead of line drawings. Such storyboards are the norm when an advertising agency is presenting possible treatments for a TV campaign to its client for the client's agreement before going into the production phase.

For whom?

Productions are obviously not created in a vacuum, but in a context of how it will be viewed and used. The notion of the audience for a piece of broadcasting may be very wide and vague, but for many productions there is a clearly defined target audience.

If the audience is a defined one, it is essential for the producer to find out as much as possible about their characteristics, expectations and needs. It is easier to convey messages, or (as we expressed it in the section above) to share meanings with people you know.

Time spent on answering those four questions before real planning begins will be time well spent.

Planning

With a clearer idea of what you are wanting to produce and why, you can begin the real work of generating ideas, researching, scripting, and planning how you will work.

Imaginative ideas leading to creative ways of using sound and/or vision make for interesting finished products. Sometimes constraints of time and resources make it inevitable that a well-tried formula is adopted. This is perhaps most consistently obvious in news gathering and reporting, where the constant meeting of deadlines, and the need for accurate unambiguous presentation, leave little scope for imagination. In contrast, if you were producing advertisements you would expect the approach to be innovative. Where possible, brainstorming for ideas amongst the team is important: what are we including, how can we present it?

Researching both the topics and sources of information is the next step. If you are planning a drama narrative rather than a more factual piece, your research might be for locations or for actors or whatever seems necessary.

Finally, you are getting to the point of committing plans to paper. We might call this a storyboard, a script, a treatment, or simply a plan. There are different ways of tackling it, but the key point is to include the sound and visual elements if it is a video, film or slide/tape production. A storyboard is a helpful format.

Before we leave this preparation and planning section, it might be useful to think about how you might go about planning for a particular production. Imagine you have the opportunity to interview and make a recording of a famous person: choose a person whom you would like to interview, and jot down in note form how you would research and prepare for doing it.

Making

This is where all the planning pays off. Other chapters in this book will deal with this at more length within various media. Here we simply want to stress a few general points.

Most audio-visual productions demand team work, probably in front of and behind the camera or microphone, so having clear tasks and roles set out saves time and should ease frustration. The more you can get it right first time, the better.

Make sure you have all the people, places and objects you need where and when you need them. This is essential. It is also vitally important to make sure you have the equipment and materials, and that they are working.

Almost inevitably, the types of production we are dealing with here require processing and editing after the initial capturing of material on camera or whatever. For example, if you are taking a short sequence of photos to illustrate an article, you hope that by taking a roll of 36 exposures that you can select, say, five that will give you what you want. Or, if you want a video sequence to show how to carry out a particular task (say, how to change a tyre) you will take more footage than you need to edit to the short sequence you want.

Viewing

We are using this term in at least two senses: first, to indicate the actual reception of the finished product by the intended audience; and secondly, to indicate the opportunity to pilot test the product with the intended audience. These situations will vary depending on the nature of the production, but before final completion, it is worthwhile to test the production with your commissioner and/or your audience to check if it is fulfilling the aims and gaining the effects you intended. A clear example of such testing would be for adverts, where they are tested out on a sample group before being broadcast. Similarly, if you were making some sort of training package, you would want to test it before going into final production and reproduction.

Reviewing

At the completion of any production project, you and the team should leave time for evaluating what has been done. The general theme might be: 'If we were to do it all again, what would we do differently?' Obviously, the actual artefact would be analysed in terms of achieving its aims and in terms of its technical success or failure, but you would also want to consider the whole process from the preparation and planning stage.

Figure 1.2 summarises the stages of making any sort of audio-visual production, from original concept through planning and production to final publication and review.

Figure 1.2
Stages of the production process

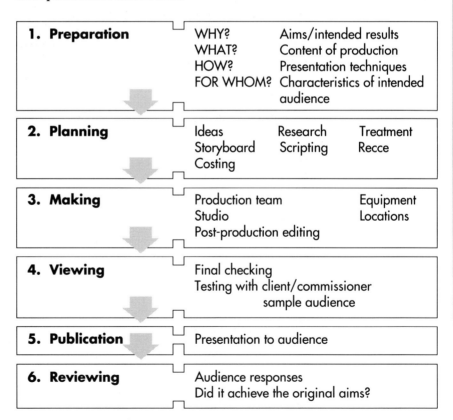

1. **Preparation**	WHY?	Aims/intended results
	WHAT?	Content of production
	HOW?	Presentation techniques
	FOR WHOM?	Characteristics of intended audience

2. **Planning**	Ideas	Research	Treatment
	Storyboard	Scripting	Recce
	Costing		

3. **Making**	Production team	Equipment
	Studio	Locations
	Post-production editing	

| 4. **Viewing** | Final checking |
| | Testing with client/commissioner sample audience |

| 5. **Publication** | Presentation to audience |

| 6. **Reviewing** | Audience responses |
| | Did it achieve the original aims? |

Types of Production

In planning and producing audio tapes, photographs, slide/tape sequences, video tapes, films or any technically based presentation, the influence of published and broadcast materials is inevitable. The conventions of technical presentation which we have referred to above have grown out of this professional tradition, so that people who view your productions in whatever context bring expectations based on their previous experience of public media. These conventions are challenged and adapted by producers who are seeking new artistic and technical effects, but they still underpin the planning and making of any production. The use of video equipment, which has become more and more accessible in the past decade, has to some extent developed its own professional and amateur traditions that do not necessarily follow the established conventions of broadcast mass productions. In both traditions, however, there are agreed types of productions that have developed their own presentational styles according to the different purposes and audiences.

In this section, we are briefly introducing the main types of production so that you are aware of the different styles and ways in which your productions might be evaluated. For example, the styles of photographic or video presentation of a family wedding record would be totally different from the styles of photographic or video presentation of a news report intended for broadcasting.

So far we have suggested that as you approach making any audio-visual production you must plan, prepare, research, script and make in the light of as precise a knowledge as possible of the aims, content, desired effects and intended audience for your production. We are now also suggesting that it is useful as you plan your productions to identify what sort of production it is. Ask yourself, What sort of production am I making?

You might characterise your production in terms of the following broad opposites, for instance:

- factual or fictional
- personal or impersonal
- artistic or scientific
- comic or serious
- entertaining or informative
- broad or narrow target audience
- conventional or unconventional

The types, or genres as they are often called, of media productions are not confined categories, and the same production might well include both sides of those 'opposites' and might deliberately mix the genres. For example, a piece of fictional drama may well include some factual documentary material and might be called a piece of 'faction' or dramatised documentary. In making such a production, however, the production team would be expected to make it clear to the audience which elements were 'real' and which were 'drama'; hence, in a documentary the producer might use a caption that indicates that a particular sequence is a 'dramatised reconstruction'.

Recognising the established genres of production enables you either to **11** work within them, or to challenge the conventions using your own imaginative and creative approach. The genres of audio-visual productions have grown out of long established cultural traditions. For example, it was Aristotle in ancient Greece around 4 000 BC who said that a story should have a beginning, a middle and an end. You might like to watch some broadcast TV programmes, both drama and documentary, to see if this notion of beginning, middle and end still influences producers. Obviously, producers and writers through the centuries have challenged that prescription, but have you never watched a film or play on TV and then heard someone say: 'That was a funny ending . . . I didn't think it would end there'? Audiences do tend to expect a production of whatever kind to end with a clear final conclusion, although a producer can deliberately leave the audience with no conclusion so that people have to come up with their own ending.

Let us the look at some broad production styles you might want, or be asked, to use.

News

This label is obviously used to categorise a type of production in any medium, whether print, radio or TV. We cannot here go into all the qualities and techniques of news production, but we want to signal some of them. For instance: the content must be topical and in some sense 'new'; there will be a variety of mixed topics; some will be rated more important than others and will be treated differently, both visually and in speech; there is a requirement of accuracy and truth; the issues of 'objectivity' and point of view and bias and opinion are all important; the selection of items (why are they called 'stories'?) has to be made against either stated or unstated criteria.

Within the broad genre of news, there are also clearly established news genres which have their own hierarchy. For example: you, as a viewer, will have clear expectations about how a news sequence on the TV will flow. It will probably go from a disaster such as war, accident or famine, to national or international political items, to crimes and legal cases, to social or scientific issues, to sport and then arts or human interest, or maybe an animal story.

Watch news broadcasts and compare radio and print treatments from different newspapers and channels. Producers bring different criteria about choice of topic and presentation, and different concepts of what their audiences want. But whatever these criteria, audiences expect an effective news production to be clear and accurate, to express complex issues in an easily understandable way, to provide direct observation of events, and to get behind the story to explain its significance.

An old definition of news is that it is 'information that someone somewhere does not want you to have'. This may not be a serious definition, but it highlights the fact that news productions should not rely only on publicity handouts, nor allow themselves to be manipulated by powerful agencies in society.

As far as production techniques are concerned, you would rarely find a news item without an interview, without visiting places where the action is happening and without a reporter to interpret the events and issues. If you seek to make news production, even if only about a small local area, these issues will still apply. If you wish your news to be taken seriously it has to follow the conventions of production.

The establishment of a 24-hour news channel on TV has reinforced the notion that 'news' is a manufactured commodity that is bought and sold around the world. Within this, there are issues of who pays for the news and who governs the dominant viewpoint on world events. At any rate, we now have a flow of non-stop talk and news images beaming around the world. News making brings a particular level of responsibility to the production team, since on a local, national or international level, the presentation of news sets an agenda for people's ideas, attitudes and beliefs. The selection of news indicates a range of topics to which we are supposed to give attention.

Current affairs documentaries

Documentaries are a slow art form within a TV daily industrial system which delivers round-the-clock entertainment and information. Within British television documentaries not only carry considerable prestige, but also exist on a substantial scale; this scale varies somewhat with definition, but British television's four conventional channels offer about 20 hours of documentary every week, mainly in the evening hours....This flood of material is made by about two hundred producers, directors and producer-directors who see themselves as factual film-makers. Each of these currently active film-makers will make between one and three hours in a year; 90 minutes (or three half-hours) would be a typical year's film-making....Documentary-making encompasses ordinary people in real-life situations of drama and pathos; but British documentary also covers science, the arts and religion, as well as natural history and the environment. Across this huge range of the ordinary and the extraordinary, documentary-makers see the acquisition of high-quality film – and its shaping into an original final form – as central.

J. Tunstall *Television Producers*

Traditionally, current affairs would be described as the background to the news. This is too limiting a view of the infinite range of topics and treatments that a documentary production can embrace, but it does signal the central difference: the scope and intention to treat a specific topic in more depth.

As with all productions, a key question is: what do I want the audience to gain from viewing this sequence of material?

The genre of documentary has been developed as a broad approach to exploring issues, topics, people or places in a wide variety of ways. You might like to think of programmes, or collections of photographs in exhibitions or magazines, that aim to share a particular personal view of an aspect of the world. Documentaries do give more scope to the individual point of view; however, they also sometimes seek to work in the tradition of the 'objective' news style.

Whatever the style, a successful documentary will collect and analyse information, opinions and evidence. The quality of research and the arranging of that research into a well-argued and well-presented sequence are keys to arresting the audience's attention and keeping their interest. Making complex issues easier to understand, or presenting the various sides of an argument through interviews, visual images and a closely argued series of ideas, are what make the documentary a most important genre.

It is useful to see a documentary as an essay. The producer needs the discipline of gathering information and of arranging it into a coherent argument with a beginning (the issues), a middle (the evidences and sources of argument) and an end (conclusions drawn for the audience to consider). However, an essay may not immediately be a stimulating way of presenting the content using sound and/or image. The essay form needs adapting to more of an 'article' form, for example by means of an arresting opening that stimulates a desire to keep listening or looking, a variety of presentational techniques and a step-by-step exposition of the argument. This may sound dull, and the challenge for the current affairs producer is to maintain a passion for the topic right to the end. Part of that passion is likely to come from some sort of conflict – conflict is often said to be the heart of drama – between different people, agencies or viewpoints.

Take the opportunity to view and listen to some current affairs broadcasting. Analyse purpose, content and presentation methods. Compare a science-based programme with a social, political, or economic programme and then with an arts-based programme. Compare a long-established flagship programme like BBC's *Panorama* with a Channel 4 documentary such as *Diverse Reports*. Do you detect that arts programmes employ ways of working and technical presentations that differ from those in science documentaries?

Sports

How can you photograph or video tape a sports contest? As a spectator, you will only have one viewpoint, although your eyes and ears will selectively range and focus over areas of activity in ways that one microphone or one camera cannot.

The technical aspects of capturing sports action, whether on still or video camera, are what make it interesting to us. A variety of cameras and camera positions and angles is what makes audio-visual presentation of sport almost an art form in itself. The audience is placed in the position of a very privileged spectator who has the wide view as well as the close-up detail of shots and personal anguish.

Sports appreciation is essentially a visual activity for the spectator, so the tradition of radio broadcast sports is an interesting one. Listen to radio coverage of athletics, cricket, association or rugby football, or tennis ... the verbal description of the action must be precise and fast but at the same time the 'spaces' of non-action must be taken up with sound commentary of analysis and time filling. Hence, cricket commentaries on British radio have become a radio art form with their techniques for filling the extensive gaps between each delivery of the ball.

We suggest that you watch and listen to broadcast productions, both live and edited, to analyse their approaches and technical presentation. You might also like to take a video camera along to a sports event and seek to capture it for later presentation.

Drama

Imagine you want to tell the story in a photo sequence of a child getting up in the morning and going to school. You are to start with the child waking up and end with the first lesson of the day. Does it sound boring already? The challenge is how to dramatise it to create an interesting series of images. Terms such as 'character', 'situation', 'story' and 'plot' come to mind. It is possible to create a mood or create conflict through selected images which would be staged.

We have suggested that you visualise how you might approach that task because it demonstrates that, via a series of images, you are required to focus closely on key expressions and moments. Film and video are particularly effective dramatic media in this sense, as personal forms in which the camera makes the character directly in touch with the viewer.

Television has successfully translated drama written for the theatre to the small screen, but production techniques are different, leading generally to more intimate, close-up and personal approaches. This perhaps accounts for why the two dramatic styles which television has particularly developed are the soap opera and the situation comedy. We suggest that you watch some of these, and for part of the time you turn the sound off to concentrate on the sequence of images. The camera is especially effective in capturing facial expression and personal interaction.

It is beyond the scope of this book to deal with the complexities of drama production. There is of course an extensive range of scripting, acting and recording techniques. If you wish to follow this up, you could look at *Constructing Television* by Sue and Wink Hackman. This book for schools grew out of a Scottish Television series. Part 1 is about making drama programmes and includes the creation of 'imaginary places . . . imaginary people . . . fictions . . . characters . . . plot development . . . storylining . . . scripts . . . camerawork . . . directing and editing'.

Advertisements

These very short productions have often cost a great deal more per second than other productions, either on TV or radio. According to newspaper advertisements by the Newspaper Publishers Association, 'The cost of making a 30-second TV commercial these days is likely to be around £120 000. That's £4 000 per second. We're not talking here about a mini-epic, just an average commercial. . . .Within the last year there have been TV commercials – naming no names – which cost £1.8 million, £1.2 million and £800 000. It's baffling how any 60 seconds of celluloid can cost such vast sums when the BBC can make a whole hour of drama for a relatively meagre £400 000' (*The Independent*, 25 September 1993).

Advertisements on TV, on radio and in the press are very concentrated **15** moments of production and therefore demonstrate artistic and technical qualities very clearly. Adverts use other production genres often almost as a form of parody, so that mini-dramas, mini-documentaries, slices of personal life or sports action, fantasy, interviews, cartoons and so on are all the stuff of adverts.

They also vividly demonstrate the planning issues we discussed above. Adverts are very conscious pieces of communication that have clearly envisaged aims, a precise target audience, and a well thought-out content, and which have tested effects from the audience. Technically, they are slick products with fast editing and no loose camera shots, and they have carefully composed scripts and carefully considered use of sound and music.

Non-broadcast productions

In addition to the broadcast production genres listed above, there is now also a tradition of different types of sound and video tapes for specific, personal, social and business purposes. Availability of automatic still and video cameras has enabled 'ordinary people' to make their own productions. Of course, some accounts of 'what went wrong' at the wedding, at the stage show, on the sports field, on holiday, in the garden or in the living room, originally recorded for later personal viewing, have become a source of material for broadcast television.

These films often look as if the camera was pointed at an activity and left running. Such a production would be very tedious viewing for non-participants except in very short extracts. If an event is to be recorded for sharing with other people, it has to be planned and designed. For example, to be successful, a 'wedding video' should not just consist of a camera pointing at each guest individually at the wedding. It needs to deliver what the participants want; and to record all the people and key moments from the most attractive camera angles. It requires prior planning and reconnaissance of the locations, complete with technical checks for light and sound.

The social and business uses of audio-visual productions are growing. Community video and the use of video in schools from primary level upwards are now established. Often these are merely ways of recording events, but a community group may well set about preparing their own documentary about a local issue, to show to others to raise awareness and to lobby for action.

Training and selling productions are now familiar to us all. Every university has its own corporate video to persuade people to apply for a place there. Every travel agent has a collection of promotional videos to sell particular holiday destinations. No training event for a company is complete without a training video. Dramatised roleplays of how to conduct a meeting or how to treat a customer depend on effective production techniques. In the UK, a company called Video Arts has created some very humorous and effective materials, not least because they have used presenters and actors such as John Cleese. Like advertisements, training videos make use of a range of production genres, from the news and documentary style, through the sitcom to the serious drama or quiz show.

As you gain experience with productions, experiment with the different styles and genres mentioned here.

Models and Theories of Communication

In this book we are not aiming to introduce all the possible theoretical and analytical approaches there might be to the production of audio visual communication. In this section we want to suggest some ways in which you can conceptualise the processes of communication in which you are engaged.

In the section on audio-visual media as a means of communication (page 3), we touched on issues of how you might conceptualise what is happening when you produce a piece of communication, when we drew some distinction between 'sending a message' and 'sharing meaning'. We believe it is useful to seek to analyse the processes that make for effective communication, and to recognise some of the issues about the nature of human communication. In order to analyse these processes, many people have formulated models to summarise the key elements in a communication transaction. These models tend to use particular conceptual terms, some of which we want to use here.

First, it may be useful to state what we mean by a model of communication. Denis McQuail and Sven Windahl in their book, *Communication Models for the Study of Mass Communications*, provide a relevant statement on models and their uses: 'For our purpose, we consider a model as a consciously simplified description in graphic form of a piece of reality. A model seeks to show the main elements of any structure or process and the relationships between these elements.' A model therefore can be helpful in identifying the main elements and how they relate when you are seeking to visualise the parts that make up the total process of communication between people and groups.

An example may illustrate how a model can be used. In the 1940s an American political scientist, Harold Lasswell, suggested that:

a convenient way to describe an act of communication is to answer the following questions:
Who?
Says what?
In which channel?
To whom?
With what effect?

(From 'The structure and function of communication in society' in L. Bryson (1948) *The Communication of Ideas* Harper and Row.)

This model or formula can be used (and has often been used) as a way of analysing the elements in a communication act. As McQuail and Windahl point out, such a formula is a simplification, but it can enable us for example to identify key elements in a production. We can use it to clarify our own thinking and planning as we suggested in 'Processes of Production' on page 6.

This particular model omits any idea of a social or cultural context in   **17** which the communicator/producer and audience/receiver may live, and it also omits the notion of a purpose that drives the producer. It does, however, highlight the concepts of communicator, content or message, a chosen channel or range of media, an audience and an effect on the audience that receives it.

This formula, and there are many similar ones in McQuail and Windahl and other books on communication, has come to be known as a *linear model*. It conceptualises the communication as a simple flow of information from one person or agency to another. According to this model, if the producer is clear about the 'what' and the use of 'the channel', the message will be received. It rather suggests a sort of bull's-eye approach to sending messages.

However, as we indicated in 'Processes of Production', on page 6, recent research lays more stress on how audiences receive and interpret (and perhaps reject) the messages that are transmitted.

Figure 1.3
Communication processes between producer and receiver

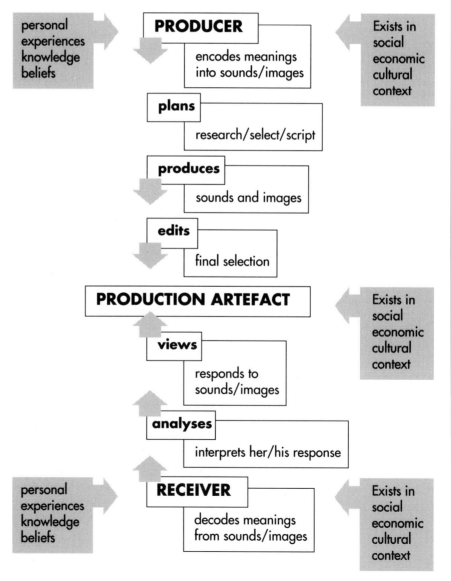

The transmission model can therefore be helpful in formulating production ideas, but we would want to use a word such as 'interaction' or 'transaction' to describe the relationship between a communicator and a receiver. The receiver is not a passive target at which a production is aimed. The receiver actively responds and interprets the sounds and images received, in terms of her/his own experiences, attitudes, knowledge and beliefs.

We referred earlier in this chapter to the 'grammar of television' in which audio-visual production is a language system with its own rules and conventions. Another concept that is often used in trying to explain communication processes is that of a 'code'. This signifies that for two people to communicate, to share meaning, they have to be able to translate their own thoughts and feelings into symbols (sounds, words, pictures and so on) which the other person can also understand, or 'decode'.

In direct face-to-face communication, people use codes of verbal and non-verbal language to express and interpret the meanings they want to share. But in producing audio-visual materials, the coding will be received and decoded by the audience normally without the producers being present. Hence, it can be said that the interaction is rather between the receiver and the product which stands on its own.

We can visualise this process in Figure 1.3. This model stresses the meeting of producer and audience only through the production. The choices made by the production team are now embodied in the text of the production for potential audiences to recreate, or rather to create newly for themselves.

In a sense, the production takes on a life of its own, independent of its makers. Another term that is used in this context to describe any sort of production is 'text', i.e. something produced according to the conventions of a code, to carry some sort of meaning for other people to take from it. In this approach, the model of communication stresses the ways in which people 'read a text', the ways in which they assign meaning to the product in terms of their own life experience and with reference to their idea of 'reality' about which the text has something to say.

This idea is based on the notion that people tend to read 'meanings' into everything they encounter. Let us take as an example an advertisement for a particular car. The makers of the ad will have a certain message to convey about the car: its appearance, its engine, its creature comforts and so on. In addition to this, they will convey notions of the potential owner or driver and her/his lifestyle and also, depending where it is presented, something about the social context in which it is to be imagined. A simple car advertisement can have a range of textual readings for producer and receiver.

John Fiske, in his *Introduction to Communication Studies* and other publications, seeks to explore the ways in which all of us draw meanings from texts of all kinds. He visualises this general process as a triangular model. Figure 1.4 (page 20) adapts this Fiske model to illustrate the processes of producing a 'text' based on content which refs to places, people, events, ideas, emotions and so on and and also the processes of reading/interpreting the text. Meanings exist in the minds of producers and audiences/readers as a result of the interplay between the text/production, the experiences and knowledge of the producers and receivers and the context (referent) in which they both live.

Figure 1.4
Meanings negotiated between producer/viewer and production/text and content/referent

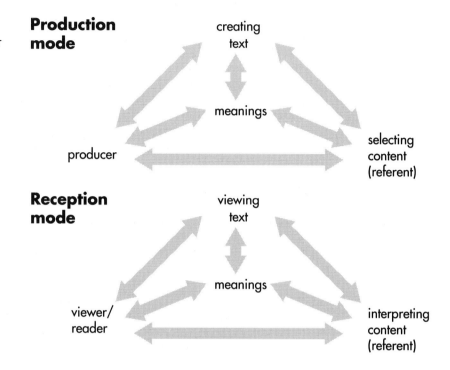

Production mode

creating text

meanings

producer

selecting content (referent)

Reception mode

viewing text

meanings

viewer/ reader

interpreting content (referent)

Readers who are interested in exploring these issues further might like to read *Television Culture* by John Fiske. However, you may feel this excursion into abstract thinking about how meaning is made from productions is a long way from the practical concerns of how to use cameras effectively, and how to edit a sequence of sounds and images. Our brief flirting with communication models and academic study of mass communication was to stress two very practical concepts:

1 in all of your production, planning and making, keep in mind the meanings you want to share, even if you may not always fully grasp a single message; and
2 keep in mind the audience and the individual receiver who will be interacting with your production.

Activities   **Advertising campaign**
Imagine that you have been commissioned to produce a series of advertising campaigns in which you can use print, posters, radio and television. You have a limitless budget. For each of the following campaigns, prepare a written outline of your treatment to include what the campaign is saying about the product, the media you will use and why, the techniques of presentation you will use and how you are seeking to persuade the target audience to purchase that product.

1 Luxury Cornish ice cream to men and women in the 16–25 age range
2 A four wheel drive vehicle to families
3 A shampoo to men
4 EuroDisney to business people as a conference venue

Presenting the fire service

The public relations officer of your local fire service has asked you to act as a communications consultant to help with some problems she has. The fire service is asked to make regular presentations of two main kinds: first, to describe the work of the brigade to various community groups, and secondly to describe career opportunities in the fire service on visits to schools and career conventions. The public relations officer has a budget to commission some audio-visual material to help in these presentations. She could seek a video production or a slide/tape production. Will one production serve both purposes?

Prepare some notes about the advantages and disadvantages of each of these media for her purposes. Also advise her whether she needs two different productions.

Further reading

BBC Television Training Materials (see Resources page 229 for the address). There is a wide range of booklets, video tapes, wallcharts etc. based on the BBC's own training courses. These include, *The Production Assistant's Survival Guide, Shooting on Location, Editing Film and Video Tape, From Script to Screen, Stand by Studio: an introduction to studio television, Filming Action, Writing Comedy, Creative Editing, On Camera: how to produce film and video.*

Burton, G. (1992) *More than Meets the Eye: an introduction to media studies* Edward Arnold.

Cotton, B. and Olover, R. (1993) *Understanding Hypermedia from Multimedia to Virtual Reality* Phaidon.

Davies, D. (1969) *The Grammar of Television Production* Revised by John Elliot, Barrie and Rockliff.

Dimbleby, R. and Burton, G. (1992) *More than Words: an introduction to communication* (2nd ed.) Routledge.

Elliott, G. (ed.) (1985) *Video Production Techniques* Kluwer.

Fiske, J. (1990) *Introduction to Communication Studies* (2nd ed.) Routledge.

Fiske, J. (1987) *Television Culture* Methuen.

Gration, G., Reilly, J. and Titford, J. (1988) *Communication and Media Studies: an introductory course book* Macmillan.

Hackman, S. and W. (1989) *Constructing Television* Hodder and Stoughton.

Hart, A. (1988) *Making the Real World: a study of a television series* Cambridge University Press.

McQuail, D. and Windahl, S. (1981) *Communication Models for the Study of Mass Communication* Longman.

Peak, S. (ed.) (annually) *The Media Guide* Fourth Estate.

Price, S. (1993) *Media Studies* Pitman.

Root, J. (1986) *Open the Box: about television* Comedia.

Silverstone, R. (1985) *Framing Science: the making of a BBC documentary* British Film Institute.

Stafford, R. (1993) *Hands On: a teacher's guide to media technology* British Film Institute.

Tunstall, J. (1993) *Television Producers* Routledge.

Watson, J. and Hill, A. (1993) *A Dictionary of Communication and Media Studies* (3rd ed.) Edward Arnold.

Winston, B. and Keydel, J. (1987) *Working with Video: a comprehensive guide to the world of video production* Pelham Books.

2 Photography

> **I**mportant though technical skill is, the camera is just the means by which a photographer expresses his creative vision … Making successful pictures means understanding what lies behind a subject's appeal, rather than just reacting intuitively. Analyse your reactions to a scene, deciding what is visually attractive and emotionally stimulating; which elements need emphasis and which should be ignored.
>
> (J. Hedgecoe, *New Manual of Photography*)

Introduction

The increasing use of the visual image as a means of communication has meant that it is more important than ever for students of the media to have a reasonable grasp of both camera and darkroom techniques. Photography can be a rewarding and fun hobby, as well as a creative tool that helps to express your own personal vision.

This chapter aims to introduce you to all types of 35mm single lens reflex (SLR) cameras, as well as medium-format, autofocus compact and large-format cameras. We shall discuss lens and film choice, using flashguns, studio lights and/or natural light to create certain effects, choosing and using filters for both black-and-white and colour photography, as well as explaining how to develop your own photographs in the darkroom. Although each section will begin with the basics, the more experienced photographer will also find material of use, as there are insights into handy techniques used by the professionals, as well as more advanced darkroom work.

Even if you have never picked up a camera before, after reading this section and applying a little of your own creative flair, you should soon be taking photographs that are something more than just 'snaps'. Taking a good photograph is not just simply about having a 'good eye' for composition; you need technical knowledge to help realise the photograph you see in your mind's eye. This chapter aims to give you the knowledge that you need, teaching you the skills necessary for technically competent photography.

What do You Need?

A typical college camera kit will normally comprise: a semi-automatic/manual camera body, 50mm 'standard' lens, 28mm wide angle lens, 70–210mm telephoto zoom lens and a semi-automatic flashgun of some description (see Figure 2.1, page 24). These items form the core of the basic kit that you need to take good photographs, but other accessories such as tripods, filters, cable releases and reflectors are necessary for certain picture-taking situations. The 28mm and 50mm 'prime' lenses can also be replaced by the versatile 28–70mm zoom lens.

This section will deal principally with the constraints of having limited access to equipment, yet will also talk about some more exotic items by way of an introduction to what is available, should your college have it. A resource list at the end of the book gives a few addresses of some hire companies should you require a special item for that perfect photograph, and we will also mention a few 'short-cut' alternatives if your budget does not stretch that far!

Figure 2.1
A typical SLR kit comprising: camera body, 50mm, 28mm, 70–210mm lenses, flash, sturdy tripod, filters, cable release, camera bag and a reflector

A Brief History of Photography

There has been some debate as to the exact origins of photography. William Henry Fox Talbot working in his laboratory in Wiltshire during the late 1830s is credited with producing the oldest known negative (taken in August 1835), while the Frenchman Louis Daguerre obtained the first 'official recognition' for photography in 1839, when his method for producing daguerreotypes was acquired by the French state, with a view 'to being in a position to make a present of it to the whole world'. Either way, photography has been with us for well over 150 years.

At first, photography was only available to a select few. Only those who could afford expensive camera and developing equipment were able to produce photographs. Cameras were large and unportable, and used exposure times of up to several minutes, making them complicated and awkward to use.

In 1887, the Eastman Corporation launched the first 'Kodak box camera', a relatively small roll-film camera which finally made photography truly available to the masses – the era of the snapshot was born. Realising the popularity of photography, Leitz of Germany launched a completely new film system in 1923, which was set to revolutionise the photographic industry. Available in sealed metal cartridges, this film was significantly smaller than the older, paper-backed roll film. The launch of the new film enabled cameras to become smaller and smaller, and today's 35mm film cartridges are a direct descendant of the first prototypes.

The Leitz Camera (the Leica) developed by Oskar Barnack initially used cut down rolls of 35mm cine film, although pre-rolled film quickly became commercially available. The smaller cameras and the possibility of 36 continuous frames meant that the new 35mm cameras could be used to record 'life' with great spontaneity. Photographers such as Robert Capa and Cartier-Bresson were great advocates of the small Leica, and their photographs taken in many different parts of the world were typical of the new style of 'photojournalism' that emerged thanks to the camera's compact and easy-to-use design.

After the launch of the first SLR camera, the Japanese quickly established a hold on the domestic 35mm camera market, with names like Canon, Nikon, Olympus and Pentax coming to the fore. During the 1970s, cameras became smaller and more automated, leading to the first wave of autofocus compacts at the end of the decade (see Figure 2.2).

SLR cameras meanwhile became lighter and more sophisticated, and all for a cheaper price. Today, a camera like the Canon EOS 1000Fn has a built-in flash, fully automated exposure, automatic film advance, autofocus and different exposure modes, for less than £400.

Figure 2.2
The Pentax zoom 90WR compact camera

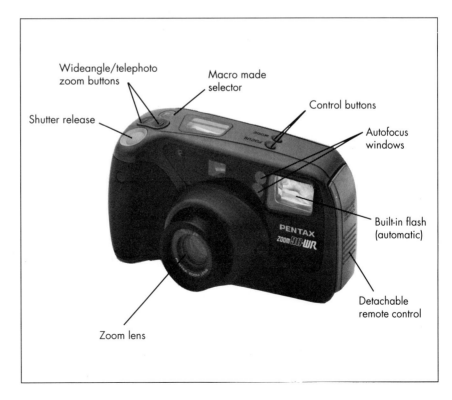

It has therefore become easier for 'the person in the street' to take photographs. Nowadays, with most modern cameras, you don't need to think about exposure, film speed or even focusing. The camera takes care of everything, leaving you to concentrate on the most important aspect of a photograph: composition. However, although you don't *need* to think about exposure and focusing, a knowledge of the basic principles is a must for taking photographs that are something more than just 'snaps'.

The Single Lens Reflex Camera

Basically speaking, there are four main types of SLR camera: the fully manual, the semi-automatic, the fully automatic/program and the autofocus program. All SLR cameras have interchangeable lenses, that enable the camera to 'see' in many different ways. A wide angle lens will take in a large field of view (it will see a lot), while a telephoto will have a narrow angle of view (it will see very little, and as a result appears to magnify distant objects). The different lenses available for SLR cameras and their many varied applications will be outlined later.

The prime advantage of the SLR camera is that the image you see in the viewfinder is the image that you actually end up with on film – you look through the lens to see what you are framing (Figure 2.3). This enables very precise composition, and allows you to ensure that the subject that you are photographing is in sharp focus. Most older SLR cameras have manual focus (you have to focus the picture yourself), whereas the majority of SLR cameras sold today tend to have an autofocus facility.

Figure 2.3
Diagram showing the path of light through an SLR camera

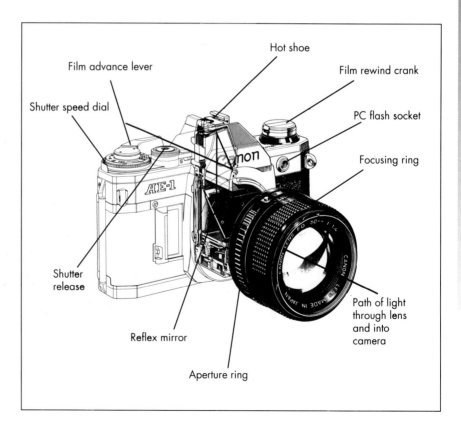

Figure 2.4a
The Canon A1 has manual, shutter priority, aperture priority and program modes

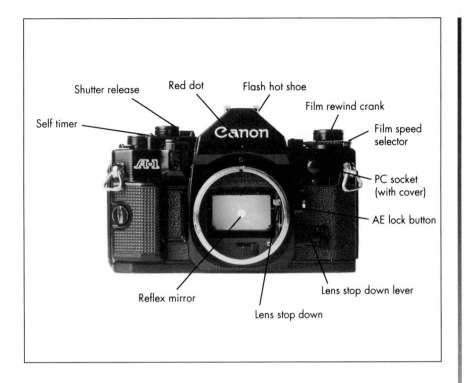

Self timer

Shutter release

Red dot

Flash hot shoe

Film rewind crank

Film speed selector

PC socket (with cover)

AE lock button

Reflex mirror

Lens stop down

Lens stop down lever

Figure 2.4b
The Pentax K1000: manual control only

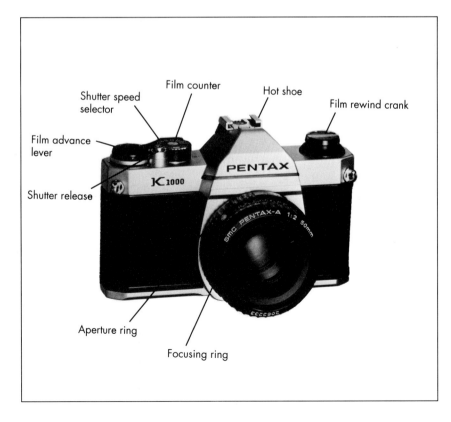

Shutter speed selector

Film counter

Hot shoe

Film rewind crank

Film advance lever

Shutter release

Aperture ring

Focusing ring

Most schools and colleges have SLR cameras with fully manual or semi-automatic exposure systems and manual focus, which allow the student to experiment and learn the rudiments of photography the 'hard way'. Although the manual or semi-automatic SLR is very good for most picture-taking situations, it can be a little slow when you want to shoot things in a hurry. With the manual/semi-automatic camera, the photographer has to set the shutter speed and/or aperture her/himself, balancing one with the other to achieve the correct exposure.

New fully manual and semi-automatic cameras are rarely available these days, although there is a healthy secondhand market for them. Typical examples that are often found in schools and colleges (and are also available for a reasonable secondhand price) are the (original) Pentax P30 (semi-automatic/manual), Pentax P30n (semi-automatic/manual, with program option), Pentax K1000 (fully manual), Canon AE1 (semi-automatic/manual), Olympus OM10 (semi-automatic, with manual function if a 'manual adapter' is fitted), Minolta X300 (semi-automatic/manual), and Praktica MTL50 (manual only). Each SLR marque (i.e. Canon, Olympus, etc.) has its own set of lenses that cannot be interchanged with another; so, for example, a Canon lens cannot be used on a Pentax camera.

A guide to the SLR camera body

Although there are many different types of SLR camera body, they have many universal features. Figure 2.4, on the previous page, shows two SLR cameras with the main features labelled. The following is an explanation of these features.

Shutter release: Your finger should rest here, as this is pressed to take the photograph. This button also serves as a trigger for the metering system, and to set the exposure you should only half-press it.

Self-timer: A time-delay device that trips the shutter after about ten seconds. It was primarily designed for family portraits where the photographer wishes to be included, yet it can also be used as an alternative to a cable-release for shake-free pictures.

Film wind-on lever: After the picture has been taken, you will need to operate this lever to wind the film onto the next frame and recock the shutter. If your camera is fitted with a motordrive (see the section 'Camera and Lens Accessories') then this lever becomes redundant.

Film rewind crank: Once the film is finished, it has to be rewound into its canister for processing. Unless this part of your camera is automatic, you will have to wind this round when the film is finished. Before doing this, you will have to release the film from tension, by pressing the film release button (normally marked with an 'R') located on the bottom of the camera.

Shutter speed dial: One of the most important parts of the manual camera. This is used to alter the amount of time the shutter remains open, and speeds typically range from 1/2 000sec to 'bulb' (see Glossary).

Aperture ring: Although attached to the lens, this is another important dial. This controls the amount of light that hits the film, and the f-stops normally range from f2.8 to f22.

Some lenses are available with higher f-stops (up to f0.95), and the smallest aperture is theoretically f∞ (infinity).

Frame counter: This registers the number of frames taken on the film.

Red dot: Although it may look insignificant, this mark helps you to locate where to mount the lens. Each lens should have a similar red dot, and you should align the two to mount the lens properly.

Film speed dial: Each film has a different sensitivity to light, which is measured in ASA/ISO and called 'film speed'. This dial is used to program the speed into the camera's metering system. Most cameras nowadays do not feature this dial, as they use a system called DX coding, which allows the camera to automatically 'read' the film speed off the cartridge itself.

Flash hotshoe: This is a mounting point for the electronic flashgun, although various other accessories can be mounted in its place.

PC socket: This is an alternative flash connection, and is primarily used for connecting studio flash.

Lens release button: When you want to change lenses, this button releases the lens from the camera. If your camera takes M42 non-bayonet screw-in lenses, you will not have one of these.

Focusing ring: Use this to alter the focusing distance of the lens.

Stop-down lever: The lens aperture remains fully open at most times, allowing the viewfinder to be at its brightest for easy focusing. When you want to see the effect the aperture has on depth of field, push this button, and the aperture will stop down (close).

Figure 2.5
The Nikon F4: a big professional camera, featuring a built-in motordrive

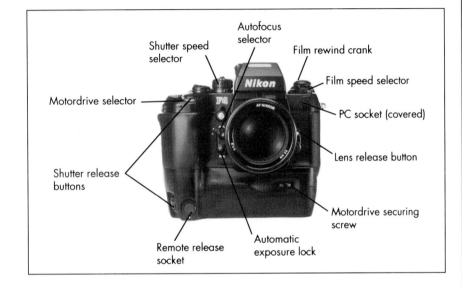

Figure 2.6
The Canon EOS 5 is a typical example of the modern SLR. It features smooth lines, a built in motordrive and a pop-up flash

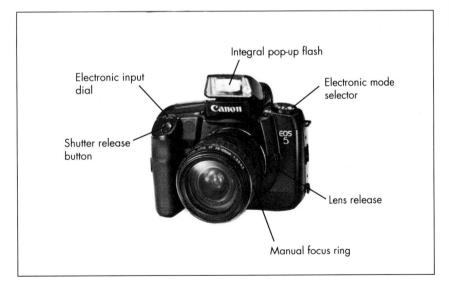

The cameras in Figure 2.4, on page 27, illustrate how the SLR has looked for nearly 35 years; yet there are many variations on the theme, with buttons and LCD displays replacing the old levers and dials. Figures 2.5 and 2.6, above, show two alternative SLR cameras that are very different from the 'traditional' SLR shape!

29

Using an SLR camera manually

Learning to use an SLR manually is perhaps one of the most important things when starting off in photography. Although many SLRs available nowadays can be used as 'point and shoot' cameras (making photography a lot easier for the beginner), it is still worthwhile to know how to use an SLR manually, as it gives you the rudiments of exposure control. This knowledge will serve you well in tricky metering situations, where automatic cameras will be fooled into taking under or overexposed shots.

The main principle of photography is to expose a piece of light-sensitive celluloid film to light, using a lens to focus the rays sharply. However, the film must be exposed for the correct amount of time according to its sensitivity, otherwise it will be overexposed (the resulting photograph will appear too light), or underexposed (the resulting photograph will be too dark).

To control the amount of light that reaches the film, the photographer has to balance two variables: shutter speed and aperture. The first governs the amount of time that the film is exposed to light, while the second controls the amount that actually reaches the film. Therefore, the less light that the aperture allows through (the higher the number on the aperture), the slower the shutter speed needs to be. The relationship between aperture and shutter speed is variable, as the combination for correct exposure depends on the brightness of the light and the speed of the film.

A manually controlled camera has a light-sensitive cell that measures the average EV (brightness) of the scene being photographed, and then translates this into a shutter speed/aperture combination that must be set by the photographer. For example, for an EV of 0, the shutter speed/aperture combination (at 100 ASA) must be 125 sec at *f5.6, and the combination can be altered accordingly i.e. 60 sec f8 or 250 sec f4).* Although the shutter speeds and apertures vary, the amount of light reaching the film is constant.

Figure 2.7
The 'match needle' viewfinder from the Pentax K1000

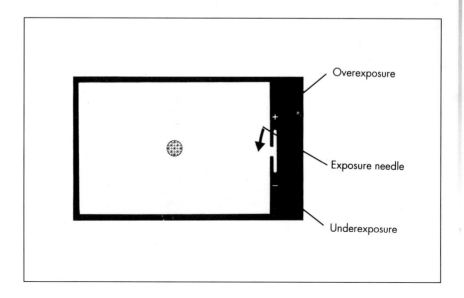

The fully manual camera uses one of two methods to illustrate the correct exposure: Figure 2.7 shows the 'match needle' type, while Figure 2.8 shows the flashing LED viewfinder.

With the first method, you have to turn the aperture or shutter speed dial to place the needle in the centre of the exposure indicator. Anything above this towards the '+' sign indicates overexposure, while anything below (towards the '−') signifies underexposure. LEDs are more sophisticated, as the full range of shutter speeds is shown, with the speed set on the camera dial flashing. The shutter speed recommended by the camera is shown by a non-flashing LED, and to achieve correct exposure you have to align the two by altering either the shutter speed or aperture. Should you wish to deliberately over-or underexpose for effect, then the manual camera is ideal for doing this.

Most cameras (even those with the latest autofocus programs) can be used manually, although the method of viewfinder display is often different from the older versions described above. If you have any doubt, consult the camera's instruction manual, which in most cases is clear to follow.

Using the semi-automatic camera

The semi-automatic camera is the next step up from the all-manual version, as you only have to set one of the two variables (shutter speed and aperture) manually. The camera automatically sets the other to achieve correct exposure. The semi-automatic system is called either shutter priority or aperture priority, depending on which variable you have to set yourself.

Some cameras are able to offer shutter priority and aperture priority modes, although it is normal for just aperture priority to be available on a semi-automatic camera. Aperture priority is deemed to be more important, as changing the aperture allows the photographer to control depth of field (explained on page 40). Shutter priority should be selected for the occasions where you want to freeze fast action using a

Figure 2.8
The flashing LED viewfinder from the Pentax P30n

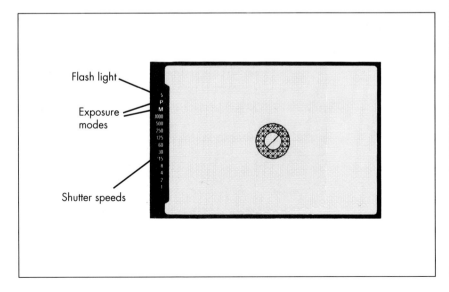

fast (high) shutter speed, or for where you want to creatively blur a subject by setting a slow shutter speed.

With shutter priority cameras, it is vital that you set the aperture on the lens to the 'A' (automatic) mark, or, if your lens does not have this, to the smallest aperture possible (the greatest number), which is probably something like $f22$. This is so that the lens can stop down to the required aperture automatically.

Using a program camera

The program camera sets both the aperture and shutter speed automatically, leaving you completely free to concentrate on your subject. Most program cameras also allow you to set semi-automatic and manual modes, so you get the best of all worlds. Like the semi-automatic camera, for the program function to work properly, the lens aperture must be set to either 'A' or its highest number.

One disadvantage of using a program camera is that you have no direct control over what aperture and shutter speed combination the camera selects. This can mean that you have more depth of field than you wanted, or the shutter speed may be too slow.

Fortunately, camera manufacturers have come up with a 'program shift' function, that allows you to change the shutter speed/aperture combination together, thus arriving at the correct exposure, but with the shutter speed or aperture you require.

The autofocus program camera

Most college or university cameras have manual focus, which means that you have to focus the image yourself using the focusing ring. However, modern technology and demand has resulted in cameras that can focus themselves, and it is rare for new cameras *not* to have autofocus nowadays.

In the viewfinder of the autofocus camera, there is a target-like box which is the focusing window. Place the subject you want in focus over that window, and then depress the shutter button halfway down to set the autofocus into motion. The subject should snap instantly into perfect focus, leaving you to just take the picture.

Most autofocus SLRs have two autofocus modes: focus lock and AF servo. With focus lock, the camera focuses on the subject you have placed over the focusing window, and will keep it in focus for as long as the shutter button remains down. With AF servo selected, the camera will change focus (if it needs to) for as long as the shutter button remains depressed. This mode is particularly useful for moving subjects, such as a car coming towards a stationary camera; although it can be irritating if selected when you don't want it.

Autofocus, despite being very sophisticated, is not foolproof. The system works by sensing the differences in contrast on a subject within the focusing window, and alters the focus until it 'sees' contrast at its clearest. Therefore, subjects with little contrast (such as smooth white wall) will be impossible for the camera to focus on. If this happens, switch to manual focus and do it yourself, or alternatively try and find some contrast in the frame (which may be, in the case of our wall, a bit of ivy growing up it, or a shadow that has been thrown onto it). Other problem areas include photographing through windows (the camera tries to focus on the reflections on the window) and in low light situations. If there is a problem and you cannot focus, just switch to the manual option.

Compact cameras

Since the end of the 1970s, compact cameras have become the most popular type of camera available. Small and easy to use, they can be useful for catching candid portraits or for taking record shots at recces. Many professional photographers have a compact in their camera bags 'just in case', as the fully automatic setting will allow you to take a photograph literally seconds after you have put it up to your eye.

Most modern compact cameras feature autofocus, which operates in a similar way to that of autofocusing SLR cameras. Position the AF 'window' in the viewfinder (normally a square or circle) over the subject you want to be in focus, and the camera will do the rest. Should the subject be out of the camera's range, then most will not take the picture until you have recomposed the shot.

If you are photographing a scene where the main subject is not over the AF window, you will need to use the 'focus lock' facility to ensure that the subject is in sharp focus. To do this, position the main subject over the AF window, and gently push the shutter button half-way down so that the green AF light illuminates. Once this has been done, keep your finger on the button and reframe the shot to how you want it to be, and take the picture. Providing the green AF light remained on while you recomposed, then the main subject will be correctly focused. If you fail to use the focus lock, then the camera will normally focus on the background, leaving your subject hopelessly out of focus.

Medium-format cameras

Figure 2.9
The Bronica ETRSi, shown here with waist-level viewfinder, 120 film back and 75mm standard lens

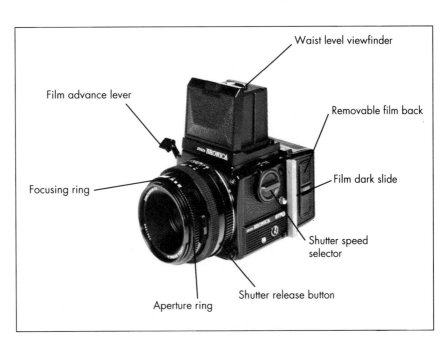

Waist level viewfinder

Film advance lever

Removable film back

Focusing ring

Film dark slide

Shutter speed selector

Aperture ring

Shutter release button

These cameras (see Figure 2.9) take 120 or 220 roll film that is significantly larger than 35mm. Their main use is in the studio, although some professional photographers use them on location when large-scale reproductions are required from the original picture.

Because the resulting negative/transparency is a lot larger than 35mm, transparencies are a lot easier to view with the naked eye, and negatives can be used for larger enlargements at the printing stage. Most medium-format cameras are manual or semi-automatic, and are able to accept interchangeable lenses. The focal lengths of the lenses are also different to those for 35mm film, with the equivalent to the 28mm wide angle being 45mm; 50mm standard, 75mm; and 135mm medium telephoto, 180mm.

Because medium-format cameras are generally heavier than their 35mm counterparts, use of a tripod is recommended.

Large-format cameras

These cameras produce very large transparencies/negatives, normally with a dimension of 5×4 or 10×8 inches. They tend to be the preserve of specialist professional photographers, and are particularly useful for producing clear, outsize prints for billboard posters.

Large-format cameras feature bellows to focus the image on the photographic plate at the back of the camera. The two sections at either end of the bellows can be moved out of line to alter perspective or create long-reaching depth of field. Large-format cameras can only be set manually, and simply cannot be used without the use of a tripod.

The future: still video and photo CD

Several attempts have been made over the past few years to usurp film as the main medium for taking photographs. So far, however, the printed image produced by a still video camera (Figure 2.10) is not of sufficient quality to be a real threat to celluloid film, although some

Figure 2.10
Is this the shape of things to come? The still video Canon Ion

newspapers have already started to use still video to input photographs directly into their page layout computers, thereby bypassing the darkroom and development stages. Still video stores all the images taken on disk, and photographs can be rejected and erased over with ease. This prevents any possibility of waste, and makes economic sense for professionals who take a lot of shots.

Computers can be used to manipulate photographic images, and are even displacing some techniques that used to be the preserve of the darkroom. Photographs can be made darker, lighter and sharper; they can be manipulated to erase certain objects, and the computer can even combine several images into one. One famous example of a computer being used to manipulate an image was devised by a German magazine, which placed a photograph of Princess Diana's head on the image of a naked woman, and used it as a cover shot. The final image was so convincing, that many people thought that the magazine had somehow acquired an exclusive nude photograph of the princess.

To counter the attack from still video, Kodak launched 'Photo CD', a process that transfers photographs taken on ordinary 35mm film onto a compact disk. The disk can be placed in a special player, and images can be recalled onto the screen at the touch of a button. We shall talk in Chapter 6 at further length about electronically scanning photographs or diagrams and the increasing use of photography in multimedia applications.

The Lens

Figure 2.11
Lenses come in various shapes and sizes

Some photographers suggest that the lens is the most important part of a photographer's equipment – the camera is just a light-proof box for holding the film. Lenses are available in a variety of shapes and sizes (Figure 2.11), and will drastically alter the angle of view that is projected onto the film in the camera.

Choosing the right lens is very important, as the same subject will look very different depending on which lens you use. Figure 2.12 shows a series of shots taken with a variety of different lenses, and demonstrates how angle of view can alter the effectiveness of an image. To keep the subject the same size in the frame, the photographer had to move back as he changed lenses, otherwise the magnification effect of the telephoto lenses would have cropped in too close to the subject.

Figure 2.12
A series of shots taken with different lenses

a 15mm fish-eye lens

b 20mm lens

c 28mm lens

d 35mm lens

e 50mm lens

f 85mm lens

g 100mm lens

h 135mm lens

i 200mm lens

j 300mm lens

k 400mm lens

l 600mm lens

The 35mm SLR camera is the most versatile photographic tool, as there are a large number of interchangeable lenses available, allowing it to be used for almost any photographic situation. Each lens has its own focal length (measured in mm) that alters the angle of view.

The higher the focal length, the narrower the angle of view, which results in a magnification of image. Wide angle lenses have a short focal length and a wide angle of view; while telephoto lenses have a long focal length, and a narrow angle of view. See Figure 2.13 to compare the angle of view taken from the same position with a 28mm wide angle lens and a 600mm super telephoto lens.

Figure 2.13a
Photograph taken with a 28mm lens

Figure 2.13b
Photograph taken from the same position with a 600mm lens

Lenses with variable focal lengths (e.g. 28–70mm) are known as *zoom lenses*, and are particularly useful if you don't want to carry a lot of equipment around with you. Lenses of just one focal length (e.g. 28mm) are known as *prime lenses*, and normally have wide apertures to let lots of light in. Lenses with wide apertures (anything less than *f*2.8) are known as *fast lenses*.

Wide angle lenses (7.5–35mm)
These lenses allow you fit a lot into the frame, thanks to their large angle of view. They tend to exaggerate perspective when used to photograph a subject close up, and offer very deep depth of field. Lenses with a focal length of less than 28mm will distort subjects placed around the outside of the frame, so be aware of this when you are using a 'super wide angle' lens.

The ultimate wide angle lens is the *fish eye*. This lens offers an incredible 180° of coverage, but has very significant distortion (see Figure 2.14, page 38) that can be used for effect. Although the fish eye lens can produce some spectacular images, you must be very careful not to overuse the effect. One or two fish eye photographs in a portfolio of 25 images is okay, but the novelty of fish eye distortion

Figure 2.14
A fish-eye lens converts
straight lines into curves

soon wears off. Fish eye lenses are expensive to buy, although a cheap alternative is the fish eye converter, which screws into the front of a 28mm lens, giving a fish eye effect.

Some photographers regard the 28mm wide angle lens as a 'standard' lens, as it is particularly good for shooting subjects at close quarters. Use wide angle lenses for shooting photographs in a crowded room, or for when you want the viewer to feel really close in with the action.

The 'standard' lens (50mm)

The 50mm (or standard) lens has an angle of view that is roughly approximate to the human eye. Up until the mid-1980s, it was normal for a camera to be sold with this lens; nowadays, the cheaper price and improved performance of zoom lenses have displaced the 50mm as the most widely purchased lens.

All 50mm lenses have fast maximum apertures (up to $f1.0$ on the incredible Canon 50mm $f1.0$L), that allow you to take photographs in low light conditions. However, depth of field is reduced, and the 50mm's angle of view is relatively narrow when compared to the 28mm. Professional photographers rarely use them, and you may find them awkward to use, especially indoors.

Telephoto lenses (85–2 000mm)

Telephoto lenses are available in a huge variety of focal lengths, and their purchase price spirals upwards as the focal length increases. As telephotos have a narrow field of view, longer focal lengths (300mm and above) magnify distant objects in the frame, although depth of field reduces substantially.

Most telephoto lenses above 300mm have relatively slow maximum apertures, thanks to optical constraints in their construction. Fast long telephotos (like the 600mm *f*4.5 – see Figure 2.15) are extremely bulky lenses to use, and you must use a camera support to minimise camera shake. Prices for these lenses run into thousands of pounds, so it is unlikely that your college or university will have one. The resource list at the end of this book lists some shops that have exotic lenses for hire.

Special lenses for special purposes

To cater for the demand to see what the eye cannot, lens manufacturers have designed several lenses that can be used for special situations.

The *macro lens* is used to photograph subjects such as insects, flowers and stamps at close range. Coupled with an extender or bellows (see 'Camera and lens Accessories', below), the macro lens allows you to fill the frame with the smallest of objects, although care must be taken with lighting.

Tilt and shift lenses allow you to correct the distortion often caused when pointing wide angle lenses up at tall objects. The front elements can be moved through several degrees to allow the converging lines of, say, a building to be straightened out so that they are parallel. This lens is used extensively by estate agents and architects.

Catodioptic or *mirror lenses* are compact and light long telephoto lenses that make use of mirrors to give clear telephoto images. The aperture is always fixed (normally at *f*8), as it is technically impossible to fit a variable aperture. Light levels can be controlled by using neutral density filters (see 'Filters' below), and highlights in the frame form distinctive 'doughnut-shaped' rings, allowing you to always spot when a mirror lens has been used (see Figure 2.16).

Figure 2.15
A super-telephoto lens: the Canon 600mm *f*4.5

Figure 2.16
Note how out-of-focus highlights create 'doughnut rings' when using a 500mm mirror lens

Aperture

As mentioned earlier, the aperture is an adjustable iris that is used to control the amount of light that enters the camera. Situated near the camera body, the aperture ring lists the *f*-stops available, and this is adjusted in click stops. *f*-stops range from *f*1.0 to *f*32, although most lenses range from *f*3.5 to *f*22.

The higher the number on the aperture, the less depth of field you will have in your photograph. However, you will probably often have to use high *f*-stops to allow plenty of light into your camera; otherwise the corresponding shutter speed may be too low, resulting in camera shake.

Depth of field

Depth of field is one of the key disciplines to learn about photography, and can be used to great effect. Depth of field is a term used to describe the 'zone of focus' in the frame: that is to say, the furthest distance that something is in focus, to the nearest distance it isn't blurred. The lower the *f*-stop you use, the longer your zone of focus will be (see Figure 2.17).

Figure 2.17
The effect of aperture on depth of field

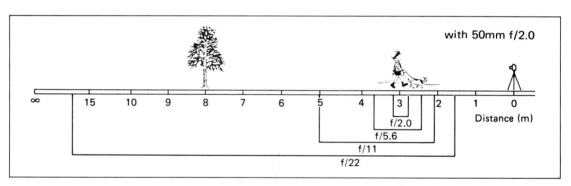

Figure 2.18a
Portrait taken with a 135mm lens at *f*2.8

Depth of field decreases with telephoto lenses, so a subject photographed at 3m with a 135mm lens at *f*8 will have a zone of focus that starts at 2.8m and ends at 3.2m (see Figure 2.18); while a 28mm wide angle lens focused at 3m set at *f*8 would have a zone of focus from 1.5m to ∞ (infinity). The wide angle lens' range of depth of field is noticeably longer than the telephoto.

Depth of field can be used to isolate your main subject from your background, and can conversely be used to make every object in the frame sharply in focus. It is tempting to shoot everything at full aperture for minimal depth of field, although you must make sure that everything you want in focus is. Some fast telephoto lenses when used at full aperture for portraits can result in the subject's eyes being in focus, while their nose is blurred. If in doubt, use the camera's 'stop down' lever that closes the aperture down, allowing to preview depth of field. However, with the aperture stopped down, light levels in the viewfinder drop, and it is unlikely that you will see things clearly. Never focus with the lens stopped down, as not only is it difficult to see the image clearly, depth of field will probably fool you into focusing wrongly to start with.

Most lenses have a depth of field scale situated near the aperture ring. This allows the photographer to check the precise area of depth of field, by reading off the distances near the appropriate aperture settings.

The lens hood

When shooting directly into the sun, it is quite likely that you will encounter 'flare' or haziness caused by the strong sunlight scattering in the lens. One way to avoid this is to use a lens hood that clips in front of the lens to cast a shadow over the front element, thereby shading sunlight from the lens. Make sure that you have the right lens hood for

Figure 2.18b
The same portrait taken at *f*8; note how the background becomes sharper

your lens, as incorrect ones will cause vignetting which will ruin your photography completely.

If you haven't got a lens hood, then position your hand to cast a shadow over the front of the lens, and stop flare. However, be careful not to get your hand in shot, and make sure that having a hand waving around in front of you doesn't cause camera shake.

Flash

At its simplest, a forward-facing, camera-mounted flashgun will produce a good, even burst of light to bring subjects out of the dark. More complex flash set-ups will include multi-flash studio work, or using Through The Lens (TTL) metering to balance flash with daylight.

The flashgun is a very important piece of kit to have, as it is like having your own instant source of daylight completely at your command. If you intend to do any amount of photography indoors, a flash is absolutely essential, and it should be the most powerful one you can get your hands on. A flash's power is measured by its 'guide number'. The higher the guide number, the more powerful the flash.

Like the camera itself, there are various types of flash: the fully manual, the semi-automatic (thyristor), the fully automatic (TTL), or a combination of all three. Flashes come in a variety of shapes and sizes, and may or may not have a bounce/swivel head. They can either be powered by conventional batteries or nickel cadmium battery packs, and may sit directly on the camera hotshoe or off to the side on a bracket as 'hammerhead' flashes, pictured in Figure 2.19.

Figure 2.19
A Metz CL4 hammerhead flashgun

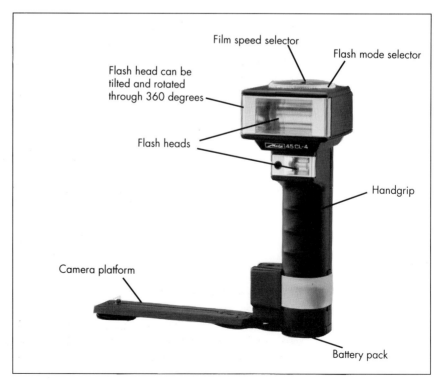

Using a flash manually

Like manual camera operation, setting a flash manually is very easy; it just takes up valuable time fiddling with the various dials and charts. If you flash is totally manual, it will feature a distance/aperture/film speed chart (see Figure 2.20) that you are supposed to consult to set the flash for the correct exposure.

Figure 2.20
Distance/film speed/aperture chart from a manual flash

ASA	DIN	m: 0.8 / ft: 2.5	m: 1.2 / ft: 4	m: 1.6 / ft: 5	m: 2.4 / ft: 8	m: 3.2 / ft: 10	m: 4.8 / ft: 16
50	18	f8	f5.6	f4	f2.8	f2	f1.4
100	21	f11	f8	f5.6	f4	f2.8	f2
200	24	f16	f11	f8	f5.6	f4	f2.8
400	27	f22	f16	f11	f8	f5.6	f4

First, set the camera to its correct flash synchronisation speed, by turning the shutter speed dial around to 'X' or 1/60sec. Most modern cameras have faster synchronisation speeds than 1/60sec, although manually operated cameras normally tend to have a flash sync. Speed of no more than 1/60sec.

Using the distance reading from the focused lens, set the appropriate aperture according to the film speed/distance combination. For example, with the chart in Figure 2.20, a subject at a distance of 3m, taken with 100 ASA film, would demand an aperture of $f2.8$ for it to be correctly exposed. A higher aperture than this would result in overexposure, while a smaller aperture would mean an underexposed and disappointing result.

If your flashgun doesn't have a manual exposure chart, then you can work out the correct aperture by using the simple formula:

$$\frac{\text{guide number (adjusted for ASA of film)}}{\text{distance between flash and subject}} = \text{aperture}$$

For example, if the guide number of your flash with 64 ASA film is 160, and your subject is 3m (10ft) away, then the correct aperture to be set is $f16$.

The semi-automatic thyristor system

This system has a sensor, built into the front of the flash, that measures the light reflected back from the subject being photographed to govern exposure. Simply set the film speed of the film you are using on the movable chart, and then read off the aperture needed for the required zone of exposure; the flash will do all the rest.

Figure 2.21
A semi-automatic flash chart

Automatic *f-stop* settings

Film speed	ASA	25	64	100	200	400	800
	DIN	15	19	21	24	27	30
YELLOW mode		1.4	2.5	2.8	3.5	5.6	8.0
RED mode		2.0	3.5	4.0	5.6	8.0	11.0
BLUE mode		4.0	6.7	8.0	11.0	16.0	22.0
PURPLE mode		5.6	9.5	11.0	16.0	22.0	32.0

Automatic operating ranges:

YELLOW mode	5ft to 43ft (1.5m to 13m)
RED mode	4ft to 30ft (1.2 m to 9m)
BLUE mode	2ft to 15ft (0.6m to 4.5m)
PURPLE	2ft to 11ft (0.6m to 3.4m)

Figure 2.21 shows a typical semi-automatic flash gun chart. Say we were using the camera and flash at a party (with 100 ASA film), where no one would be further away than 4.5m while being photographed. Before photographing, simply set the flash sync. speed (see above) and the appropriate aperture (in this case the 'blue mode' and *f*8), and you will not need to alter it at all for as long as you stay within the minimum and maximum range of the flash (in this case 0.6–4.5m).

Through the lens flash control

To take advantage of the benefits offered by TTL flash metering, you will need a camera and flashgun that are capable of TTL metering. Cameras with TTL flash metering measure the amount of light hitting the film during the exposure, and turn the flash off once enough light has entered the camera. This results in perfectly exposed flash pictures with little user effort.

TTL flash is particularly useful for daylight fill-in situations, as it allows you to balance flash exposure with the background. Fill-in flash is normally used to balance dark foreground subjects with bright backgrounds (see Figure 2.22), and can be used, for example, to remove harsh facial shadows in portraits.

If your flash has a TTL mode (and your camera can accept TTL flashes), you can use it to balance the flash with the background. First, take a meter reading from the background with the flash switched off. You should then manually set the camera with this shutter speed/aperture combination and switch on the flash. Providing your main subject is within the flash's range, the flash will automatically calculate the exposure necessary. A few TTL flashes have a red or orange 'exposure OK' light that comes on after the picture has been taken, to confirm that everything was correctly exposed.

Bounce flash

Direct flash photographs, although correctly exposed, can often look a bit harsh. The strong, cold beam from the flash tends to illuminate the foreground subject strongly, but leave the background in the shadows. To overcome this, many flashguns have movable heads that allow you to direct the light away from the direction of the lens. This is known as *bounce flash*, and results in a softer, more uniform balance of light between foreground and background.

When directing the light away from the subject in this way, it is important that you bounce the light off something (preferably white). A low ceiling is recommended, although a reflector (see Figure 2.30, page 50) can also be used. Make sure that the item that you are using to reflect the flash off is white, as this gives the best reflectivity and 'natural' colour. Using a yellow wall or orange piece of paper will colour the reflected flash, and can be used for effect.

Setting the exposure for bounce flash is tricky, as you must take into account the increased distance that the light has to travel, as well as the reflectivity of the surface you are bouncing from (see Figure 2.23). TTL flashguns will work all this out for you automatically, but if you haven't got access to one of these, mentally work out the increased distance that the light has to travel and open the lens up two stops to allow for badly reflecting surfaces. The best angle for bounce flash is around 45°, and bounce flash should never be used for subjects further than 2.5m away.

Figure 2.23
Remember to take into account the increased distance the flash has to travel and the reflectiveness of the object being bounced from, when using bounce flash

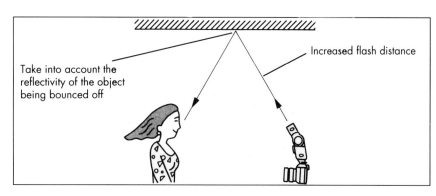

Take into account the reflectivity of the object being bounced off

Increased flash distance

Multiple flash

Occasionally you may want to use more than one flash to cover a wide subject that cannot be easily exposed by using one flashgun. There are several ways of approaching this, and we will deal with each separately.

■ You can connect the flashes together using extension cables that trigger each flash from the single camera hotshoe. When using this method, it is important to ensure that the cables are concealed from view, as a wide shot of a house interior will be ruined by black cables running everywhere. Remote flash leads can either be TTL (in which case the exposure will be worked out automatically), or just a simple trigger. With the latter, you will have to use a flash meter (see studio lighting on page 67) to work out the correct exposure, although you might like to experiment with using the automatic thyristor setting on your flash if you haven't got access to a flash meter. Providing all the flashes and the camera are set to the same aperture/distance setting, then the sensors in the flashguns should take care of exposure automatically, although bad connections can cause problems.

■ If your university or college hasn't got remote flash cables, another way of firing many flashguns simultaneously is by using *slave units*. These are photoelectric cells that sense when the master flashgun has fired, and then set off the flashgun to which they are connected. Slave units are particularly useful for situations where cables cannot be concealed, although you must make sure that the slave unit is in a position where it can sense the master flash. Exposure is calculated in the same way as above.

■ If you've only got one flashgun, it is possible to simulate multiple flash using the automatic sensor on the flash. Set the camera up on a tripod, with the aperture set to the automatic distance setting (normally $f5.6$). Hold the shutter open for around 30sec (using a cable release and the 'bulb' setting), and move around your subject firing the flash at the appropriate places using the flash 'test' button. This is known as 'painting', and providing you are not wearing bright clothes and move quickly, you will not register on the film.

Before using this technique, you must make sure that your flash and camera are set correctly, and that the subject is dark enough not to be overexposed by a long shutter speed. Be careful not to stand still for too long in one place while in view of the lens, and do not obscure the path of the flash, otherwise your shadow will show up very clearly.

Camera and Lens Accessories

For most picture-taking situations, a camera body, a selection of lenses and a flashgun will be adequate. However, some situations call for specialist camera accessories that are vital for the success of the shot. Your university of college may not have all the items listed here, although many can be hired from camera hire shops for a nominal charge. Consult the Resource section at the back of this book for a list of hire shops.

Tripods

This accessory should be seen as more of a necessity than a luxury. Tripods come in a variety of shapes and sizes, and as a general rule you should always use the heaviest and most sturdy version you can find. Some camera shops sell small plastic tripods that are next to useless, and if your tripod is fitted with a quick release head, make sure that it is solid when secured to the baseplate.

Always use a tripod made a by a reputable manufacturer: Manfrotto, Gitzo, Slik and Benbo are all tripods used by professional photographers, and they're all very sturdy. Most tripods feature three-dimensional heads that allow you to move the camera to any angle for that perfect shot. Some versions also have legs that spread out to allow you to do tripod-mounted low angle shots.

If you cannot manage to take a full-size tripod along with you on a shoot, try and take a mini 'table-top' tripod instead (Figure 2.24). This small camera support can be slipped into your camera bag very easily, and will probably prove to be invaluable for getting shots that would have otherwise been ruined by camera shake.

Figure 2.24
A useful accessory to have in your camera bag: a tabletop tripod

The monopod

When using long telephoto lenses, you must be extra careful to avoid camera shake from ruining a picture (see 'Tips for good photography', below). Professional photographers on location normally use an extendable monopod (see Figure 2.25) to rest the lens and prevent camera shake.

Monopods can also serve as 'camera poles' when used in conjunction with a remote control. After attaching the camera firmly to the monopod, you can raise it above your head for high angle shots, or hold it down over water for low angle shots that would be impossible without getting wet.

Figure 2.25
The extendible monopod will help prevent camera shake with telephoto lenses

The camera bag

Your college or university will probably have a camera bag to carry all your SLR kit around with you, without which lenses can easily become damaged or stolen. When choosing a camera bag, make sure you select something that sits comfortably on your shoulder: you may be carrying its weight for a considerable amount of time. Specialist manufacturers like Billingham, Fogg and Camera Care Systems all produce well-padded, comfortable and waterproof bags, and we strongly recommend you use one of these to carry your expensive camera kit around with you.

47

Cable/remote release

Cable/remote releases allow the shutter to be fired without direct contact with the camera body. Before the advent of modern electronic cameras, all SLR cameras had a manual cable release socket into which the plunger-type of cable release could be screwed. By turning a nut, the cable release could be locked to keep the shutter open in the 'bulb' setting; it can also be used as a remote release to completely avoid camera shake while the camera is on a tripod.

Cameras made nowadays use an electronic switch to do the job of a cable release, and although they are more reliable, they are also much more expensive.

Cleaning kit and useful non-photographic accessories

It is vitally important that you keep your camera kit spotlessly clean at all times. Not only will dirty lenses impair the quality of the image, grit inside the aperture or underneath the focusing ring is likely to damage the lens. A typical cleaning kit to keep your camera in good condition will include: a blower brush, lens tissue, soft cloth for wiping camera bodies, lens-cleaning fluid, canned air under pressure and some cotton buds.

Never try cleaning the camera's shutter blinds or the mirror, as you are likely to damage them – leave it to a professional who is trained in the job. When cleaning a lens, you must be careful not to scratch the glass. To avoid this, only use optical grade lens tissue and fluid – you should never try wiping a lens with your jumper or handkerchief.

Other useful bits and pieces to take along to a photoshoot are: a pen, small notebook, gaffer tape, masking tape, pocket torch, a penknife and a set of jeweller's screwdrivers. You never know when you might need them.

The handheld meter and grey card

Before the days of through-the-lens metering, photographers had to use separate handheld meters to tell them what exposure to use. Nowadays, most metering systems are sophisticated enough not to need a separate meter, although there are times when the backup is useful.

Handheld meters (Figure 2.26) are more flexible than built-in metering systems, as they are capable of taking both reflected and incident light readings. A reflected reading is where the meter calculates the exposure from the light reflected off the subject (in a similar manner to most cameras), while an incident reading samples the light actually falling onto the subject through a translucent cover.

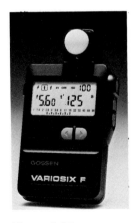

Figure 2.26
A handheld meter

To use a handheld meter in reflected light mode, set the film speed on the meter at the ASA rating for the film you are using, point the light-sensitive cell at the subject being photographed, look at the position of the needle, and read off the exposure from the dial. For incident readings, use the same procedure, but remember to slide the translucent dome over the light-sensitive cell. When taking an incident reading, remember to hold the meter in the same lighting conditions as your subject: it's no good holding the meter in shadow, if your subject is under the sun. Remember also that incident light readings do not take into account the subject's reflectivity. They are particularly useful, therefore, for photographing white or black objects.

The Kodak Grey Card is a sheet of thick card coloured 18% grey, which is the average reading that your camera's metering system uses to ascertain the exposure. When photographing bright or dark subjects, meter off a grey card to prevent your metering system being fooled by the high or low reflectivity of the object in frame.

Bellows and extension tubes

Even if you use a macro lens to get in close to your subject, it is unlikely that you will be able to get a better reproduction ratio than 1 to 1. If, however, you use an extension tube between your lens and the camera body, then it is possible to get extremely close to your subject.

Figure 2.27
The Canon FD bellows unit, fitted with an ML-3 ring flash

Extension tubes do not impair the image in any way, they simply allow you to magnify objects at close range by enormous proportions. A bellows unit (Figure 2.27) is like an extendable extension tube, as it allows you to precisely move the lens away from the camera body, and also focus at that exact point. Extension tubes limit you to just one close-up distance, while bellows can be positioned infinitely.

Ringflash

When photographing objects in macro, you are likely to be very close to the subject, which can mean that the camera's own shadow cuts down on the amount of light reaching the subject. To overcome this, a ringflash is positioned around the lens, to provide a direct shadowless light. Medical photographers make great use of the ringflash, as it enables them to photograph objects like teeth (Figure 2.28) with great ease.

Figure 2.28
Using bellows and a ring flash allows you to take photographs at very close quarters

Most ringflashes work automatically at a fixed aperture, although you may need to use a tape measure and work out the exposure manually.

Motordrives

Motordrives (Figure 2.29) bolt on to the camera to wind the film on automatically. Their frame speeds range from two frames per second (fps) to over 7fps on specially designed professional cameras. Some versions also feature an automatic film rewind mode as well.

Motordrives are far from an expensive luxury. Indeed, with certain types of photography (portraits, action photography and sport) they are an absolute necessity. Motordrives allow you to keep shooting without having to take your eye away from the viewfinder, and also allow you to record action that may be over in just a few seconds.

Figure 2.29
The Nikon F3 fitted with a high-powered removable motordrive

After the launch of the Canon T50 in 1984, built-in motordrives have become common in many modern SLRs. One disadvantage with this, however, is the lack of a manual film wind-on facility: what do you do if your batteries run out (always keep a spare set of camera batteries with you, just in case), or if you have to keep quiet?

Straps, lens caps and body caps

A good strap is very important for the photographer on the move. It should be comfortable to wear, and not dig into the neck or shoulder.

Try and keep the strap as short as possible, as this prevents the camera swinging about when you are running, or walking over difficult terrain. A short strap will also keep out of the way when using the camera on a tripod, and the Op-tech strap imported by New-Pro can be instantly detached through the use of secure quick-release clips.

To ensure that your lenses or camera body don't get damaged while they are sitting in your camera bag, always remember to fit front and rear lens and body caps. If your camera hasn't got any, try and get hold of some as quickly as possible, as it surprising how quickly lenses can get scratched when they are dirty.

The waterproof housing

Cameras and water don't mix, although there may be times when you want to get a shot below the waves; especially if you are a keen diver or snorkeller. To do this, use a special watertight housing that fits over the camera and lens to keep them dry.

Underwater light is very different from that on the surface, and it is advisable to use a flash if you can. As flashes give out high voltages, it is imperative that your underwater housing is completely watertight. Set the flash to TTL (if your flash has it), although you may find that using the flash manually will give you better results under certain lighting conditions. Kodak also make a special slide film called Ektachrome Underwater, which virtually eliminates the excessive blue cast normally obtained with photographs taken underwater.

Reflectors

Figure 2.30
Three reflectors are being used here to bounce light back onto the subject, although she is adopting a somewhat outdated pose

Figure 2.31
Although it looks cumbersome, the flash softbox allows you to take flash photographs without harsh shadows

The reflector is one of the most underrated pieces of photographic equipment available (Figure 2.30). A reflector is especially useful when shooting a subject positioned in shadow, as the reflected light will lift out your chosen subject from the gloom.

Most reflectors are available with double sides: one side white, with the other side gold or silver. Use gold for warm reflected light when shooting portraits, while silver should be used when you want the ultimate reflectivity. Reflectors are also useful for bouncing the light emitted from a flashgun.

The flash diffuser
As mentioned earlier, direct flashlight can be a little too harsh for some subjects, and a way of overcoming the problem, apart from bounce flash, is by using a flash diffuser or 'softbox' (Figure 2.31).

These devices fit over the flash head, and spread the flash out over a wider area through diffusion. The resulting light is softer and less intense, and should be used for all indoor portraits taken using a flash.

Filters
A filter is a piece of optical grade glass or plastic that is placed in front of the lens to alter the image in some way. Filters are either square (which you hold in place using a special holder), or screw-in circular, and are available in a variety of different sizes.

If you have a lot of lenses with different diameter filter threads, it is worth using the large square type of filter, as otherwise you will have to buy several sizes of the same circular version. Square filters are available from Cokin, Lee Filters and Jessop, and you should always buy the large 'professional' versions, as these are more adaptable for a large variety of lenses.

Some long telephoto lenses have lens diameters that are too big to accommodate even the largest square filters, and in this case, you will probably be able to use specially made drop-in filters that fit into the lens body. Unfortunately, graduated, polarising and effects filters are not available in the drop-in type, and all 'drop-ins' are very expensive.

The various types of filter and their uses are listed below:

Skylight and UV filter
Skylight and UV filters have little effect on the image, and they should be attached to the lens at all times for protection. Say, for example, you dropped a lens accidentally. In most cases only the filter would be damaged, and it is a lot cheaper to replace a £20 filter than a £300 lens!

Skylight filters are coloured slightly pink, although there is little distinguishable difference between a photograph taken with and without the filter attached. UV filters cut the amount of ultraviolet (UV) rays entering the camera, and are especially useful for taking pictures at high altitude, where UV light can make things appear unnaturally blue and hazy.

Polarising filters

Like sunglasses with polarising lenses, polarising filters are particularly useful for removing unwanted reflections from glass and water (see Figure 2.32). They also make clear blue skies very blue, and darken colours under bright sunlight, giving them better contrast and saturation.

Most polarising filters consist of two lenses sandwiched together, and you should turn the ring furthest away from you to alter the amount of polarised light entering the camera. Polarising filters reduce the amount of light entering the camera by two stops, so if you are using a

Figure 2.32a
Note how the polarising filter cuts reflections from the surface of the water

Figure 2.32b
This is the same photo taken without a polarising filter

handheld meter, remember to open the aperture up two stops more than the meter suggests. If you are using the camera's meter, then this adjustment will be made automatically.

Two types of polarising filter are available: a linear version and a circular type. Generally speaking, linear polarisers should only be used for cameras with manual focusing, while circular polarisers are suitable for all cameras. Consult your camera's handbook if you have any doubt.

Graduated filters

Graduated filters are coloured for only half of the filter, and the colour gradually diminishes into nothing. These filters should be used to colour dull grey skies, or to add extra colour to an otherwise bland photograph. They were used extensively in the film *Top Gun* to colour skies pink, yellow and blue.

When using a graduated filter, set the correct exposure before putting the filter in place, as the darker area may fool the camera into overexposing your subject. Use graduated filters with care, as there is a danger of detracting from the photograph if the colour used is too extreme. Similarly, don't overuse them, as their effect will become repetitive if used too often.

Good colour graduated filters to have are: light blue, tobacco, dark grey, green and dark yellow.

Colour conversion filters

Although it is indistinguishable to the human eye, there is a vast difference between the colour of daylight and the colour of artificial lights. This is due to the difference in *colour temperature*, which is measured in °K (Kelvin). Natural daylight has a colour temperature of 5 400°K, and is predominantly blue, while tungsten artificial lights typically have a colour temperature of 3 200°K, and give off orange-coloured light.

Most types of photographic film are colour balanced for daylight, so if you use them under artificial lights, the resulting pictures will have an orange cast. Similarly, if you use a film balanced for tungsten light outside, the pictures will be very blue. To overcome this, you can attach a colour conversion filter over the front of the lens, and this will correct the colour temperature and balance. For daylight films used under tungsten lights, fit a dark blue 80A filter; for pictures taken outside with tungsten balanced film, use an 85B orange filter.

You should be aware that a colour correction filter reduces the amount of light entering the camera, so you will have to adjust the exposure by approximately one stop for correct exposure. If you are using the camera's built-in exposure meter, this adjustment will be made automatically.

Other colour conversion filters include the light blue 82A for balancing colour under a late evening sun, and the light orange 81A for correcting colour when daylight conditions are too blue. The FL-Day filter should be used to correct the green colour emitted by fluorescent light.

Effects filters

If you want to set up some really bizarre pictures, then you will probably want to use one of the variety of effects filters that are available. Like effects on video, you must be extremely careful not to overdo it, as some of the effects are quite clichéd. If in doubt, shoot one picture with the filter and one without. That way, you will at least end up with one usable shot.

Effects filters available include: *soft focus/fog filter* (that diffuses the light entering the lens, making the shot appear slightly out of focus and dreamy), *precut shapes* (that allow you to position a circle, star or keyhole over the image), *starburst filter* (that turns any highlights into 4, 6, 8 or 12 pronged stars), *centre spot clear* (that puts everything except a small circle in the middle into soft focus), and the *multiple image filter*.

With the multiple image filter, you can make it seem as though a person has an identical twin. Using the camera's 'multiple exposure' function (if fitted – consult your handbook), you place the filter over the lens, so that half of the image is obscured. After setting the camera manually without the filter in place (to ascertain the correct exposure), take the shot and then reposition the filter so that the other half of the image is obscured. Providing the camera doesn't wind on the film, you can then take the other half, so that the resulting image consists of the two halves joined. You must use a tripod with this filter to ensure that the background remains in the same place, and be careful not to overlap the two halves of the filter, which would result in an underexposed strip in the middle.

Close-up filters

Close-up filters allow you to take macro shots of small objects, without having to go to the expense of extenders or a bellows unit. The close up filter screws into the front of the lens, and magnifies the central part of the image by up to 4×. Exposure is not affected, so there is no need to carry out any exposure adjustments, although depth of field will be extremely shallow unless you use a small aperture.

Neutral density filters

Neutral density (ND) filters cut down the amount of light entering the camera, without altering the colour balance of the image. They are particularly useful for when you would like to use a slow shutter speed or large aperture (for blurring water or isolating a subject from the background, for example), but the lighting conditions and the sensitivity of the film will not allow it.

ND filters are available in several different strengths, the strongest of which is nearly visually opaque. You may find it useful to focus before attaching the filter, as the smaller amount of light entering the camera will make focusing difficult with the ND filter in place.

Filters for black and white

So far, all the filters we have been talking about have been suitable for both colour and black and white photography. However, there are some filters available that are exclusively designed for black and white work, and if used correctly will drastically alter the black, white and grey tones of the final print.

Red filters prevent any red light from entering the lens, so anything red will appear very light grey or white. When photographing someone with skin blemishes it is worth using a red filter, as this will remove all but the worst spots. Clear blue skies are darkened by the red filter, to the extent that they appear almost black, with white clouds providing a stark contrast. Many landscape photographers who shoot in black and white very rarely take the red filter off their cameras.

Green filters should be used for photographing people, as skin will appear healthy and tanned with a green filter attached. A dark green filter is especially effective when shooting a portrait under tungsten lighting.

A *yellow filter* is used for a clear contrast between blue sky and landscape. Some photographers like to leave a yellow filter on their cameras permanently when using black and white film.

Orange filters increase the contrast between reds and yellows, so are particularly useful for sunsets and autumn scenes.

These coloured filters for black and white work can also be used with colour film for startling effects. As with all types of photography, don't be afraid to experiment.

Film

Film, of course, is vital for all photography, and it is important that you choose the right type of film for your choice of subject. For example, an exhibition for a local business would demand shooting on colour print film, so that the resulting pictures can be enlarged and displayed; while a slide/tape sequence for the same exhibition obviously requires shooting on transparency film.

Film is available in a variety of different sizes and formats (Figure 2.33), ranging from 24×36mm (35mm) to 10in by 8in (10×8). Most SLR cameras take 35mm film rolls, that are normally available in 12, 24 and 36 exposure lengths. The other commonly used format is 120 roll film, which is paper backed and can give from eight to 15

Figure 2.33
Fuji Velvia in the many different film formats

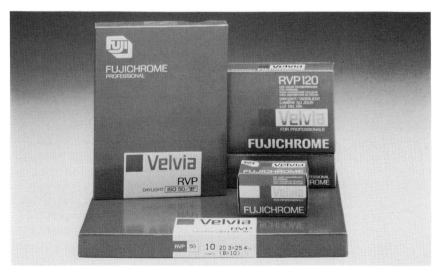

exposures depending on the frame size of your camera. 220 roll film gives double the amount.

A film's sensitivity to light is measured in ASA or ISO, and the higher the number, the more sensitive the film is to light (the 'faster' it is). Film speeds range from 6 to 50 000 ASA, although the normal range is 100, 200 and 400 ASA.

A film works by light-sensitive crystals forming after it has been exposed to light. The faster the film, the greater these crystals lump together, causing images that seem to be made up of thousands of little dots called 'grain'. As film speed increases, the photograph will become more grainy, and this can be used for artistic effect. Grainy photographs cannot easily be enlarged, as a large amount of grain will result in a print that is unclear.

Black and white (monochrome)

Black and white negative film was the most commonly used film up unto about 20 years ago, when its popularity declined among 'snappers', who prefer colour film. However, black and white film is still immensely popular amongst enthusiastic photographers, as, through the use of the darkroom, images can be manipulated to produce 'arty' photographs. Black and white darkroom work is relatively easy, and monochrome photography makes you think more about the use of light rather than colour, so trying your hand at black and white photography will teach you a lot about the importance of light and composition, as well as the intricacies of developing and printing your own photographs.

Black and white film is available in a huge variety of different speeds and formats, and we recommend using any of the following: Ilford Pan F Plus (25 ASA), Ilford Delta 100 (100 ASA), Ilford FP4 Plus (125 ASA), Kodak TMAX 100 (100 ASA), Ilford HP5 Plus (400 ASA), Ilford Delta 400 (400 ASA), Kodak TMAX 400 (400 ASA), Ilford XP2 (400 ASA), Fuji Neopan 1600 (1600 ASA), and Kodak TMAX 3200 (3200 ASA).

Ilford XP2 is an odd one on this list, as it is a black and white film that can be developed using colour C41 chemistry. This allows you to hand in your film to a 1h colour laboratory, and receive up to 36 6 × 4 sepia-toned proof prints an hour later. XP2's film speed can also be rated at up to 3200 ASA with very little decrease in quality. Altering the speed of a film is known as 'pull' or 'push' processing, and we shall talk about this in 'In the Darkroom', p. 71.

Colour transparency or slide film

Transparency film produces a positive on the film, so that pictures can be viewed without the need to produce prints. It is heavily used by professional photographers working for magazines, as the colours on transparency film are much better than print, and no colour balance or quality is lost through a secondary printing stage.

Transparency film is very easily under or overexposed, as the 'latitude' of the film is very small. Correct exposure is therefore very important, and you may like to 'bracket' your exposures. To do this, shoot several shots of the same scene with identical shutter speeds, but with the aperture set one stop above and below what the camera is suggesting. This way, you will have a selection of differently exposed shots to choose from.

Transparency films are available in professional and amateur versions, the difference being that professional films are guaranteed to be of the optimum colour balance, and should be kept in the refrigerator to keep that them way. Amateur films are cheaper, and do not need to be stored under 15°C.

Amateur transparency film is normally 'process paid'; in other words, you do not have to pay anything extra for the film to be processed, providing you use the film mailer supplied with the film. If you are in a hurry for the processing, however, you can use a professional laboratory, who will generally be able to process your film within a couple of hours, although the cost will be comparatively high.

Recommended films we use include: Kodachrome 25 (25 ASA), Fuji Velvia (50 ASA), Kodachrome 64 (64 ASA), Fuji Provia (100 ASA), Agfa CT 100i (100 ASA), Ektachrome Elite (100, 200 and 400 ASA), Fuji RHP (400 ASA), Kodak EES (800/1600 ASA). Choosing an ideal transparency film is difficult, as each of the above have their own particular colour balance and characteristics. As a general rule, Kodak slide films are generally more blue under daylight, while Fuji films (especially the remarkable Fuji Velvia) give superb results under bright light conditions. Try a few before shooting anything important so that you can develop your own preference.

Colour print

Colour print film is readily available, cheap and easy to get processed, although the quality is not as good as equivalent speed transparency film. Nevertheless, if you need a large quantity of general prints for an exhibition, you will need to use colour print film, as making prints from slides is expensive.

Unlike slide film, colour print film has a wide exposure latitude, so it is particularly good for use in tricky lighting conditions. It is also good for push processing, and prints are much easier to view than 35mm slides. Most high street photographic retailers or chemists offer an overnight or 1h developing service, although it is worth shopping around for the best quality of printing. If a colour print film is developed badly, the results can be terrible. Generally speaking, you get what you pay for ...

As print film is so widely used, there is a huge variety of makes, speeds and lengths of film available. Any film produced by Kodak, Fuji or Agfa will be very good, although it is worth trying out some of the 'own brands' of colour print film, as they are always made by big manufacturers. For example, Jessop colour print film is allegedly made by Agfa, while Boots' own brand film is supposed to be bought in from Fuji. For the ultimate print quality, try using any film from the Kodak Ektar range (25, 100 and 1 000 ASA) or Fuji's Reala (100 ASA). Remember, however, to have these high-quality print films developed at a good processing lab – the resulting prints will only be as good as the lab's printing abilities.

Specialist film

There are several types of specialist film available, and if used correctly, they will produce stunning and different results. The films we have listed are: Kodak HIE black and white infra-red film, Agfa Dia Direct and the variety of Polaroid instant films available.

Kodak HIE black and white infra-red film is one of those types of film that every enthusiastic photographer should try at least once (see Figure 2.34). Skies taken with infra-red film are deep black, foliage turns white and human skin takes on a pale 'glowing' appearance that looks slightly eerie.

The first thing to remember about using black and white infra-red film is that you cannot see the light that the film senses. Infra-red rays are undetectable by the human eye because they are beyond our visible colour spectrum. For this reason, you can never be 100% sure what the black and white tones in the final photograph will be like.

Figure 2.34
Infra-red film makes skies very dark black and turns grass white

The camera's light meter also cannot detect infra-red rays, so don't bother trying to use it when taking a photograph with Kodak HIE. Instead, try experimenting with exposure using the guidelines below, although it is worth bracketing a couple of stops either way to obtain a negative of the correct density.

- Bright sky, direct sunlight: 1/125sec *f*11
- Cloudy, yet still bright: 1/30sec *f*11
- Overcast, or open shade: 1/15sec *f*11
- Heavily overcast: 1/8sec *f*11

As you can see, these exposure times are unusual for the lighting conditions, and you should remember to use a tripod with the slower speeds: infra-red film is just as susceptible to camera shake as any other film.

Another 'must' with infra-red film is the use of a filter in front of the lens. You can use two types: a standard red filter (normally used for darkening skies with conventional black and white film), or a specially made infra-red filter, that can only be used for infra-red film. The latter is visually opaque, so you have to frame and focus before you attach the filter. You cannot use Kodak HIE without a filter, as the film will be badly fogged by blue light and the negatives will be unusable.

Apart from exposure and the need for a filter, infra-red film also needs care in focusing, as infra-red rays are not on the same wavelength as normal light, for which most lenses are corrected. Each lens's focus must be slightly adjusted to obtain sharp results. Most modern lenses have marks showing where you should adjust the focus on the lens. But if your lens has not got this feature, then just move the focusing dial so that the focus reading is slightly closer. For example, with the Canon FD 28mm *f*2.8, when the subject is 1m away, the adjustment needed for infra-red film shows the mark on the conventional focus scale at 0.8m. However, because the aperture being used is generally *f*11, depth of field will cover most focusing discrepancies.

Handling and developing infra-red film is fairly tricky, as you have to be careful of daylight fogging the film. The camera should be loaded in *absolute* darkness, so unless you have a portable changing bag, you cannot load or unload Kodak HIE out 'in the field'. Similarly, the film must be developed in a metal developing tank, because plastic ones tend to 'leak' infra-red rays, which are harmless to ordinary films. It is best to have infra-red film developed by a professional, and Jessop Photocentre offer a reasonably priced specialist infra-red developing service in their nationwide chain of photographic shops.

Agfa Dia Direct is the only black and white transparency film available, and many of the photographs taken in this book were shot with this film. Dia Direct can only be processed by Agfa in London, so the price of the film includes the processing cost. The film boasts very fine grain, as it is rated at an incredibly slow 12 ASA! This necessitates the use of a tripod for all but the brightest of light, and, as with all transparency films, correct exposure is critical. If you are intending to produce a slide/tape sequence including black and white pictures, then Dia Direct is the only slide film that you can use.

Polaroid is the only manufacturer of 'instant' films, and these produce 'proof prints' that are particularly useful for checking exposure and composition on location or in the studio. Available in 35mm, 120 and 5×4 versions, Polaroid instant films have to be developed using their own special chemistry, although they are available for inspection within a couple of minutes. 35mm Polaroid films have to be developed using a special wind-on device, while the larger format films have peel-off backs that start the development process. Pictures produced on Polaroid film are not really suitable for exhibition or publication, although they can be used to create unusual or bizarre prints.

Tips for Good Photography

Camera shake and how to avoid it

Camera shake is the photographer's worst enemy – it can ruin a photograph that would otherwise be perfect. Camera shake is caused when there is enough camera movement to show up in the final photograph, and this results in blurred and unsharp photographs.

One simple rule to overcome camera shake (apart from using a tripod) is to never use a slower shutter speed than the focal length of the lens in use. So, for example, a 50mm lens should never be used handheld at less than 1/60sec, while a 500mm should never be used with a shutter speed of less than 1/500sec.

Telephoto lenses are much more susceptible to camera shake, as their narrow field magnifies any movement that may already be there. Hold up and look through a 300mm lens for a minute – after that time you will probably find the view shaking all over the place. If possible, use some kind of camera support (a monopod, tripod or rifle grip) with telephoto lenses, rather than attempting to hold them by hand.

You will probably have to experiment to find out what the lowest shutter speed you can safely hand hold a lens at. You can generally handhold a 28mm lens without camera shake for up to 1/15sec, although anything lower than this will probably result in appalling camera shake.

Methods of metering

Correct exposure is vital for all photography, as incorrect exposure will ruin even the most precisely composed image. Some sophisticated 35mm SLR cameras feature several different types of metering mode (centre weighted average, partial and spot), although most only offer the facility for an average exposure reading.

Average exposure is satisfactory for most situations, although when your photograph contains a large proportion of sky or objects that are bright white or dark black (see Figure 2.35), the camera's metering system will be 'fooled' into over- or underexposing the picture. To obtain the correct exposure, you will either have to compensate for the camera's tendency to over- or underexpose (this needs a certain amount of experience), or rely on other methods to get you out of trouble.

One way to avoid badly exposed photographs is to use a separate handheld meter with an incident setting or a Kodak Grey Card (see

'Camera and Lens Accessories', above). However, if you don't have access to either of these bits of equipment, you will have to use the camera manually or operate the camera's 'exposure lock' feature.

When faced with a difficult metering situation, find an object that reflects an average level of light for the scene being photographed, take a meter reading from it, and either set the camera manually or use the camera's exposure lock feature (if fitted) to lock the exposure into its memory. Be careful not to take a reading in the shade if your subject is in bright light, and avoid metering off bright subjects like sand or a white wall.

Metering difficulties will also be encountered when shooting a subject that is strongly backlit – a portrait against a window, for example. In this case, you can either use fill-in flash (see 'Flash' above) or the exposure lock/manual setting as above. If your subject can be easily approached, fill the frame with a portion of the subject (a face, for example), and lock in the exposure that way. Alternatively, find an object of the same reflectivity under similar light, and meter off that.

As with all the techniques talked about in this book, there's no substitute for experience, and we recommend experimenting with average exposure and exposure lock/manual under typical tricky lighting situations as mentioned above. That way, you will gain the experience without having to worry about messing up the photographs for an important assignment.

Figure 2.35
The photographer had to meter off a grey card here to prevent the camera being fooled by the large expanse of white

Composition

Some people seem to simply 'have an eye for what looks good', and there is no doubt that good composition makes the difference between a good photographic image and an amateurish 'snap'. Take a look at some photographs that you find pleasing. Ask yourself why they look good: is it the colours; the shape of the objects in the frame; the patterns they produce? How would you have approached the same subject? Is there anything you would have added or taken away?

Figure 2.36
How would you improve the composition of this 'snap'?

Generally speaking, you can't really go too far wrong if you remember to fill the frame all the time. Take a look at the average 'snap' (Figure 2.36) – why did this photographer allow the subject to be so small in the frame? And why were the bottoms of his legs cut off? Note all that wasted space around the sides of the frame – wouldn't it have been much better if the photographer had taken the time to move in closer to their subject?

Another assured route to good composition is to think about what you've got in the frame, and weigh up the possible alternatives. Why not use a telephoto lens to compress the background, or a wide angle to get really close to your subject (see 'The Lens', above)? What would the picture look like taken from a higher or lower viewpoint? How can you make the image form interesting patterns? How can you use colour to the best effect? It may seem that all this thinking will take a long time, but once you begin to think about how you are composing a shot it'll soon become second nature to you.

Panning to show movement

Still photography is relatively ineffective at showing movement, unless you know what technique to use. Panning during a relatively slow exposure will result in the background being blurred, while the moving subject remains (fairly) clear, giving the impression of speed and fast movement (see Figure 2.37).

Figure 2.37
Although not completely sharp, this panning shot conveys a great sense of movement

You will probably have to experiment with the panning technique before you get good results, as it is fairly tricky to follow a fast-moving subject at a constant speed. The best results come from shooting with a telephoto lens (anything greater than 135mm), although as Figure 2.37 demonstrates, a wide angle lens can also be used for really dramatic shots. The shutter speed selected can range from 1/15sec to 1/60sec, depending on how easily you can hold a camera steady and how fast the subject is moving. As we've suggested before, practice before trying the technique out during an important shoot.

Picture-taking Situations

This section talks about typical photographic situations and how best to approach them. It talks about the lenses, film and accessories you should use, as well as tips to help you get better results when faced with that particular picture-taking situation.

Outdoor portraits

Few people really enjoy having their photograph taken, and it is up to you, the photographer, to put them at ease, and end up with the most natural and flattering shot possible. Talk to your subjects while you are photographing them; make them laugh; reassure them that the image you can see in your viewfinder is good, and, above all, appear competent. There's nothing worse for a nervous subject than a photographer who doesn't really seem to know what s/he is doing.

For flattering portraits always use a telephoto lens. Note how the portrait photographed in Figure 2.12 becomes more and more flattering as the focal length becomes longer and longer. However, be careful not to use too long a lens, as this will mean that you will be too far away from the subject to strike up a rapport. Of course, telephoto lenses do not have to be used all the time. A wide angle lens can be used to place more emphasis on the background (see Figure 2.39, on page 64), although be wary of venturing too close for fear of distorting the face.

Figure 2.38
Turning your subject at an angle to the camera, but having them turn their head towards you, creates a more interesting portrait than shooting head on

Portraits outdoors (Figure 2.38) are best shot with the subjects facing away from the sun, as this prevents them from having to squint, and the sun in their hair will create highlights (Figure 2.40) that are pleasing. Take care when shooting into the sun, as you may have to contend with flare and awkward metering situations. Where possible, situate yourself in shadow to avoid flare, and meter from the subject's face to get the best exposure possible.

For flattering portraits, it is best to position subjects at an angle of around 45°, turning their head so that they look over their shoulder at the camera (see Figures 2.38–40). Having your subject positioned square on to the camera will look awkward and unflattering, especially as you will have difficulty finding a body 'cut off' point that doesn't look silly.

When using a telephoto lens, use the widest aperture possible, giving you minimal depth of field to blur the background. Focus in on the eyes, as this is the most important part of the face, possibly even to the extent that part of your subject's hair isn't in focus, as in Figure 2.40.

Decide whether to shoot your portraits in black and white or colour – black and white often produces more flattering shots than colour. Soft focus filters and fill-in flash can also be used well, and a reflector (see 'Camera and Lens Accessories', above) is recommended to prevent too many harsh shadows.

Figure 2.39 'left'
Although telephoto lenses
are recommended for
portraits, wide-angle
lenses can often be used
effectively

Figure 2.40
Cropping in close to your
subject will often produce
a flattering picture.
Remember to use a wide
aperture for minimal
depth of field, and to
focus on your subject's
eyes

Group shots

Group shots are perhaps one of the most difficult photographs to
shoot, as you are in effect taking several portraits all at once. Tips for
good group shoots include the following.

1 Make sure that you are in control, which can be achieved by talking
   to the group as a whole.
2 Tell everybody when you are about to shoot, and shoot two in quick
   succession. This (hopefully) will prevent everyone from blinking at
   the same time.
3 Arrange the group so that is as narrow and deep as possible. Use the
   classic convention of 'tall ones at the back, small ones at the front'
   to make sure that everyone can be seen.
4 Shoot from a higher angle than your subjects, as this will make
   everyone seem as though they are of a similar height.
5 Make sure that everyone is holding their hands in the same way.
   There's nothing worse than a group photograph with three people
   with their arms folded, and the rest with their hands in their pockets.
6 Tell a joke to make everyone smile!

Action or sports photography

With action photography you will probably want to freeze the action still. This can be done by using as fast a shutter speed as possible. With an aperture priority camera this can be done by selecting the widest aperture the lens will allow. To get in close to the action, you will probably have to use a telephoto lens, so a fast film (say, 400 ASA) would be advisable. During the darker winter months, a film like Kodak Ektar 1000 may be necessary.

As well as freezing action, you can also pan with moving subjects to create interesting images (see Figure 2.37, page 63).

Shooting on location

You will probably have to shoot on location fairly often, and this necessitates taking all the right gear with you, including plenty of film and spare batteries. Always take more film than you think you will need, with a fair selection of film speeds just in case the lighting isn't quite what you expected. Spare batteries are always handy, as you can never be sure when your camera's power supply is going to let you down.

Depending on what you are shooting, take all the gear that you think you are likely to need, plus a few extras 'just in case'. Your camera equipment should be clean before you start a shoot, and cleaned immediately afterwards if you were shooting in a dusty or dirty environment. All your equipment should be carried in a comfortable camera bag, that also carries a notepad and pen/dictaphone, as well as the other bits and pieces mentioned on page 48.

The Studio

The photographic studio provides an ideal environment for complete control of lighting and background, and is particularly suited for still lifes and controlled portraits. Some studios use a mixture of daylight and artificial light, and there is no reason why you shouldn't convert a large room in your house into a temporary studio. All you need is the right equipment and a bit of knowledge.

Studio equipment

Many photographers use a tripod while in the studio, as not only does this allow them to frame their photographs accurately, it also provides a convenient rest for the camera while they make adjustments to the lighting or background. For really awkward positions, a G-clamp or camera mount can also be used. Nevertheless, don't feel chained to your camera support – if you feel that your tripod is getting in the way, lose it.

When using a studio, you will need to have a suitable background for the subject you are shooting. Manufacturers like Colorama and Lastolite make a wide range of background rolls, ranging from conventional portrait 'splatter' backgrounds, to coloured grids that can be used for effective product photography. A large roll of white paper (normally around 3m long) also provides an excellent background for all sorts of subjects and situations.

Other bits and pieces that are useful to have in a studio include:

reflectors (see 'Camera and Lens Accessories', above) gaffer tape, staple gun, Plasticine (for supporting objects in still life) and scissors.

Studio lighting

Artificial studio lighting is divided into two categories – tungsten photofloods and studio flash – that are both mains powered. Tungsten lights are cheaper and easier to use than flash, but they will soon get hot and are easy to break. Studio flash produces a consistent crisp light, although it can be difficult to view the effect the flash will have on the subject before taking the picture, due to the short burst of light flash gives out.

Whatever type of light you use, you will need to have holders and stands to support them, as well as a complement of reflectors and diffusers to control the output and intensity of the light given off. Figure 2.41 shows a variety of reflectors and diffusers, and you should experiment with them all before carrying out your first 'real' studio photographic shoot.

Figure 2.41
A variety of reflectors and diffusers for studio lights

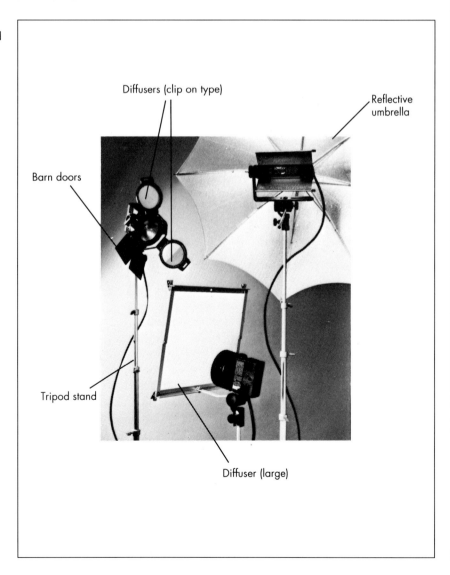

Lastolite reflectors (see Figure 2.30) are easy to bounce light off, and this results in a soft, even light that is particularly flattering. Aiming a light through a diffusing screen will give a similar effect. For studio flash photography, silver or white umbrellas are used to give off soft light, although an alternative is the large 'softlight', a lamp in a large reflective bowl that must be positioned near a subject to give almost shadowless light (see Figure 2.42).

Figure 2.42
The softlight is particularly suited for studio still-life work

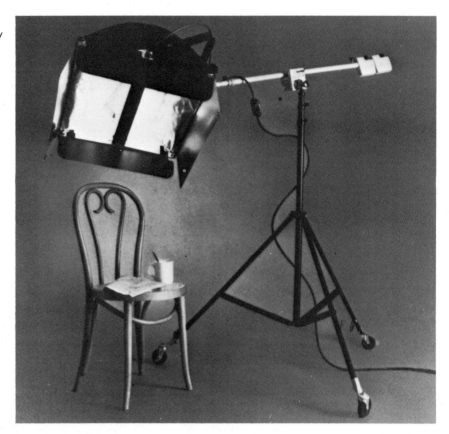

You will probably be using several sources of light in the studio, so care will need to be taken over metering. With tungsten lights, meter with all the lights in position and switched on. Take care that your camera isn't fooled into over- or underexposing with dark or light backgrounds, and it may be worth bracketing your exposures to get the best results. Most professional photographers in the studio use Polaroid instant film to check that everything is as it should be, and remember to place a blue filter in front of your lens if you are shooting under tungsten lamps with daylight film.

When using flash, you will need a separate flash meter to work out the correct exposure for the photograph. Place the flash meter in front of the subject facing the camera, and use a remote trigger to fire all of the flash heads at the same time. Make sure that the flash meter is set to the same ASA as the film in the camera, and then set the aperture as indicated by the meter. The camera's shutter should be set to the flash ('X') sync speed, which is normally around 1/60sec. Plug the main flash into the camera's flash PC socket (see Figure 2.4) to set it off when the shutter is pressed, and the other flash heads should be synchronised with leads or separate slave units (see 'Flash', above).

Typical lighting set-ups

As with all photographic disciplines, experimentation is the order of the day as far as studio lighting goes. Below we list a few of the conventional methods of shooting portraits and still lifes.

Lighting for *studio portraits* depends very much on the subject and style of photograph you are after. Figure 2.43 was shot with a single tungsten light aimed straight at the subject, resulting in very harsh, contrasty lighting. To prevent the shadows from being so harsh, the photographer could have bounced the light off a reflector, or used a diffuser to even the light off a little. The background was a simple piece of black cloth, and the subject wore a black top to isolate her hand and head.

Figure 2.43
This dramatic picture used just one direct light and a black background

Figure 2.44
A more typical studio portrait. A key light and a fill placed on either side of the subject provide an even and effective light

Figure 2.44 shows a photograph taken with a more conventional lighting set-up. It uses a reflector to fill in shadows on the opposite side to the light, although it is possible to use a secondary light source in place of a reflector. When using this method, care must be taken to balance the two lights, ensuring that the 'key' (main light) gives off a stronger light than the 'fill'. Care must also be taken when using light coloured backgrounds, as you may need to illuminate this as well to prevent it from appearing too dark in the final picture.

To give an attractive 'catchlight' in the hair, a third light can be added to the lighting set up, to give a result that is similar to 'three point lighting' for video.

The *still life* is probably the most controlled and composed photograph you will ever take, therefore you will have plenty of time to experiment with various different types of lighting. The most common type light used for still life work is the large 'fish fryer' diffuser (see Figure 2.42), that gives off an even light with soft shadows. Set the object up on a table, with a graduated sheet of background paper placed behind it so that it forms a curve around the object. The fish fryer should be placed above the object, with a secondary light aimed directly at the object to fill in any shadows. Figure 2.45, which is a promotional shot for Panasonic, was taken using this technique.

Figure 2.45
The softlight positioned above the subject (here, a Panasonic Palmcorder) creates pleasing highlights and background 'fall-off'

Figure 2.46a
Taken with just one light aimed at the subject, this still life has too many harsh shadows

Figure 2.46b
Using a reflector to bounce back light onto the subject removes the shadows and makes the still life much more attractive to look at

Figure 2.46 again shows the usefulness of a reflector. In the first shot, the still life is ruined by harsh shadows, but with a reflector in place to bounce back light, the contrast evens out to look much better. Reflectors can often get you out of trouble, particularly if you only have access to one source of light.

In the Darkroom

Some photographers suggest that taking the picture is only a small part of photography. Developing and printing the image to the best effect requires just as much skill as getting the exposure right and composing the shot well, and is arguably the most creative part of photography.

In this section, we will show you how to develop and print a black and white film, and give you tips on how to get the best from your negatives. We have decided not to cover colour printing in this book, as the automatic equipment used by high street colour labs will often produce better results than prints you make yourself. Colour printing in the darkroom is quite complex and more expensive than having prints enlarged at a laboratory, so it probably isn't worth the time and effort spent learning. If, however, you want to have a go at colour printing, we have listed a few books at the end of this chapter that will help you get started.

Figure 2.47
Some of the equipment needed for black and white developing and printing

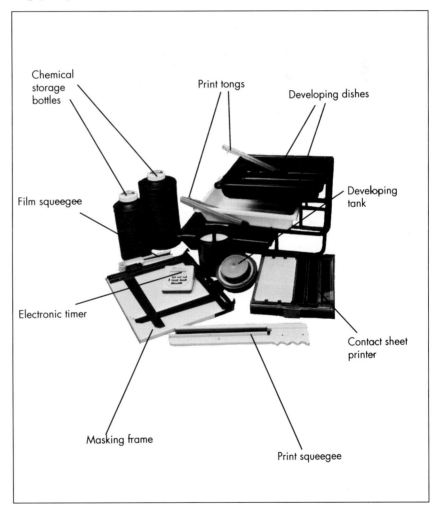

Chemical storage bottles

Print tongs

Developing dishes

Film squeegee

Developing tank

Electronic timer

Contact sheet printer

Masking frame

Print squeegee

The equipment
Developing a black and white film requires two sets of processes: one to develop the negatives, and the other to physically print the picture onto light-sensitive black and white paper. All processing must be done in complete darkness, although a red-coloured safelight can be used

when printing black and white negatives.

A light-tight developing tank with a film reel is necessary to develop the film; an enlarger, darkroom timer, developing dishes, print tongs and a safelight are needed to print the negatives. All this equipment (Figure 2.47, page 71) must be kept free from chemicals and dust, otherwise you risk contamination to the prints or negatives you are developing.

Processing a film

For the purposes of this book, we shall talk about developing a typical black and white film, in this case Ilford HP5 Plus. Developing colour slide film is almost as easy as this once you have mastered the technique, although the temperature of the colour chemicals needs to be a lot higher than for black and white film.

Most developing tanks use a plastic semi-automatic loading spiral to hold the film in place during development, and mastering the technique of getting the film in place is fairly difficult. It is worth practising with a roll of waste film before trying the 'real thing' in complete darkness.

After removing the film cassette lid, insert the film into the reel using the two large flanges as a guide (see Figure 2.48). Once the film is in, turn the two sides of the reel until the film is fully loaded, and then cut off the empty film cassette. Place the reel(s) into the developing tank, and ensure that the lid is firmly in place. Once this has been done, it is safe to turn on the lights.

After doing this, mix up the chemicals according to the manufacturer's instructions. It is very important that the chemicals are mixed at exactly the right temperature (normally 20°C for black and white film), and that the temperature is kept consistent throughout the developing process. Failure to do so may mean that the film will be incorrectly developed. Each 35mm reel needs around 300ml of diluted chemical,

Figure 2.48
Loading film into the reel

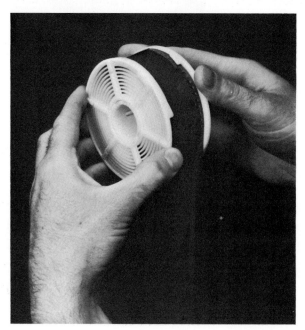

so if you are developing three films in one go, you should mix up 900ml of developer and fixer. We recommend using Kodak D76/Ilford ID11 for general purpose developing (i.e. for films from 100 to 400 ASA), and Ilford Hypam fixer. These chemicals are well proven, and are used widely by universities, colleges and professional photographers because they give good results.

Once the chemicals are mixed, pour the developer into the developing tank quickly, ensuring that you either note the time on your watch or start a darkroom timer. Tap the tank on the table to dislodge any air bubbles that may be trapped in the film, and wait until the development time has elapsed. During this period, invert the tank a couple of times every minute, to make sure that the developer gets sufficient agitation.

Start to pour out the developer about 5–10sec before the development time has finished. After giving the tank a thorough rinse-out using water at 20°C (*not* water straight from the tap), add the diluted fixer, and wait for the film to fix. You may like to add some Ilford Rapid Hardener to the fixer, as this will protect your negatives once they are dry, as well as allowing easier drying.

Once the fixer has been poured out, place the film under running water for at least 15min, so that all traces of chemical are removed. Add Ilford Wash Aid or washing up liquid to help clean the developed negatives, and hang them up to dry in a clean, dust-free area. Make sure that both ends of the film have a film clip or clothes peg hanging from them, as this will help straighten the film as it dries.

After this, cut the film into strips of six, and carefully slide them into a neg. bag to prevent them becoming dusty or scratched. Before storing them, you may also like to make a contact sheet (see Figure 2.49), which is done by resting the negatives on top of a piece of photographic paper (using a sheet of glass to hold them down), and exposing the

Figure 2.49
A contact sheet allows you to look at pictures before enlarging them

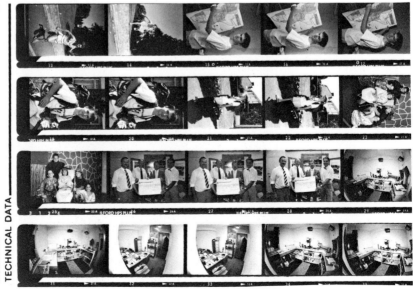

SUBJECT
TECHNICAL DATA

paper to white light from an enlarger. The contact sheet will allow you to see your images in positive form, to allow you to make a selection.

Push processing

Occasionally you may have film that is too slow in your camera bag, especially if you are shooting in changeable light conditions. Every film (especially print film) can be uprated to give faster shutter speeds by manually changing the ASA rating on the camera. However, doing this will mean that you will have to alter the development time to compensate – this is known as *push processing*.

For example, if you choose to rate Kodak TMAX 3 200 at 12 500 ASA, you will need to increase the development time at 21°C from 11min to 15 ½min. Of course, increasing the film speed will mean a significant increase in grain – but if it is a case of getting the shot or not, it's definitely worth it.

Unfortunately, you cannot just push process part of the film, so if you intend to upgrade the normal speed rating, you'll have to stick to it throughout the whole roll. Consult your film information leaflet (enclosed with most types of film) for push processing development times.

Basic printing skills

Figure 2.50
The Durst M370 black and white and colour enlargers

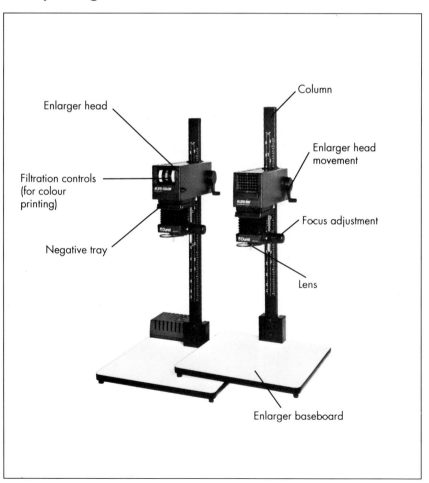

Figure 2.50
The Durst M370 black and white and colour enlargers

Before starting any work with the enlarger, you will need to set up the chemicals to develop the photographic paper. You will need three developing dishes of the appropriate size: one that contains developer; another, stop bath; and the remaining one, fixer. These should be kept at 20°C, and there should be a final water bath with running water, in which the developed prints should be washed. We recommend using Ilford Multigrade paper developer, Ilford IN-1 stop bath and Ilford Hypam fixer, although there are other brands of chemicals available.

After choosing which shot you want to enlarge, you must place that strip of negatives into the enlarger (see Figure 2.50). The enlarger head can be moved up and down the column to reduce or enlarge the image, and the focus must be adjusted with each move. A special enlarging lens is placed underneath the enlarger head, and the aperture must be altered to suit the density of the negative being enlarged. You should always focus at maximum aperture (normally $f2.8$) to give the brightest image for easy focusing, and you should use a special tool called a *focus finder* for really accurate results. The focus finder magnifies the grain on the film, allowing you to make sure that it is completely sharp.

Once the image is in sharp focus, stop the aperture down to around $f8$, and place a piece of light-sensitive black and white photographic paper onto the enlarging easel (providing the room is darkened and the red or yellow safelight is switched on). The easel allows you to frame your prints with a white border, as well as ensuring that the paper remains completely flat during the exposure.

Black and white photographic paper is available in different grades, and these alter the contrast of the print being made. A print made with grade 0 paper (the 'softest' grade) will be very flat and grey (Figure 2.51, page 76), while the same shot made with grade 5 (the 'hardest' grade) will be much more contrasty (Figure 2.52, page 76). You should print thin, underexposed negatives on hard grade paper, and dense, overexposed negatives on soft grade paper. For average density negatives use an average grade, around grade 2 or 3.

Some photographic papers like Ilford Multigrade allow you to change grades without having to change your box of photographic paper. A special set of coloured filters alters the grade of the paper, allowing you to experiment with the effect that different grades have on an image. One box of Multigrade is much cheaper (and more flexible) than several boxes of graded paper, so try to use Multigrade if possible.

Once your piece of photographic paper is in place, you will have to work out the exposure necessary to make the perfectly exposed print – you will have to make a test strip (Figure 2.53, page 77). To do this, cover about ⅚ of the paper with a piece of card, and make a 5sec exposure. Slide the card along to reveal the next strip, until all the paper has been exposed. You will need about six 5sec exposures to give you a good range, allowing you to assess which exposure gives the best black and white tones.

Place the exposed paper in the developing tray quickly, ensuring that all of the paper is covered by chemical as quickly as possible. Keep the print in each developing dish for no longer than is recommended by

Figure 2.51
A photograph printed on grade 0 paper

Figure 2.52
The same photograph printed on grade 5 paper

the chemical manufacturer, and especially do not be tempted to keep the print in the development tray for that little bit longer, as this will mess up any possible exposure accuracy. If a print is too dark or too light, alter the exposure on the enlarger, as this will produce much better results.

Once you have decided the correct exposure from the test strip, make a straight print at that exposure, and develop it as before. After it has been in the fixer for about 30sec, it is safe to turn the main light on (ensuring that the unexposed photographic paper is safely in its closed box), allowing you to assess the print under 'proper' lighting conditions. Any exposure alterations can be easily accommodated, although you *must* make all alterations on the enlarger, rather than extending the development time in any way.

After washing the print for at least 15min, it can be hung up to dry or dried using a specially designed automatic dryer. If you are drying the print naturally, make sure that it is kept flat, and that air can circulate all around it to speed up the drying process.

Figure 2.53
A test strip is vital to ascertain the correct exposure. Note how the image becomes darker from left to right, where the paper has received longer exposure times. The optimum 'basic' exposure for this print is 15 seconds

Advanced printing skills

As you become more and more skilled in the darkroom, you will gradually find yourself being able to 'read' a negative before printing it. You will notice that each area of the negative has different density, that should be taken into account at the printing stage. To do this, you will have to expose certain sections of the negative for longer or shorter than the average exposure, and this is known as 'dodging' and 'burning in'.

Dodging is where you hold back the exposure of the print by shading it from the enlarger's light, while *burning in* is where the exposure is increased, by letting light only go to that section of the print. These techniques should be used to darken areas that are too light, or lighten areas that are too dark. Burning in is particularly useful for making dramatic skies look dark, while dodging can prevent faces from going too dark in portraits. Figure 2.54, page 78, has had the sky burnt in, while the foreground grass in shadow has been dodged to prevent it from going too dark. The car was exposed for the average time, which was worked out from the test strip.

You can use your hand to dodge or burn in, but you must make sure that it is in the right shape to create the correct shadow. Some photographers use specially constructed shapes stuck on wires to dodge and burn in, and you may find these useful when doing small areas.

Figure 2.54
The sky in this print received 40 seconds of exposure, while the car had 18 seconds, and the grass, 8 seconds. Dodging and burning was used to alter the exposure times

While dodging or burning, make sure that you move the object casting the shadow backwards and forwards over the print, as holding it still will result in a stark shadow between the different exposures.

To ascertain how much dodging and burning in a print needs, make several test strips over the various densities of the negative. This way, you will know exactly how much exposure the print needs in each section.

Dodging can also be used to create the vignette effect that was popular in the days of Edwardian photography. Cut out an oval shape from the middle of a piece of cardboard, and use this as a mask when making the print. Move the mask backwards and forwards as the exposure is being made to give exposure 'fall off' around the edges, causing the vignette effect.

To really recreate the effect of old photographs, you can also use sepia toner to stain black and white photographs yellow or brown. The sepia toner is applied to developed and fixed prints, so there is no need to use the darkroom for this process. However, the chemicals used are highly toxic, so take care when handling them.

Retouching

Even in the cleanest darkroom, minute particles of dust can settle on static negatives, resulting in small white marks on the developed print. Although you can blast each negative with compressed air before making a print, this is still no guarantee for blemish-free prints. Remember that too much cleaning with a blower brush can scratch the negative. By far the best way to stop blemishes ruining prints is to retouch them after the developing stage.

Retouching prints is a skilled art, as it is all too easy to apply too much Spot On ink. If you have never tried retouching before, you should practice on some spare prints first. Using a small '00' sized brush, dip the end into a jar of Spot On retouching solution, and thin out the density of the black by brushing on a piece of blotting paper first. Gently apply the ink to the print, gradually building up the density so that it matches the grey tone around the blemish. Retouching really does make an incredible difference to a marked print, and it is a skill well worth developing if you intend to do a lot of black and white printing.

Solarisation

This is a technique that was accidentally discovered by the famous American photographer Man Ray in the 1920s. The effect turns certain areas of the negative into positives, which, when printed, results in a print that is half negative and half positive. Solarisation is a risky effect, as it involves opening up the developing tank half way through the development stage. If you leave the tank open for too long, the film will be ruined.

For an Ilford HP5 film, open the tank up for 3sec two thirds of the way through the development process, and then continue developing the film as usual. The fixed film may look slightly more opaque than normal, but as long as it isn't completely black, it should be easy to make prints from. Solarisation is a technique that everyone should try at least once, although only try it on a film that you don't really mind loosing, just in case things go wrong!

Storing and Presenting Photographs

Slide storage
Slides should be kept in plastic wallet files that can be bound in ring binders. This will not only keep your slides clean, it will also allow you to make a selection easily by holding the slide page up to the light. If you have developed your own slide film, you will need to place the resulting transparencies in plastic mounts for ease of viewing. Gepe slide mounts are available in packets of 100, and the two halves of the mount clip together easily, clasping the transparency in place. Alternatively, large cardboard mounts can be used to really set off the 35mm transparency.

Mounting prints
Mounting your prints will really set them off well (see Figure 2.55), and buying cardboard mounts is a lot cheaper than you may think.

Figure 2.55
Mounting your prints will really set them off well

Regardless of whether your finished print is black and white or colour, black mounts seem to work best, although, if care is taken, coloured mounts can also be effective.

The print can either be placed in front of the mount or behind it, using a cut out 'window'. When mounting the print in front, use either aerosol Scotch Spray Mount or Ademco mounting tissue to bond the print to the mount. Spray Mount is easier to use, although the mounting tissue will give a more permanent bond. When using mounting tissue, you have to use a special heated mounting press to 'melt' the tissue onto the card, and care must be taken to get the print straight on the first attempt. To remove an incorrectly mounted print, simply reapply the heat, and, with care, the print should lift off.

Staging an exhibition

An exhibition is a chance to show off your photographic talents, and almost as much care must be taken to set up the exhibition, as the amount spent on taking and developing the images. Each print displayed should be given a title, that should be placed alongside: the date it was taken, where it was shot, and any other relevant technical information.

The prints should all be mounted and framed, using identical frames to ensure consistency. Borderless glass frames are fairly reasonably priced, and some specialist frame shops will offer a special price for large numbers of prints framed identically. Hang the prints using secure 'mirror mounts' and screws to ensure that they cannot be knocked off or stolen.

If possible, produce a small booklet to accompany the exhibition, and this can be done using some of the techniques talked about in Chapter 6 (page 186).

Glossary

Listed below is a selection of photographic terms and what they mean.

120/220: The number designated for medium format roll film. 220 film is twice as long as 120.

35mm: The most commonly used film format. Available in metal cassettes, one frame measures 24×36mm.

AF: Abbreviation of *autofocus*.

Aperture: Adjustable iris that controls the amount of light entering the camera through the lens.

ASA: Abbreviation of *American Standards Association*. This measures film speed, i.e. the film's sensitivity to light.

Bellows: Adjustable extender between the camera and lens used for extreme macro photography.

Blower brush: Camera accessory that allows you to clean lenses and camera. Consists of a brush and a mini-bellows to direct a jet of air at dust.

Bounce flash: Bouncing light from a flash gun off a reflective surface, to eliminate harsh shadows.

Bracketing (exposure): Making several exposures of the same subject, which is recommended for tricky metering situations. You should take one exposure using the camera's suggested aperture/shutter speed combination, and two more, one each that is over- and underexposed by one *f*-stop.

Bulk film loader: Allows you to roll your own film using 30m rolls. Buying bulk film in is cheaper than buying individual rolls.

Burning in: Increasing the exposure of part of a photographic print under the enlarger.

Cable release: Provides a remote shutter release to avoid camera shake.

Camera clamp: A clamp with a screw thread, allowing the camera to be attached to most solid objects.

Clip test: Developing the first few exposures of a roll of film, to ascertain the development time needed (useful for push processing).

Compact camera: A small camera without an interchangeable lens. Normally small enough to be put in a pocket.

Crop: A darkroom technique to exclude (or 'cut off') part of the image on the negative.

Databack: An interchangeable back that allows you to print the date and/or time on the photograph. However, once on the negative, it is impossible to remove.

Depth of field: The zone of focus, controlled by altering the aperture. The higher the *f*-stop, the greater the depth of field.

Developing tank: Lightproof tank for developing films. Normally contains reels to hold the film in place.

Dodging: Decreasing the exposure of part of the image in the darkroom. Otherwise known as 'holding back'.

DX code: A system for selecting film speed automatically. The camera 'reads' a series of metal 'bars' on the side of the film cartridge to ascertain the correct film speed setting.

Enlarger: A device for printing from negatives or transparencies.

Enprint: A 6×4 inch print. The standard size produced by most colour laboratories.

Extension tubes: Fixed tubes placed between the camera and lens for macro photography.

Fibre-based paper: Photographic paper that has the non plastic protection for the emulsion. Fibre-based prints take a long time to dry, and must be dried completely flat (see *Resin-coated paper*).

Fill in flash: A burst of flash to 'fill in' shadows during daylight hours. Normally done to balance foreground exposure with background exposure.

Filter: Placed over the lens, this alters the colour and/or type of light that enters the camera body.

Graduated filter: A half-coloured filter that can be used to alter the colour of skies.

Grain: The 'dots' that make up a photographic image. Grain increases with faster speed films, and can be used for effect.

Grey card: A grey board for accurate exposure measurement.

Guide number: Measures the power output of a flashgun. Can be used to work out manual exposure values.

Hotshoe: A 'cradle' to accommodate a camera-mounted flashgun. The contacts between flash and camera are integrated into the hotshoe.

Incident light: A direct exposure reading, taken from the source of light.

Large format: Any film format that is larger than roll film (normally 5×7 or 10×8 inches).

LED: Abbreviation for *light emitting diode*.

Lens hood: A built-in or detachable lens shade, that prevents stray light entering into the camera and causing flare.

M42: The lens fitting for screw-in type lenses.

Macro lens: A lens that allows you to focus in very close to your subject.

Masking frame: A base for placing photographic paper under the enlarger. Through the use of movable straight edges, borders and cropping can be carried out.

Medium format: Cameras that take 120/220 type roll film.

Mirror lens: A telephoto lens that uses a series of mirrors to produce the image. Also known as a Catadioptic lens.

Monopod: A solid one-legged camera support that is particularly useful for holding telephoto lenses steady.

Motordrive: A device permitting automatic film advance very quickly. Some motordrives are capable of advancing the film up to seven frames per second.

Mounting board: A piece of (normally) coloured cardboard for mounting prints for display.

Multiple exposure: The act of making several exposures on one frame of film.

ND filter: Abbreviation for *neutral density filter*. Neutral density filters reduce the amount of light entering the lens, without adjusting the colour balance.

Ni-Cd batteries: Abbreviation for *nickel cadmium* batteries. These are rechargeable, and are extensively used by photographers. They are particularly well suited for use in flashguns, as they offer quicker flash recycling times.

Overexposure: The act of letting in too much light into the camera, which results in negatives/transparencies that are too light. Overexposing photographic paper under the enlarger results in prints that are too dark.

PC socket: A female flash socket for attaching remote manual flashes.

Polarising filter: A filter that only lets in light of one wavelength. Useful for darkening skies and cutting down on reflections on water, glass, etc.

Pull processing: Decreasing a film's development time when a roll has been exposed at a lower ASA rating than recommended.

Push processing: Increasing a film's development time when a roll has been exposed at a higher ASA rating than recommended.

Rangefinder camera: A camera with a separate viewfinder. The opposite of the SLR, where you actually look through the lens to see what you are framing.

Reciprocity failure: The colour change in a film when it is subjected to a long exposure time (more than 3sec) and it tends to become less sensitive.

Red dot: A coloured dot to make lens mounting easier.

Red-eye: A common occurrence when photographing people with direct flash. Caused by light bouncing off the subject's retina, it can be avoided by using bounce flash, or by making your subject look at a bright light for a couple of seconds before taking the photograph.

Reflector: A piece of reflective card or cloth that is used to 'bounce' light back onto a subject

Resin-coated paper: Photographic paper that has a plastic coating on the emulsion side for protection and easy drying.

Ringflash: A flash tube that fits over the end of the lens, especially suited to macro photography.

Sepia toning: A post-printing process that changes white tones to brown/beige. An effect often used to make photographs appear 'old'.

Silica gel: Moisture-absorbing crystals that should be kept in a camera bag, to prevent condensation or moisture building up in lenses and cameras. Lenses that are stored in damp conditions are likely to develop fungus growth that will impair the image.

Slave unit: A device for triggering flashes remotely. The slave senses when a master flash has been emitted, and fires the flash it is attached to immediately.

SLR: Abbreviation of *single lens reflex*. This describes cameras that let the user look directly through the lens for precise composition.

Spot metering: Very precise exposure reading taken from a subject. Normally measures light emitted from just 3% of the whole picture area.

Teleconverter: A device placed between the lens and camera body to magnify the image produced. With a 2× teleconverter placed on a 50mm lens, the lens becomes a 100mm. However, the maximum aperture is halved, so *f*2.8 becomes *f*5.6.

TLR: Abbreviation of *twin lens reflex*. These cameras have separate lenses for the viewfinder and shutter.

TTL: Abbreviation of *through the lens*. Can be used to describe metering under flash or daylight conditions.

Underexposure: The act of letting in too little light into the camera, which results in negatives/transparencies that are too dark. Underexposing photographic paper under the enlarger results in prints that are too light.

Variable contrast paper:
Photographic paper that has adjustable grades. This saves you from having to have large amounts of graded paper in stock.

Wratten filters: A series of coloured filters made by Kodak, that can be used to correct colour balance problems caused by tungsten lights, reciprocity failure, etc.

X-sync: Another way to describe the flash synchronisation speed of the camera.

Zoom lens: A lens with adjustable focal lengths. A wide angle zoom lens normally has a range from 28 to 70mm, while a telephoto zoom normally ranges from 70 to 210mm. There are zoom lenses available that can cover focal lengths from 28 to 210mm, but these normally have slow maximum apertures, and may produce 'soft' images.

Further Reading

Calder, J. and Garret, J. (1989) *The Traveller's Photography Handbook* Pan Books.

Farndon, J. (1986) *Understanding Photography* Marshall Cavendish.

Freeman, M. (1980) *The 35mm Handbook* Leisure Books.

Hedgecoe, J. (1989) *New Manual of Photography* Weidenfeld and Nicolson.

Monk, B. (1991) *1000 Photography Hints* Octopus Books.

3 Audio and Radio Techniques

Introduction Since the beginning of time, sound has been the principal means of communication. Early life forms soon learnt to make sounds by grunting or banging things together, and as time evolved, humans developed language to communicate with each other. To send messages over longer distances, prehistoric man used drums fabricated from animal skin and branches.

It was not until the late 1800s, however, that devices to record and relay sound were being explored and developed. Bell's invention of the telephone was one of the first major steps forward, and this new medium of communication enabled people to communicate over large distances by the use of wire.

At the beginning of this century, ways of recording sound were being investigated, and these led to the invention of the phonograph. This device etched sound 'waves' onto a waxed cylinder, and a needle relayed these scratches to a large horn which amplified the sound.

Up until the discovery of electricity, devices for recording and relaying sound were mechanical. The First and Second World Wars helped advance communications, with the 'wireless' or 'radio' being developed for both military and civilian use. This was the first time that electronics had been used to amplify and record sound, and from those simple beginnings, the long play (LP) record, audio cassette, compact disk, FM radio and more recently digital audio tape (DAT) have been developed.

Understanding the Basics of Sound Before embarking on the practical use of sound, it is necessary to understand how sounds are made, heard and transmitted.

To use a simple example, if an elastic band is stretched across a matchbox and plucked, a noise is generated. As the band vibrates, it displaces air around it, generating a wave which can be heard. A sound wave pushes the air in front of it, creating 'ripples' that can be likened to the surface of a pond after a stone has been thrown in. From the centre of impact, the ripples spread outward, decreasing in strength as they move out from the centre. Using this analogy to represent sound waves, large peaks are loud noises, while smaller peaks, further away, are quieter. This series of peaks for measuring sound is called a *sine wave*.

The distance between each peak in a sine wave will vary. A small distance between each peak shows a high frequency sound, while a large distance between each peak depicts low frequency. The human voice produces a range of frequencies with short and long sounds. For example, the letters 't' and 's' are high frequency sounds, while 'm' and 'n' have low frequencies.

A sine wave of a typical human voice would look something like the one shown in Figure 3.1. There is a significant frequency difference between the male and female voice: a male voice will typically produce a range of sounds from 100Hz to 8kHz, whereas a female has a higher range: between 200Hz and 10kHz.

Figure 3.1
A sine wave of the human voice. Note the range of frequencies

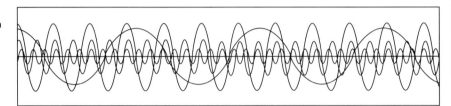

Musical instruments can produce a large range of frequencies. A cymbal has a range of 500Hz–20kHz, while a timpani drum produces a lower frequency: 50Hz–500Hz. The piano has a very wide range: typically 25Hz–5kHz, which is created when a hammer hits a string. Each string varies in thickness: the thicker the string, the lower the frequency.

There many ways of producing sounds, but not all can be heard by the human ear. In theory, we can hear a range of frequencies between 20Hz and 20kHz, but a more realistic range is 30Hz–17kHz.

Measuring sound

The 'loudness' of a sound is measured in decibels (dB) and all sounds are measured from a standard reference of 0dB. The louder the sound, the higher the decibel reading, and the pain threshold of the human ear is around 120dB.

The Microphone

As we discussed earlier, sound is created by pressure waves, and a microphone is a device that converts these waves into electrical energy. Basically speaking, a 'dynamic' microphone consists of a diaphragm that vibrates when sound waves hit it, and these are converted into a small electric voltage via a coil sitting between two poles of a magnet.

The 'condenser' microphone works on a similar principle, although it uses a fixed back plate to create the electronic charge. Condenser mikes have to be battery operated, or they can be powered by an external 'phantom' power source. Generally speaking, condenser microphones have a higher frequency range than their 'dynamic' equivalents.

Apart from the difference between dynamic and condenser microphones, microphones are available with differing 'pickup' ranges, and each one is designed for a particular function.

The Omni-Directional Microphone

As its name implies, the omni-directional microphone picks up sound from all directions (see Figure 3.2). It is ideal for interviews, but is not recommended for recording instruments in an orchestra. Omni-directional mikes are widely used with portable tape recorders, as they are easy to handle and are less prone to 'rustling' (where the noise of the microphone case being handled is recorded).

The Bi-Directional (figure of eight) Microphone

This microphone (Figure 3.3) will pick up sounds from two directions, and is ideal for studio interviews where two people are sitting opposite each other.

The Cardioid (Uni-directional) Microphone

This microphone records sound from one direction only (see Figure 3.4). The pick-up area, therefore, is relatively narrow, so the microphone is especially suited for speech from a single person. Cardioid microphones are prone to accentuating bass frequencies, and have a tendency to 'pop' if not positioned correctly.

Figure 3.2
Polar diagrams of an omnidirectional microphone

Figure 3.3
a bi-directional microphone 'right'

Figure 3.4
and a unidirectional microphone 'far right'

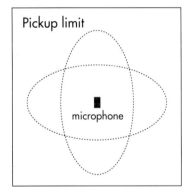

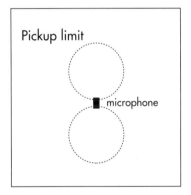

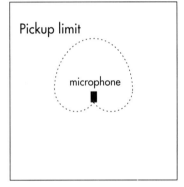

The Gun Mike

Gun mikes are widely used in television and electronic news gathering (ENG) roles and are very directional. The pick-up area is quite small, and care needs to be taken when directing the mike at the subject. Gun mikes normally come with a fury cover (a 'Dougal') which is used to reduce wind noise.

As well as these four categories of microphone, microphones are available for specialist applications. Hypercardioid microphones, for example, have acceptance angles of as little as 30° for extremely directional recording; while miniature tie-clip microphones are particularly useful for the television studio (see page 107).

The Portable Tape Recorder

There are two standards of portable tape recorder in common use at present: audio cassette and reel to reel. Another format, digital audio tape (DAT) is becoming increasingly popular, although the method for recording the sounds to tape is very different, and shall be discussed in 'Using a DAT Recorder'.

Reel to reel tape is very easy to edit, as the tape can be physically cut and rejoined (see 'Audio Tape Editing', page 97). Although cassette recorders are smaller and more portable, recordings made on them are normally copied onto reel tape for easy editing. Nevertheless, crash editing can be achieved by using two cassette machines: one as a recorder and the other as a player. However, this type of editing is fairly inaccurate.

How the tape player records sounds

Magnetic tape is a thin vinyl ribbon coated with a metal oxide on one side, and this can be magnetised or demagnetised. The particles of metal oxide lie in random bunches until a magnetic field is applied, and this changes them into organised vertical magnetic lines.

When recording using magnetic tape, the electronic pulses from the sound input source (a microphone, CD, etc.) are converted into differing magnetic fields, and these organise the metal particles on the tape as it moves past the recording head. Once the recording is complete, these newly arranged particles can be read by the playback head, which reconverts the signals into electricity to be outputted through speakers or headphones.

You must be very careful not to let any magnets come into contact with the metal particles on a tape, as the foreign field will rearrange the particles on the cassette and the recording will be lost.

Setting the levels on a portable cassette player

All 'professional' portable cassette recorders have record level controls, which use the standard volume unit (VU) meter (see Figure 3.5) or an LED/LCD alternative to show the level of sound being recorded. Before recording, point the microphone at the loudest sound you are likely to record, and alter the level meters up or down, so that the needle (or LED) 'peaks' at around –3dB. Any sounds that peak above 0dB (i.e. into the red band) will distort badly when they are played back, so be very careful when setting the levels.

While recording, keep a close eye on the VU meter. Should it start peaking into the red band frequently, adjust the levels to suit. Similarly, if the sounds you are recording are below –10dB, raise the levels to take this into account.

The next three sections will discuss the various differences and operational techniques of reel to reel, audio cassette and DAT portable recorders.

Figure 3.5
Diagram of a VU (volume unit) meter

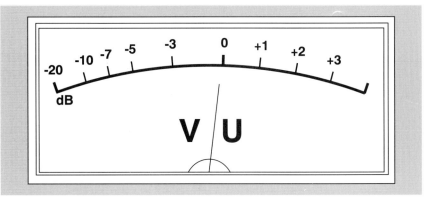

The Uher Reel to Reel Recorder

Figure 3.6 shows a typical reel to reel tape recorder with its controls and level meters. The magnetic tape (wound on separate reels) passes from left to right, allowing it to be dragged across the erase, record and the playback heads respectively.

The erase head consists of a coil wound on non-ferrous metal, and it is used in the record mode to remove any previous recording on the tape. The record head is very similar, except that the voltage applied to it varies with the sound that is being fed into the recorder. The playback head 'reads' the magnetic signal off the tape, and this is then amplified and 'translated' back to an audio frequency via headphones or a loudspeaker.

Figure 3.6
The Uher reel to reel recorder

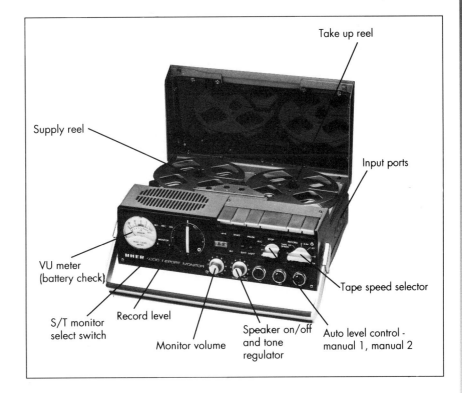

The speed at which the tape is pulled through is controlled by the capstan and pressure wheel/idler. The standard speed for music and speech is either 7.5 or 15 inches per second (ips), although some machines are capable of faster speeds: up to 30/60ips. A fast tape speed gives a higher quality recording with very little 'wow' and 'flutter', which is distortion in recorded sound caused by fluctuation in tape speed. Speeds in excess of 30ips are normally used for high quality recordings of music or speech. Wherever possible, set the fastest tape speed your machine is capable of – although be careful that you don't run out of tape before the end of your recording!

Overleaf is a handy reference guide to the features of a Uher (or similar) portable recorder, such as the Marantz professional cassette recorder shown on page 91 (see Figure 3.7).

Auxiliary output: A plug for connection into an amplifier or mixer.

Input socket: For recording from an external source (CD, record deck, radio etc.).

Slide/tape synchroniser: For use in a tape/slide presentation.

Illumination light for the VU meter: One press will switch the lamp on for about 10sec, two presses will leave the light on continually.

Battery check: The VU meter shows the state of the batteries when this button is depressed. Providing the needle moves to the green section in the VU meter (marked 'BATT'), the batteries are okay for use.

Monitor: This switch allows you to monitor the sound level as it is recorded ('S'), or (as the Uher has a separate playback head) 'T' can be selected to hear the signal coming directly from the tape. Using the 'T' monitor setting during recording can be a little strange at first, as there is a slight delay between reality and what is recorded, creating an 'echo' effect. Monitoring what is recorded directly from the tape does allow you to detect any imperfections ('wow' and 'flutter').

Tape speed control: Most Uhers have four settings: 0.94, 1.88, 3.75 and 7.5ips (marked as 2.4, 4.7, 9.5 and 19cm per second (cm/s) on the machine). Setting the speed switch control to '0' switches the power off.

Level control: Most Uhers offer two manual settings and an automatic level control. Automatic control constantly monitors the sound level, adjusting the sensitivity so that the meter will not 'peak' above the maximum record level. Similarly, the recorder will increase the levels automatically should the sounds being recorded be quiet. Using the automatic level control does have its drawbacks, however, especially when there is a sudden loud sound (an explosion, for example). When the automatic level control detects this and lowers the levels, there is a quiet patch after the noise has finished while the machine resets itself. If you expect to be recording extremes of sound, try and use the manual level if possible.

Tape control buttons: Fast forward, record, start, pause, stop and rewind. The 'Record' button must be pressed with the 'Start' button to roll the tape.

How to use a Uher recorder

The first thing to do is to load the tape onto the recorder. The tape spool should be put onto the lefthand spool carrier, and a few inches of tape should be wound off and laid through the slit in the centre of the machine. The tape should be then wrapped around the spare spool on the right, and secured by pulling the end through the slit on the spool.

Next, connect the microphone into the 'Mic.' socket on the side of the machine, and select the tape speed, the most common being 7.5ips (19cm/s). Zero the tape counter, and set the monitor switch to 'S', which is the source position. Push the pause button down, and then depress the start and record buttons together to set the record level manually (see 'The Portable Tape Recorder', above). To do this, select manual record setting 1, and adjust the knob until so that the loudest sound peak does not exceed –3dB on the meter.

If the monitor/speaker level control is turned up, there will be a loud high-pitched howl which is called *feedback*. This is caused by sound from the speaker being fed back to the microphone, and can only be prevented by turning the speaker off. In practice, the speaker/tone control should always be set to zero to avoid this embarrassing noise, and pulling the tone control out will switch the speaker off completely.

If you want to make a test recording, release the pause control and record a sample to check that everything is in order. Don't hold the microphone too close or too far away from your subject when recording: an ideal distance is about 12in or 30cm. It is much better to re-adjust the levels than have a microphone too close to someone you are trying to interview. The only exception to this rule is when there is a lot of background noise around you. Here you will have to have the microphone as close to your subject as possible, and you will have to alter the levels to suit.

When you are satisfied that everything is correctly set, zero the tape counter and start recording. It is always advisable to use a pair of headphones to monitor the sound as it is being recorded, although in an interview situation this is rude and clearly not feasible. If you cannot use headphones, do not be tempted to use the loudspeaker as a substitute, as you risk creating feedback (see above).

Playing back the tape

When you have completed your recording, press 'Stop' and rewind the tape to the start of the recording (which should be easy providing you remembered to set the counter to zero). Press in the tone control to switch on the loudspeaker, set the monitor level control to about halfway and switch the monitor switch from the source (S) position to tape (T). When start is pressed, the recording will be replayed through the loudspeaker, and the levels can be checked on the VU meter.

The Portable Cassette Recorder (Marantz)

The Marantz-type of portable cassette recorder (see Figure 3.7) is very similar to the Uher, with the exception that it uses standard audio cassettes in place of reels, making it smaller and easier to use.

Some versions of the Marantz feature three heads (record, playback and erase) like the Uher, allowing the user to monitor sound as it is actually recorded onto the tape. Most Marantz machines are limited to the standard tape running speed, although the CP130 mono machine offers a slower speed for low-quality logging applications.

A checklist before recording

1. Always check that the batteries are OK before starting a recording
The state of the batteries can be checked by pressing the battery check

Figure 3.7
A Marantz professional cassette recorder

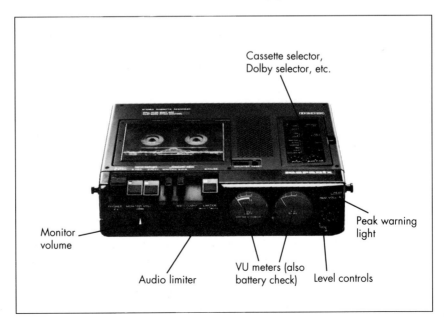

- Cassette selector, Dolby selector, etc.
- Peak warning light
- Monitor volume
- Audio limiter
- VU meters (also battery check)
- Level controls

button, with the amount of power left being shown on the lower scale of the left-hand meter. Two letters indicate the levels for ordinary batteries ('D') or rechargeable ones ('R'). Always carry a spare set of batteries with you, and if the levels are low, replace them.

2. Have enough tape for the recording
Audio cassettes are available in various lengths:

- 60 minute–30 minutes of continual recording on each side.
- 90 minute–45 minutes each side.
- 120 minute–60 minutes each side.

We recommend that you use the shortest tape possible, as tapes with a longer running time are much thinner, and intensive use can stretch the tape causing 'drop outs'. These are gaps in the recording which occur when oxide is missing from the tape surface.

3. Place a tape into the machine
Press the 'Stop/eject' button, which will open the trap door. The cassette is placed into the machine with exposed tape facing you.

4. Set the mode switch
Set it for mono operation, plug a microphone into the left socket and set the microphone attenuator switch to zero.

5. Turn the playback volume control down and press down the pause, record and play buttons together

6. Set the record level
Ensure that the VU needle does not go into the red area of the meter by adjusting the peak adjustment for the correct level (–3dB).

7. Release the pause control
Make a test recording, as this will help to check that the machine is working properly. Should the meter pointers not move, check that the microphone is in the correct socket and the right buttons have been pressed.

As mentioned in the description of the Uher operation, if a howl is experienced, turn down the monitor level control.

8. Check what you've recorded
Rewind the cassette, turn up the monitor level control to about half way and make sure that the speaker switch is turned on. Push 'Play' to check the test recording, and if everything sounds all right you are ready for your assignment.

Take care of the recorder at all times. For example, don't let the machine get wet in the rain or leave it in strong sunlight, as this can often melt the cassette. Never leave the batteries in the machine if it is not going to be used for some time.

Using a DAT Recorder

Although the set-up and basic operation of the DAT portable recorder is very similar to that of the Uher or Morantz, the method of recording the sounds to tape is radically different. Based on a similar principle to the compact disk, DAT differs in the fact that sound can be recorded digitally as well as played.

Figure 3.8
The Sony professional
DAT recorder

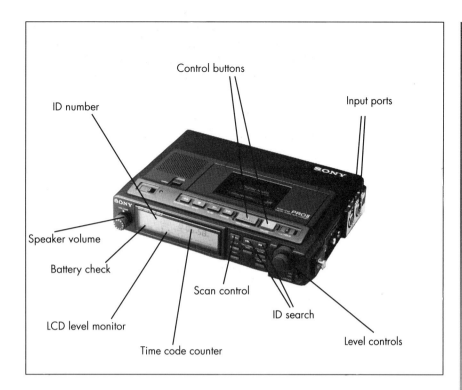

Control buttons

Input ports

ID number

Speaker volume

Battery check

Scan control

ID search

LCD level monitor

Level controls

Time code counter

Tapes are available in 30, 46, 60, 90 and 120min versions, although unlike conventional audio tapes, there is no need to turn the tape over to record on both sides. Like other audio tapes, however, it is best to select the shortest running time possible to prevent tape stretch or wear.

The sound is recorded to tape digitally, which means that you have to select a 'sampling rate' which should be 48kHz for the highest quality. Similarly, the digital system allows you to set 'start IDs' which allow you to locate the start and end of each recording at the touch of a button. The tape is logged in hours, minutes and seconds, and DAT players are remarkably quick at fast forwarding and rewinding. For example, a 2h tape can be rewound or fast forwarded from start to finish in 1min, and the search speed for 'start IDs' normally runs at 16× normal speed.

On the Sony D10PRO II (see Figure 3.8), a liquid crystal display (LCD) replaces the conventional VU meter as the nerve centre of the machine. The display shows level meters, battery indicator, index ID code and the tape counter. By pressing the 'Counter mode' button, the display will show how much time remains on the tape, while the 'Recorded time' button allows you to see how much you have recorded on the tape.

Using the DAT recorder
Sound levels should be set in an identical way to the Uher or Marantz, and to start recording you should press the 'Pause' and 'Record' buttons down together. Once the 'Pause' button has been disengaged, the machine will automatically write a silent ID code at the beginning of the recording, allowing you to relocate the beginning very easily.

Once you've finished recording, re-engage the 'Pause' button, and the tape will stop.

With your recording successfully recorded to tape you may want to check that it was okay. Simply push the 'Rewind search' button (*not* the standard rewind button), and the machine will locate the start of the last recording using the ID system. At the end of the recording (i.e. where you re-engaged the pause button) most DAT machines will stop automatically, ready to record on the next section of tape.

Like the Marantz and Uher, the DAT machine is also reliant on batteries, so make sure that you take enough spares to last for the entire recording session.

Editing with DAT
Editing DAT is very similar to editing video, as you use two machines (a source machine and an edit machine) coupled to an edit controller. 'In' and 'out' points are set using DAT's inbuilt time code, and as all the sound information is relayed digitally, there is no loss in quality. See Chapter 5 (page 119) for further details on video editing.

Audio Interview Techniques

Now that you are familiar with the three main media for recording audio, we shall discuss the various methods for recording sound 'on location'.

Unlike the case of video location recording, there is seldom any need to carry out a pre-recording recce, although you should avoid trying to record at locations with a lot of background noise, or in echoey rooms without carpet or with little furniture.

Recording an interview
1 Put the recorder down within easy reach, so that you can press the necessary buttons and can see the record level meters. If you are outside or standing up, use the recorder's shoulder strap to carry the recorder on the opposite shoulder from the hand that you are holding the microphone with.
2 Check the area for noise and echo, and if it is unsatisfactory ask politely if you can move to another location. Often this is not possible and the best has to be made of the situation. Here are a few basic guide lines.
   a) In areas with a lot of background noise, place the microphone close to the interviewee's mouth – although don't go too far and embarrass or intimidate her/him.
   b) In echoey rooms, position yourself so that the interviewee speaks into a corner, and ask your interviewee to speak quietly. Remember to increase the sound levels to take this into account.
   c) In both cases, try and make a test recording before the interview. This will help you make the best of the situation.
3 Before the interview, research the subject and have some knowledge about your interviewee.
4 Prepare a few basic questions and use a 'key reference' in the first question. This is often referred to as the 'hook', and is used to provoke and keep your audience's interest throughout the piece. Your 'list' of questions should by no means be fixed. The best

interviewers add and develop their questions as the interview progresses.

5 The position of the microphone is very important. It is preferable to place the microphone in a stand on a table, as this eliminates any possibility of 'rustle' which is caused by your hands holding the microphone. If you have no choice but to handhold the mike, form a small loop of cable around your hand, and hold the microphone firmly but not too tightly. Don't fidget with the lead, as this will cause rustling noises on the recording which are very difficult to edit out.

6 Get your interviewee to sit or stand in a comfortable position, and hold the microphone between you, so that you both talk across it, just below chin level. If you are handholding the mike, it is best to point it at the person who is talking. If the balance between each voice is vast, then move the microphone nearer or further away. Try to avoid continually re-adjusting the record level, as this will be distracting for your interviewee, and will make it difficult for you to concentrate on what they are saying.

7 Mistakes often occur, although it is up to you whether they warrant starting the question again. If you do want to ask the question again, keep the tape running, and reassure the interviewee that you will edit it out.

8 Give your interviewee the chance to comment on the interview at the end, as s/he might want you to edit some sections out. Whether you do or not is up to you, of course!

9 When the interview is over, record a few minutes of 'silence' or background noise. This is called a *wild track* and is often useful when it comes to editing. Every environment has a background noise of some sort, and the wild track should be recorded with the same levels as the interview, and with the microphone still plugged in.

Remember: The length of the interview should always be longer than what is required for the final piece, as it is better to have too much than too little. If you have time at the end of the interview, play back the tape (without the interviewee still there), and note down what has been said. This will be useful when it comes to editing.

Problems caused with outside recordings

On a windy day, the microphone may pick up wind noise which is distracting and cannot be edited out later. Most microphones come supplied with a wind shield that reduces wind noise, but by far the best solution is to find a place that gives protection from the wind. Remember, recordings with excessive amounts of wind noise will be unusable.

When you have large amounts of background noise to contend with, use the techniques recommended above, and check a section of recording afterwards using a pair of good quality headphones. If necessary, you may have to carry out your interview again, although this should be avoided, as the interviewee's answers will probably lack spontaneity the second time around.

Radio Techniques

It goes without saying that your approach towards making a radio 'programme' should be very different from similar tasks you may have carried out with video. Radio, by its very nature, does not have any pictures to back up your story, and you should bear this in mind at all times. Phrases like 'as you can see' or 'what you can see in front of me' should be avoided at all costs.

When on location, you will have to rely on descriptive words and atmospheric sound to allow your listeners to imagine where you are. However, don't overdo the description, as this will become tedious and may even seem inane to the listener. The best radio presenters leave a lot to the imagination, and only provide a very basic 'scene setter' that gives the listener an idea of the where they are.

There are various methods for doing this. You can describe where you are briefly in an introduction to an interview, or use atmospheric sound (that can be 'borrowed' from sound effects CDs if you wish) to give the listener a idea of your location. For example, a radio piece recorded on a building site may use the sounds of a hammer against metal, lorries turning or a pneumatic drill to give the listener an impression of where the piece was recorded. All these sounds could be played for a couple of seconds at the beginning of the piece before the presenter starts speaking – although they should fade down to the background when s/he starts speaking.

All radio reports should have a 'hook' that commands the attention of listeners, drawing them into the 'story' and making them want to hear more. To use our building site example, the presenter could say something along the lines of: 'Most people have heard about accidents in building sites, and some of them have appalling safety records. I've come to this one just outside Brighton to find out what measures they use to protect their workforce.' This short sentence starts immediately with an attention-grabbing hook, and then goes on to set the scene. Backed up with background noise of a building site, the listener knows within a couple of seconds what the piece is about and where the reporter is.

It has been suggested that, because of the lack of pictures, a radio listener's attention span is shorter than that of a television viewer. You will probably have to compete with the listener doing something else while they are listening, so you should keep the report as short as possible, and add background music or sound effects to liven up your presentation. A report produced without background sound will appear very boring indeed – although don't be tempted to overdo background noises. An interview, for example, should only rely on the background noise that was recorded while the interview took place.

Be very careful to use the same microphone and recorder when producing a piece for radio, and always make sure that your levels are set correctly. A report that contains an interview that is very 'bass-y' and loud, followed with a commentary that is too quiet and 'trebly' will sound inconsistent and amateurish.

If you are on location, try and record all your pieces (including the commentary) while you are there. The same voice recorded on location and in the studio will sound very different. Although to a certain extent you can correct mistakes like these with a professional mixer, it is much better to avoid mistakes in the first place if you can.

A checklist for good radio recordings

1 Remember that your listeners can't see what you are talking about. Use description and atmospheric sound to paint a picture in their imagination.

2 To grab the listeners' attention and to tell them what the report is about, use a short introductory 'hook' that gets straight to the point, but leaves them wanting to know more.

3 Listeners may have a short attention span. Keep your reports short and interesting.

4 Make sure that your recording levels are consistent. Too much fluctuation between different recordings will appear strange.

5 Use background sound sparingly, and avoid being tempted to use the same wild track over and over again.

6 If you make a mistake while speaking a commentary, start again. Remember: listeners cannot see your lips, so your diction will have to very clear. Remember also not to speak too fast, and use your voice to convey emotion; e.g. smiling while you speak will give a feeling of happiness to your listeners.

Audio Tape Editing

As explained earlier, there are two main types of audio editing: one where the tape is physically cut and then rejoined to create an edit, and the other where material is taken from the original recording and copied to another tape in the correct order. This is known as dub editing.

Good editing practice

Editing allows you to give your audio programme a structure, and it can be also used to remove unwanted pops and bangs, coughs, ums and ahs etc. Mistakes made by the speaker can also be removed, although you must be wary of continuity.

If you are editing a piece for radio, then you are likely to have a time constraint (normally 60–120sec) that must be rigorously observed. Nevertheless, beware of overediting, as there is a possibility that the piece will lose its naturalness and original spontaneity.

Before starting to edit a tape, listen to it several times and make a note of the sections that will be needed for the piece. Have a stopwatch handy, as this will help you to time each sequence. If you don't have access to a stopwatch, you can use the tape counter as an alternative. This is less accurate, however, and should only be used as a guide.

When you have decided which sections you require from the original tape, you will need to organise them into the correct order for the final piece. It is good practice to copy the relevant sections to another tape in the correct order, as this not only speeds up the editing process, it also provides useful backup should the original become lost or damaged. When editing the original tape, great care must be taken, as mistakes can often not be easily put right. Similarly, if you are editing on reel to reel, never throw any of your unwanted material away until you have finished editing. Often the bits that you thought were worthless can be invaluable after reflection.

If you are adding a commentary, music or sound effects, these should be recorded onto another reel of tape, and labelled separately. When recording a commentary, try and use the same machine as the one you used for your original recording, as other machines may have different settings or biases. If you have to record your commentary in the studio, you may like to mix in the wild track you recorded on location during the editing process. If done carefully, this will make it seem as if you recorded the commentary on location.

Editing reel to reel tape

Reel to reel editing requires you to physically cut the tape, sticking it back together with a piece of specially designed splicing tape. Figure 3.9 shows you the process to do this. To edit reel to reel tape you will need: a (safety) razor blade or scall, an editing block, a Chinagraph pencil (yellow or white), some ¼in splicing tape and some red and green leader tape.

Never attempt to use Sellotape to join two pieces of tape together, as it is much thicker than splicing tape and will probably damage the heads. Similarly, you should never try to cut the tape while it is close to the record or playback heads, as this is sure to damage them.

When cutting tape, use only a scalpel and a specially designed splicing block. The splicing block has a groove into which the tape is placed, and there is a marked cutting line set at 45°. The angle of the cut is important, as a straight splice would create a 'pop' on the tape when it is played back. Using an angled splice reduces this noise to a minimum.

Figure 3.9
Reel to reel editing and splicing

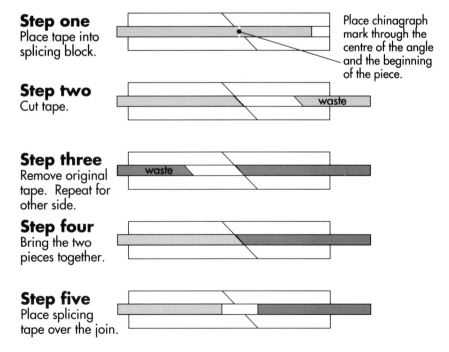

Step one
Place tape into splicing block.

Place chinagraph mark through the centre of the angle and the beginning of the piece.

Step two
Cut tape.

waste

Step three
Remove original tape. Repeat for other side.

waste

Step four
Bring the two pieces together.

Step five
Place splicing tape over the join.

Before starting to edit, however, you will need to attach some green leader tape to the beginning of tape before the first edit. This clearly marks the beginning of the piece for playback later, and also gives you a 'leader' with which to start your editing.

Place the green leader into the right-hand side of the splicing block and cut it across the marked angle with a scalpel. On the left-hand side of the block put the audio tape, and again cut it across at 45°. Take a 15mm piece of splicing tape and lay it across the join where the leader and audio tape meet. To provide a firm join, gently smooth it down, being careful not to cause any air bubbles or grooves. With the tape securely joined together, your edit is complete, and the finished product can be replayed on the recorder.

Figure 3.10
The Tascam reel to reel player and editor

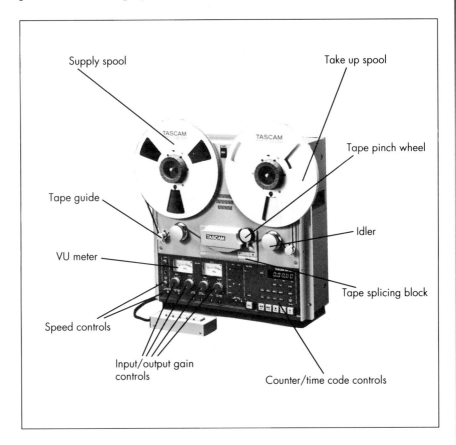

With the machine in play, cue up to the start of the first section to be edited and stop. Most reel to reel players (Figure 3.10) are fitted with a lever that engages the tape to the heads without running. This lever should be pressed down so that the tape is contact with the heads, but the reels are in freespool. This will allow you to cue up precisely where the cut should be made.

Place your left hand on the left spool and your right hand on the other, and gently rock the tape backwards and forwards until you hear the beginning of the part you want to edit. The part you need to mark should be at the centre of the playback head, so with the Chinagraph pencil gently mark a vertical line down the tape. Slacken the tape and lay it onto the left-hand side of the splicing block, centring the line in the middle of the 45° line. You should now cut the tape with the scalpel.

Next, play the tape until the next edit point is reached. To take an example, we will edit out a cough that would be distracting to the listener.

With the tape playing on the machine, find the start of the cough and mark it with the Chinagraph pencil in the same way as before. Advance the tape to the end of the cough and mark it once again with the Chinagraph – there should now be two marks on the tape. Slacken the tape and place the first mark across the cutting line on the editing block and cut. Move the tape onto the next mark and again cut. There should now be a small piece of tape cut out which was the cough. Place both ends into the editing block and slide them so there is no gap between them. Taking a piece of splicing tape, lay it across the join and press down firmly as before. Reload the tape into the recorder, and play it to see if your edit was successful.

As we suggested earlier, never discard pieces of tape that you have cut out, as they may come in useful later. If your edit was unsuccessful, simply remove the splicing tape and start again, using blank leader tape to feed the audio tape onto the spool.

Playback Devices

Like the microphone, the playback device relays electronic pulses that it 'reads' from the tape, CD or record. The output of these are much higher than a microphone, although in most cases an amplifier will be needed to bring the sound up to an acceptable level.

The CD Player

CD players 'read' digitally encoded signals written on the compact disk, converting them to electronic pulses that are converted into sounds. They offer superb sound quality (providing the original recording was digital), and you can find and change tracks with very little delay.

The Record Turntable

Although the CD player has made LP records almost obsolete, many older recordings and sound effects are only available on vinyl. Professional turntables have rotating bases that can be moved up to the record being played, thereby removing any necessity for cuing up. To cue up a section of record to be played in advance, place the needle on the head and play the LP. Once the section has been located, disengage the rotating base, and manually move the turntable (with the needle in place) until you hear the beginning of the section. When you require the section, simply raise the rotating base, and the section will start.

The Tape Player

Standard audio cassettes are widely available, and offer a convenient method for recording and playing back material. Professional tape players (see Figure 3.11) offer variable speed (pitch) controls, and instant playback when 'Play' is pressed. Dolby noise reduction suppresses some of the treble 'hiss' caused by tapes coming into

Figure 3.11
A Tascam professional
cassette player

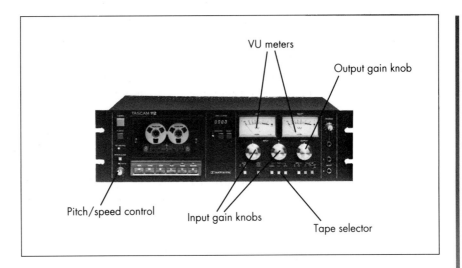

VU meters

Output gain knob

Pitch/speed control

Input gain knobs

Tape selector

contact with the head, although some recordings tend to sound to 'bass-y' with this function engaged.

DAT

The DAT player offers CD-quality recordings, but with the convenience of a recordable audio cassette. Basic functions and operation are similar to the portable DAT recorder, and the use of ID codes makes finding sections of recordings quick and easy.

The Mixer

The mixer (Figure 3.12) is perhaps one of the most important elements in a sound studio, as it allows you to merge, separate and 'balance' many different inputs. The inputs may be a CD player, a microphone, a DAT player or a record, and if two or more inputs are played simultaneously, the mixer allows you to balance and mix the sources together, outputting the end result to a recording device.

Figure 3.12
A 16-track Yamaha
professional mixer

Figure 3.13
A Tascam 6-track mixer

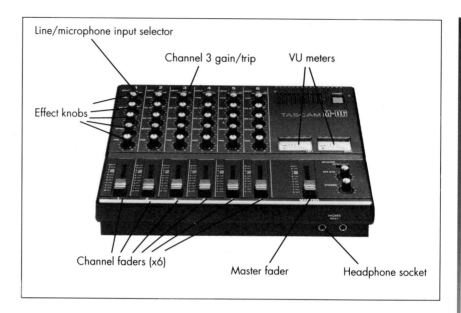

A sound mixer can be manufactured with any number of channels/inputs to suit particular uses (see Figure 3.12), although, to keep things simple, our example in Figure 3.13 has six. All sound mixers will include the following components: channel inputs, VU meters, various sound compensation/effects knobs and the master fader.

Before starting to record, several knobs must be preset. Firstly, the input to each channel must be set to either the microphone ('Mic') or 'Line' input. The need to be able select a different input is important, as a microphone has a lower output signal than a playback device. The output from a record deck, CD or tape player should be connected to a line input.

Mixer functions and labels explained

Channel Input Selector: The channel input selector must be set for the correct input (see above), which can either be 'Mic' or 'Line'.

Preset Gain: This must be set to even out the discrepancy between input variations of the different sources. Throughout this chapter we have referred to an 'average' dB reference of −3dB, and this should be used to set the gain. On some machines, the preset gain knob may be marked as 'Trim'.

Prefade Listen Switch (PFL): This is an important facility on any mixer, as it allows you to cue up a CD or record, and listen to it before mixing to the main output. The level from channel can also be checked and

adjusted as necessary before committing the source to tape. This switch is imperative for recordings that are being made live.

Pan: With stereo recordings, the pan knob allows you to adjust the signal to accentuate the left or right hand output.

Clip: This automatically 'clips' recordings that peak over a certain preset dB rating.

Bass control: Used to accentuate the low bass frequencies.

Treble control: Used to accentuate the high treble frequencies.

EQ: An abbreviation for 'equalisation'. Similar to the

domestic graphic equaliser, this allows you to accentuate or diminish treble, mid-range and bass frequencies.

Mute: By pushing this button, the signal is automatically cut to zero.

Output Monitor: The mixed output can be listened to on loudspeakers or through headphones. The latter are useful, as they reduce distracting noises and help you to keep your concentration.

Channel Fader: Unlike the preset gain control, this allows a much finer adjustment of the channel level. Channel faders are used during the mixing process to increase or decrease the level of sound smoothly.

Sound Level Monitoring

On all professional sound mixers the level of the output is monitored by a *peak programme meter* (PPM). Some mixers have VU or LED meters on the input sources, which can be used to alter the preset gain before recording. It is essential that the output of the mixer, which is fed to the recording equipment, is monitored constantly: if the needles/LED start moving into the red band, the sounds will distort badly. If you find that your sound output levels are entering the red band constantly, reduce the master fader.

VU Meters

When setting a mixer that uses VU meters or an LED display, use the standard reference tone (0dB at 1000 cycles 0.775Vrms) to adjust the master fader to the optimum level. With the fader set at the maximum position you intend to use (normally represented by a figure 7 on the fader scale), the VU meters should read –3dB on the scale, this will give the correct output level. The standard reference signal can either be prerecorded on a tape, or the mixer may its own signal generator (normally a button marked 'OSC').

Peak Programme Meters

PPMs differ from VU meters, as their scale is divided into four decibel divisions, with the reference level (0dB at 1 000 cycles 0.775Vrms) set at number 4 on the scale (see Figure 3.14). Following the guide above, set the master fader with the PPM so that it peaks at number 4 on the scale.

Figure 3.14
The peak programme meter on this professional mixer is different from the standard VU meter

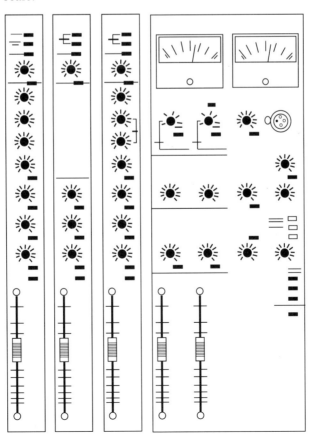

Set-up and operation

To use an example, we will talk through the procedure needed to set up a mixer using four inputs: one microphone, a tape player, a compact disk player and a record deck.

Checking Sound Levels

The first and most important procedure is to set the output level of the mixer, and most have a built-in oscillator (marked 'OSC') to generate the standard reference level of 0dB. Set the master fader to the number 7 mark, and connect the mixer output to the recording equipment. With the oscillator switched on, adjust the master gain so that the master meters read 4 on a PPM and –3dB if using VU or LED.

When using a PPM, it is normal practice to set music levels to peak between 3 and 4, and for speech, between 4 and 5. With the mixer level set, the levels on the recorder should now also be adjusted to the optimum position. Most recorders use a VU meter to set the levels, so the setting should be adjusted to –3dB with the mixer on full output. Once the master levels have been set on the mixer and the recorder, they should not be adjusted until the recording is over.

Setting up the Channels

Using our example, the mixer will be set up with the microphone connected to channel 1, the CD player to channel 2, the tape player to channel 3, and the record deck to channel 4.

- *Channel 1:* As the output from the microphone is low in comparison to other playback sources, channel 1 should be switched to 'Mic' input. With the subject being recorded at its loudest, the level should be set with the channel fader set to number 7. This enables the fader to be 'ridden' to cope with variations of voice level. The preset gain should now be adjusted to produce a voice level that peaks between –3 and 0dB on the meter scale. Once the preset gain has been set, the sound level should only be increased or decreased by the channel fader, hence the term 'ridden'.
- *Channels 2–4:* As the CD player, tape player and record deck have a larger output level than the microphone, the channels should be switched to 'Line' input. Unlike the setting of the microphone in Channel 1, the fader switch should not need to be ridden during the recording, as when the CD/tape/record was recorded the correct sound levels were maintained.

To set the preset gain, play the source machine and adjust the preset gain knob to give a meter reading between –3 and 0dB at the loudest point of the recording. Once this has been set, you should only need to adjust the fader switch to fade the recording up or down.

The mixer in the example has six channels, and the same procedure should be used for the remaining two channels if extra microphones or other source players were being used.

Figure 3.15
Four pages from a radio
drama script

RADIO SCRIPT:

"The Early Train"

PAGE ONE OF TWENTY

CAST OF CHARACTERS

Husband on train
Wife on train
Young man on train
Stuart
Olivia his wife
Narrator

SOUND EFFECTS (SFX):

Interior of moving electric train.
Train horn.
Interior of a steam train.
Whistle.
Sliding door.
Mobile phone.
Newspaper rustle.
Plates, knives and forks, glasses.
Bottle being opened and drink being poured.
Modern telephone ringing.
Title music.
Background music

RUNNING TIME:
20 minutes.

"The Early Train"

PAGE TWO OF TWENTY

RUNNING ORDER:
Scene 1: Train
Characters: Husband and wife
Action: Moving train. Reading an evening newspaper and New Scientist.

Scene 2: House Interior (dining room)
Characters: Stuart and Olivia
Action: Setting table for dinner

Scene 3: Train
Characters: Moving train. Husband, wife and young man.
Action: Young man enters in old fashioned army uniform.

Scene 4: House interior (dining room)
Characters: Stuart and Olivia
Action: Olivia enters from kitchen. Pours drink.

Scene 5: Train
Characters: Husband, wife and young man
Action: Young man pointing a gun

Scene 6: House interior (dining room)
Characters: Stuart and Olivia
Action: Stuart reading a newspaper.

Scene 7: Train
Characters: Husband and wife
Action: Train stopped

Scene 8 : House interior (dining room)
Characters: Stuart and Olivia
Action: Telephone rings

"The Early Train"

PAGE THREE OF TWENTY

TIME: 10"

1. *Introductory music faded under (10").*

2. **Narrator:** This is the story of a journey. Not an ordinary journey, but one that is unusual to say the least. Recently, a husband and wife were on a train going to visit friends for dinner. Little did they know what they were about to experience. (13")

3. *Music out... (03")*

4. **SCENE ONE:** *Fade up sound effect of electric train. Run under throughout scene. (05")*

5. *Fade up husband and wife in conversation.*

6. **HUSBAND:** "I see old Braithwaite's still rabbiting on about his radiation field theory. He was writing papers about that when I was doing my Ph.D. What a load of rubbish. His arguments were flawed from the word go. Main reason he didn't get that job at Cavendish Laboratory was because he knew more than anyone else in the field." (20")

7. **WIFE:** "What theory is that darling ?" (02")

8. **HUSBAND:** "Oh, he claims that time is actually a form of oscillating energy, and that all events are synchronised in time by their sensitivity to field. His theory is based on some work done in the 50s by an American called Charles Muses Braithwaite. He did some purely theoretical studies on events which seemed to contain anomalies in time." (17")

CONT.../

"The Early Train"

PAGE FOUR OF TWENTY

9. **WIFE:** "I thought I wouldn't understand it." (02")

10. **HUSBAND:** "I'm not sure that I understand it either, but he based a lot of his theories on things like precognition and reincarnation. I recall he got quite involved with some Hindu chappie. As you know Hindus are heavily into that sort of thing." (13")

11. **WIFE:** "What's that mean?" (02")

12. **HUSBAND:** "Oh just another way of saying that time at a particular place could jump from one point to another. He never managed to prove it though because no-one was prepared to pay for the experimental work. One of his papers in the early 60s suggested that he wanted to move two 50 ton containers past each other at 100 miles an hour." (16")

13 **WIFE:** "Sounds rather dangerous to me." (02")

14. **HUSBAND:** "Probably would have been. People were a lot more nervous about nuclear material in those days. Today, we wouldn't give it a second thought. Did you know that we have 50 ton containers of nuclear waste moving around the railways every day. I believe they use this line quite often." (14")

AND SO IT CONTINUES...

(This extract was used with the kind permission of Alan Lindfield).

Script Writing

When producing an audio play or a piece of narration for a radio documentary, it is vital that the script includes sound and effects cues as well as the dialogue.

Use one side of A4 paper to write your script, leaving a wide margin on the left for extra information such as effects, music etc. The script should be double spaced to allow alterations and to make it easier to read. Each page and item should be numbered, and sentences should be completed on the same page, so that the reader will not need to turn the page half-way through a sentence.

Narration

When writing a script for narration, use a typewriter or word processor and avoid lengthy sentences. This is so that when you or your presenter read it, it doesn't sound as though it is being read. By far the best way to check that your piece is appropriate for radio is to read it through several times aloud, or record the script on tape. This will enable you to make alterations to the dialogue, adjust the speed of delivery and make decisions where pauses should be made. At all times radio dialogue should flow naturally and be clear, as listeners are relying on their sense of hearing alone.

When recording a narration or dialogue to tape, it is a good idea to treat the microphone as a person. Use hand gestures as you would in normal conversation, as this will help you to control the speed and style of delivery. With several pages of script, spread them out in front of you, so that you can read two or three pages at a time. If you do make a mistake, go back to the beginning of the last sentence, leave a short pause (this will help in editing) and start again.

Drama

Audio drama requires a different approach to narration, as plays written for radio normally include sound effects and music, which help to create a feeling of reality. Unlike stage drama, where voice projection is needed to reach those sitting at the back of the theatre, radio is much more intimate. Careful use of the microphone and the way the dialogue is delivered are very important. Remember that the listener cannot see you, and actions such as 'smiling' to portray happiness can only be achieved in the delivery of the dialogue.

Figure 3.15 (on page 105) which is part of a 20min play, shows the layout of a script. Note the use of timings, references and item numbers.

Sound Effects

Most sound effects (crashing waves, birdsong, ticking clock, etc.) are available on record or CD, although it can also be fun to try making some effects yourself. Brown paper crumpled together can sound like a fire; opening and closing an umbrella simulates the flapping of wings; two coconut shell halves sound like the clip-clop of a horse; for squeaks, try rubbing a cork on piece of glass. By experimenting you can create novel sound effects quite simply by using everyday materials and a bit of imagination.

Music

Remember all recordings are regulated by the copyright laws, so you must get clearance from the copyright holder before using any.

Buying rights to a piece of music can be expensive, although there are some CDs and taped recordings that are copyright free. All you have to pay is the purchase price of the CD or tape.

The Resources list at the end of this book gives some of the sources for cheap or copyright-free music.

Television Sound

As we will see in Chapter 5, sound is just as important in television as the pictures. Any production can be ruined by the poor use of sound, so it is advisable to read this chapter before embarking on any video project.

Unlike radio, video and television demand that microphones are hidden away from the camera whenever possible. This can create problems, although there are special microphones available to help you surmount them.

The Lavalier or Tie Clip Microphone

This miniature microphone should be clipped to a piece of the presenter's clothing about 45cm away from her/his mouth. Most tie clip mikes have a cable connecting it to a mixer, and these should be hidden underneath clothing. Tie clip mikes are ideal for television presenters, but impinge on the 'reality' of drama. They also tend to suffer from the rustling if placed too near loose clothing.

Radio Microphone

Radio microphones are very convenient, as they allow the performer complete freedom of movement. Most consist of a small radio transmitter and a receiver and have no cable. The performer carries the transmitter in a back pocket, making sure that the wire aerial is left outside. The receiver is placed on the sound desk and connected up to the mixer like a conventional microphone.

The radio mike's range is variable, and it is at its best when used on the principle of 'direct line of sight'. Beware of interference and variable signal levels when radio mikes are used to their limit.

Gun or Rifle Microphone

Microphones of this type are used extensively for drama and outside location work. They are very directional and have to be positioned with some care. When fitted to a boom pole, they can be moved fairly rapidly by the operator, although they can suffer from wind noise. Be careful not to cause shadows with the microphone on a sunny day, and always be aware of the camera operator's frame. A visible microphone dangling above performers in a piece of serious drama will ruin the film for sure.

Conference Microphone

As its name implies, this microphone is mainly used for groups of speakers as it has an all round pickup angle. Mounted on soft rubber to reduce noise, the microphone is placed on a table in the centre of a group and will give a reasonable level from all the participants.

Glossary

Below is a list of technical terms and what they mean.

Ambient Noise or Wild Sound: This is the normal background noise of a room or environment.

Amplifier: A device used to increase the output level of a signal.

Balance: The position of the microphone for the best pickup.

Bi-Directional Microphone: A microphone that responds equally from the front and back.

Cans: Jargon for headphones.

Capstan: The drive spindle of a tape recorder for driving the tape through at a constant speed.

Crossfade: A slow shift from one sound source to another.

Cue: This is the common signal to start. When recording, this is normally made silently by the dropping of the director's arm.

Cut: A command to stop.

dB: An abbreviation of *decibel* – a measurement of sound. The standard reference level is 0dB at 1kHz 775Vrms.

DIN: Abbreviation of *Deutsche Industrie Normen*. This is the European standard of equalisation and plugs and sockets.

Dolby: A noise reduction system. When a tape is played with Dolby operative, the treble levels are lowered and tape hiss becomes less noticeable.

Drop out: Where the oxide on the tape is missing. This causes a gap in the recording.

Dubbing: Copying from one recorder to another.

Editing: To place sections of a recording into a different order.

Erase: The removal of signals on magnetic tape.

Erase Head: The magnetic head that rearranges the metal particles on a tape, effectively erasing any previous recording.

Fade: Method of increasing or decreasing sound levels.

Feedback: A high-pitched whining sound, caused when a microphone and loud speaker are too close together.

Flutter: Distortion in recording caused by a fluctuation in tape speed.

Foldback: The choice of selected sounds fed to the studio.

Frequency: The numbers of vibrations per second. Measured in cycles per second (cps) or Hertz (Hz).

FX: Abbreviation of *effects*.

Gain: Amplification.

Gain control: A fader for controlling the level of sound.

Grams: Record deck.

Head: A device for recording or playing back onto or from magnetic tape.

Hiss: A high-frequency noise associated with tape recording.

Hum: Low-frequency noise.

Idler or Pinch Wheel: In conjunction with the capstan, this drives the tape through a recorder.

ips: Abbreviation for *inches per second*.

Leader: Uncoated non-magnetic tape for splicing onto the beginning and end of a recorded piece.

Limiter: A method used to control the level of sound automatically.

Line-up: The checking of all equipment to the standard reference level and setting all equipment to it.

Master Gain: Controls the main output level of sound from an audio mixer.

Microphone: A device for converting sound waves from a diaphragm into a small electrical voltage.

Mic/mike: Abbreviation for *microphone*.

Mix: To combine a number of different sounds.

Mixer: A desk containing a number of channels which can be individually faded to a combined output.

Mono: Single channel of sound.

Monitor: Another word for a loudspeaker. This is used to check the quality of a recording.

Omni-directional Microphone: Sensitive to sound coming from all directions.

Polar Diagram: A diagram showing the pickup range of a microphone.

Pot: Another name for a fader or volume control.

PPM: Abbreviation for *peak programme meter*. This is normally the master meter on a mixer.

Producer: The person with overall responsibility for a production.

Radio Microphone: A cordless microphone which comprises a transmitter and receiver.

Splicing Block: An editing and cutting block for ¼in magnetic tape.

Splicing: Joining of one piece of magnetic tape to another in editing.

Stereo: Sound that is picked up through pairs of microphones and recorded onto separate channels: Left and Right.

Take: To record a particular sequence.

Unidirectional Microphone: Will only respond from one direction.

VU meter: Abbreviation for *volume unit.* This needle-type of meter is found on all professional recorders, mixers and players.

Windshield: A foam cover placed over a microphone to reduce wind noise.

Further reading

Alkin, G. (1993) *Sound Recording and Reproduction* (2nd ed.) Focal Press.

Borwick, J. (1993) *Microphones, Technology and Technique* Focal Press.

Huber, D.M. (1993) *The Microphone Manual* Focal Press.

Smith, M.T. (1993) *Broadcast Sound Technology* Focal Press.

Taylor, P. (1989) *A–Z of Radio Production* BBC.

Watkinson, J. (1988) *The Art of Digital Audio* Focal Press.

Audio and Radio Techniques

4 Slide/tape Productions

Just outside Dorking is the unlikely sight of a vast acreage of grape vines parading in neat files on the sun-catching chalk slopes of the North Downs. It is in fact Denbie's Wine Estate, the largest commercial vineyard in the country, which will be producing a million bottles of wine a year from 300 000 vines stretching across 250 acres....Media Projects International have produced a multi image show that illustrates the activities of the vineyard through the different seasons. Shown in a dedicated sit-down theatre, the programme uses three Hasselblads and six Carousels projecting onto a 7 by 2.9 metres screen area to display the impressive results of a photographic shoot that was staggered over a full twelve months. Narrative is provided by Denbie's personnel, both those involved in tending vines and those employed in the winemaking process.

With so few stand alone A/V's now being produced, it provides a sharp reminder of the ability of the medium to provide the gloriously sharp big image and intrigue the audience with its distinctive visual feel and rhythms. The more outstanding images are on display as purchasable prints in a separate photographic exhibition.

(Audio Visual Communications for Business magazine, August 1993)

What Is Special About Slide/tape Productions?

A slide/tape production is a sequence of synchronised sounds and images. As the quotation above indicates, these productions are now less common because video productions have become more prevalent. However, there are still attractions in slide/tape technology for some purposes and situations.

The basic slide/tape presentation consists of a collection of slides with an accompanying sound tape which is synchronised through the recording of electronic pulses to change the slide at a preset point. The sound tape can of course include a mix of voices, music, dramatic dialogue and sound effects.

It is possible to use a single unit comprising a slide projector and cassette deck with pulse recording mechanism which makes it extremely easy to produce a single projector presentation (see Figure 4.1). Such machines, made by Bell and Howell or Elf, can also contain a microchip so that the slide order can be pre-programmed to access the slides randomly. For example, if one wanted to repeat the same establishing slide several times within the sequence it would not be necessary to provide several copies of the same image but simply to select the relevant slide as needed. That same slide can be returned to as often as required.

In this chapter we shall confine ourselves to a single projector and single screen presentation. Figure 4.1 shows a simple integrated unit consisting of slide projector, cassette recorder for recording both sound and pulses to change slides, and back projector screen. (Slides can also be projected onto a large-scale separate screen.)

The production referred to at the head of this chapter uses six carousels and can be used for multi-images. A professional slide/tape exhibition is likely to use stacked projectors with a dissolve unit to change slides without there being any blank screen between images. Images can also be built up or sequenced to provide an animated movement effect. The sound tape can also be multi-tracked. Such presentations are often part of a permanent display accompanied by lighting sequences on dramatic sets and by 'speaking' life-size figures that are 'audio animatronic'.

An example of such a state of the art multimedia presentation built around sound and images can be experienced at Madame Tussaud's in London. The article which was quoted at the start of this chapter describes five recently installed audio-visual projects. At Madame Tussaud's there is now a £10 million dark ride depicting 400 years of the history of London. Visitors first enter Elizabethan London and then move on to the Plague and the Great Fire, the rebuilding of London and St Paul's Cathedral, Nelson's Column and the opening of Trafalgar Square, the Industrial Revolution, the Victorian workhouse, the Blitz, swinging London and back to the 1990s. All this in just 5 minutes through a bombardment of bright lights, sounds and images. Phil Pike, head of audio visual at Madame Tussaud's who was responsible for this audio-visual environment, commented: 'It's very

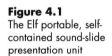
Figure 4.1
The Elf portable, self-contained sound-slide presentation unit

effects-led and there are lots of Pepper's Ghosts, lots of fibre optics, water and smoky smells.' It also demonstrates heavy utilisation of Tussaud's expertise in figure making. There are 73 individual figures of which 32 are audio-animatronic, i.e. an acrylic body that is computer controlled with pneumatics to move with synchronised recorded speech.

Such a created environment with stimuli for all five senses is a long way from a simple single projector tape/slide production. However, the qualities of such a production are the basic ingredients of these large-scale multi-image, multi-media shows. Key qualities of slide/tape include the following.

- Flexible use, from small-scale, intimate personal viewing to large-scale, mass presentation. It can vary from tiny screen and headphones for individual viewing to auditorium scale with a giant screen and amplified sound system.
- Creation of a total environment through compelling sound and images, especially when presented in blackout.
- Visual quality of slides that can give sharp images and detail not yet possible in video. The photographic quality of beautiful and precisely composed pictures lies at the heart of a successful slide/tape presentation. Recent technology to extract still images from video cameras, such as the Canon ION system, still reinforces this impact of the still image. Each image can be left on screen for as long as necessary and detailed focus on elements of the same image can easily be used. If the subject is a painting then specific elements from the total canvas be displayed and described.
- Ease of updating and editing the visual element simply by replacing a slide from the magazine.
- High sound quality of pre-recorded and scripted tape which can develop arresting dramatic impact through voices, sound and music. In the Madame Tussaud's show, each 'viewer' sits in a 'taxi cab' style vehicle and listens to a CD player. Via a personal headphone set it is also possible to use different sound tracks for the same slide sequence; for example, you can produce tapes to accompany the same slide sequence in several languages.
- Comparative ease of production and use make a simple sequence an attractive option for a tourist exhibition or a trade fair, although video productions are increasingly being used. Slide/tape productions can be transferred to video if that is the desired format – in a well-produced multiprojector sequence it may take the video viewer some time to realise that the images are all still!

In summary, there is still something special about slide/tape as a medium. The use of dissolve techniques to maintain an uninterrupted flow of images obviously enhances the basic format considerably. It has even been suggested that 'A good dissolve show is the most impressive and comfortable visual medium for the viewer – free of flicker, excessive noise, and degradation through tape wear. Slide dissolve has high impact combined with the ability to convert information; it can move very quickly in time with exciting sound tracks, or build up complex diagrams gradually to match technical explanations' (*Video Production Techniques*, slide/tape section by David Kilpatrick).

Making a Slide/tape Presentation

We shall confine ourselves here to hints on how to produce a single projector show since the principles remain the same in producing technically more complex multiprojector dissolve productions. If you want to find out more about equipment and techniques for multi projector shows, you could contact a company such as Imatronic Audio Visual of Chelmsford (details are in the Resource section, on page 228) who specialise in slide projector control equipment. Figure 4.2 shows the configuration of equipment for a multi-projector dissolve production: in this case four slide projectors, a controller for the dissolves and a computer programming unit.

Figure 4.2
The configuration of equipment for multi-projector dissolve production

Getting Started

We are not talking here about a random collection of holiday slides which are shown to friends and family in the same way we use a family photo album. We are describing a carefully planned, researched and scripted production. The general advice on how to approach productions in Chapter 1 applies just as much to slide and tape as it does to video tape. Similarly, the information on creating sound tapes and taking photographs in the previous chapters is essential for successful production of synchronised slide/tape presentations.

The more clear and precise you can be about the following elements the better.

1 Why am I producing it? What effects do I want to gain?
2 Who will view it? What types of audience is it intended for?
3 Where will it be viewed? A large-scale screen in a darkened room demands a different approach from a small screen seeking to attract attention in a trade exhibition or retail outlet.

4 What subjects and content are needed? What approach to the subject is needed? For example, if you are presenting a particular town or area, your approach will change depending on whether you making the presentation for local residents, for potential tourists, or for business people you want to invest in the area.

5 What sources of sound and visual information do I have access to? What is the budget available and the time scale? If you are preparing a presentation on a full year in the life of a place, an industry, a farm, a college then you would find it difficult without having a year to record the sounds and images throughout the year – unless you have access to suitable archive material.

6 Will the final product have to stand alone or be operated by someone on site?

7 How long should the finished presentation last?

As we stressed in Chapter 1, initial research, 'recce', planning and preparing an outline 'treatment' or draft script are all essential if only to save time later.

Researching

When you have answered the questions listed above, and maybe a few more specific issues, you are ready to start the real preparation.

A recurring theme of this book is that any audio, visual or audio-visual production begins with *ideas*, with having something that someone or some group wants to convey to some other group. All of the finally selected and arranged sounds and images will contribute to those ideas you are seeking to convey to the target audience.

The quality of the finished photographic images is a key to an impressive and memorable presentation, so we suggest you begin with visual research. But at the same time keep your potential soundtrack in mind too, so that voices and sounds accompany the sights in your mind's eye.

You have already drafted a treatment or outline script and we suggest that you also think of possible dialogue, commentary, music or sound effect alongside that script. You might find it helpful to use a storyboard to visualise your treatment. Sketching stick diagrams is an effective way of ensuring that your sequence of images is varied. If you are using a shot of a building or a machine it will be more effective as you describe it to have several images from different angles and with different details.

We are assuming that you are the only member of this 'production team', but you may have to commission and brief someone else as your photographer so you need to indicate your plans and requirements in advance. A storyboard treatment can be useful for such a briefing.

The aim of your visual research is to ensure visual variety. Think about as many visual sources as possible: locations, people, places, animals, machines, pictures, diagrams, cartoons, maps, plans, books . . . use of graphics or computer-generated images, titles and captions, and so on.

Titles, captions or indeed slides of short text can be generated in various ways. It is possible to use computer software to generate them;

they can also be photographs of previously set lettering.

As an exercise in visual research, take your place of work or place of study and imagine you are preparing a sequence of images to promote the place for new employees or students. Walk around and list the images you would want to use. In contrast, imagine you are also producing a sequence to put people off coming to your place of work or study – what images would you now seek? Or could you use some of the same promotional images and change their impact through the commentary script?

Chapter 2 of this book has indicated some ways of working to achieve well-composed photographs. With slides, it is important to capture in the frame the actual image you want. Unlike printed photographs, slides do not offer the facility to crop or work on the image at the printing stage.

When taking the slides, it is important to keep in mind their eventual use as part of a sequence. For example, if your production will include the movement of a car or any other vehicle through a short sequence of images, the movement must be in the same direction. The guidelines on picture composition for still photography and for video all apply to slides.

For multi-projector shows, it is essential that all slides are 'landscape' rather than 'portrait' so that the outline on screen remains the same as the images dissolve. For the same reason, it is advisable to keep to landscape format for any slide/tape sequence. 'Landscape' format means that a rectangular-shaped image is presented with the longer sides at the top and bottom, i.e. lengthways on the page. The cover of this book shows a 'portrait' image, with the longer sides being vertical.

This leads us to the issue of research for appropriate sound. Obviously, the final script will consist of words, either for a single voice or for several voices. You might want to capture natural conversation or you might want scripted dialogue to express specific ideas. For synchronised sound with the slides, you need timed conversation, but you may want a track of background conversation to play unsynchronised with the slide sequence. Atmospheric sound such as traffic noise for street scenes or machine noise for a factory can accompany the slides of those places.

Sound recordings appropriate to the slides are also important, as is appropriate music to create the desired atmosphere and mood. Copyright on music for public presentation is an issue and we have referred to that elsewhere in this book (see p. 106).

For guidance on scripting and the layout of scripts, see page 106 in Chapter 3. Here, we simply want to stress that the commentary, or any dialogues or interviews played over the slides, must be understandable to the listener/viewer at first hearing. This means that the language must be simple and direct, in short sentences with the easy flow of spoken, rather than written, structures. For instance, if you were describing a church it would not be appropriate simply to read from a guidebook: the content of the book would need to be rewritten into direct and easy-to-listen-to sentences.

It is also important not to state the obvious. If you were showing a slide of the church tower it would be crass to say, 'This is the church tower', but you might comment, 'The tower, built in the fourteenth century, is one of the finest in Somerset'.

As you write any script, read it aloud to ensure it reads and flows easily. Leave space between sentences to be filled by sound, music or, when appropriate, silence.

Putting It Together

Having planned and researched, and obtained your initial collection of slides and your sounds and draft script, the next step is to select the slides to make the final sequence.

If your final presentation is limited to one magazine of 80 slides, you should have more than that to select from, but you may also not want to use as many as 80. Each slide should have a point to make and not be there to 'pad out' the presentation.

It is very useful, if not essential, to have a light box to enable you to preview all your slides and to select and arrange them into the numbered sequence. This selected order will follow your script but at this stage you may well revise your outline script to reflect the final choice of images.

It is important to view the slides as a series of mini-sequences and not as individual slides. Watch for movement of people and things in the same direction (the crossover effects on video apply to a slide sequence as well), keep the horizon on the same level, do not change immediately from a dark slide to light one (unless for dramatic effect) and look at the colour patterns of the sequence to develop some visual harmony.

When you have made your first selection of the sequence, the slides must be mounted (if they have not been already). For repeated professional use and for precise focusing, slides are best mounted in glass mounts. If you were using multiprojectors dissolve systems you would also want pin registration mounts for precise alignments of each overlapping slide in the frame.

With your slides in the correct order, you can either place them in sequence in plastic suspension-file sheets and view them in order on the light box, or you may prefer to place them in the carousel to project one at a time. At this stage, place a dot in the top right corner of the mount to ensure they are always loaded the correct way round and the correct way up. When your selection is final, also place a number next to the dot so you always have the correct running order.

The next phase is to run through the sound script whilst viewing the slides. At this point it is important to time the projection of each slide to ensure the pace is neither too slow nor too fast. Generally, a fast-moving slide show has more impact – a time of 7–8sec will allow about 25 words for each slide. The tempo of any music you use must also complement the speed of slide changes. If you want to create a gentle romantic atmosphere from beautiful landscapes, the music has to reinforce the mood. The key thing is to familiarise yourself with the script and slides and to experiment before you settle on final synchronisation and record your tape. It is essential to record whilst viewing the slides either on a light box or, preferably, while they are being projected.

For information on laying down a recorded tape see Chapter 3.

The final process is of course to record the electronic pulses on the sound tape so that the slides change at the correct moment of sound. As with all synchronised productions, the precise timing is essential or the effect of sound and image juxtaposition can create comic effects. The audience would not want to hear something like 'One of the first things you will do when you join the college is to become familiar with the library . . . ' whilst viewing a slide of a television studio which is still on screen from the previous section.

The opening title slides and closing end slides are crucial for most impact and the music or voice-over at those start and end points are also important. Be clear how you want to leave the viewers. Always start and end a slide/tape production with a black slide, not a white screen. It gives much greater impact.

Piloting and Reviewing
Having completed the final synchronisation, always test the finished presentation with sample viewers from your target audience. Ideally, you will have left time now to make some final amendments in the light of their analysis. Depending on the nature of the production, you can pilot the presentation at the slide selection and final script stage before recording and pulsing the tape.

A Note on slide projectors
All slide projectors work on basically the same principle to enable even, bright light to shine through a slide and through a lens so that the image can be projected and focused on a screen. Some projectors load from the side and some from above. The advantage of top loading is that the slide falls into position without the need for force and therefore with less chance of jamming.

All slide projectors have the same basic parts:

■ The lamp to illuminate the slide. These are now usually low-voltage quartz halogen lamps taking 24 volts from a transformer which is built into the body of the projector.
■ A fan to draw air over the bulb to keep it cool. It is also important that the slide does not become too hot or it may buckle and lose focus.
■ A concave mirror to reflect the light forward. This is often coated to reflect only the visible light and to absorb infra-red radiation: this helps to keep the temperature down.
■ Two or more condenser lenses which collect light from the bulb and mirror reflector and focus it in the projector lens. They provide an even brightness over the whole image.
■ A heat filter, usually between the condensers, which allows visible light to pass through but stops infra-red. It helps to keep the illuminated slide cooler.

117

■ The slide carrier, which varies in operation according to the make and design of the projector.

■ The projector lens, which usually has a focal length of 85mm and an aperture of *f*/2.8 or *f*/2.5. The lens is mounted in a threaded tube to enable focusing on a screen in various sized rooms.

■ A remote control device is now also usual. This is essential for a synchronised slide/tape presentation, since the pulsed tape will feed in here.

■ A slide magazine, which will vary according to the make and design of the projector; it may be either circular or straight. The circular carousel developed by Kodak has become the most common standard. A carousel holds 80 slides.

As indicated above, it is possible to purchase an integrated projector, cassette recorder and back-projector screen in one unit which enables the producer to record the sound track and pulses very easily. These are also available with a microchip which enables the pre-selection and repetition of slides with random access from the magazine.

Activities

Commission from the Fire Service

As a result of some advice, the public relations officer of the local fire service has commissioned you to produce a single projector and tape production that can be shown from a single machine to community groups in town and village halls. It should last about 10min and show the range of work of the Fire Service. Prepare an outline treatment for her to consider.

Additionally, she wishes to use some of the same slides in a 45sec sequence that can be part of the display screen that is used at careers conventions to attract young people into careers in the fire service. You may not want to use a commentary but may want optional music. The purpose is to attract and hold the attention of people as they pass the stand. Prepare a storyboard showing the types of images you would want to use.

Work and live in the place that has everything . . .

You have been asked by the Economic Development Unit of a local council to make a proposal for a 5–10min sequence of sound and slides to promote its area at national conferences to attract companies to relocate there. They want you to show why that location is more desirable than others and to include such things as transport access, current business and industry, local skills, social and leisure amenities, education and training services, and available sites and grants.

Choose an area you know fairly well and prepare a treatment to show the council how you would present the location through a slide/tape production.

Further reading

Gration, G., Reilly, J. and Titford, J. (1988) *Communication and Media Studies: an introductory coursebook* Macmillan.

Kilpatrick, D. and Elliott (eds.) (1985) *Video Production Techniques* Kluwer.

5 Video and Television Production

Introduction The first television cameras were very bulky and relied on the use of valves and tubes to produce a black and white picture. Space exploration and the desire for technological progress encouraged the development of cameras that were small, light and reliable enough to be carried aboard shuttles and satellites across vast distances.

The first black and white television pictures from the moon and, later, colour pictures of the planets from a satellite gave the first close-up look at parts of our solar system that had previously only been seen from Earth through a telescope. Since those early days technical progress has continued, with the valves now replaced by microprocessors, and the tube replaced by an electronic chip with millions of individual light sensors incorporated into a charged couple device (CCD). The CCD has reduced the physical size and weight of

Figure 5.1 'above'
A typical TV studio

the modern television camera, producing high picture quality and portability.

Nowadays there are few situations in which a television camera hasn't been used. Underwater housings allow video cameras to be taken below the waves, while fibre optic tubes and 'minicams' allow pictures to be obtained from almost anywhere. Fibre optics have helped the medical profession look at the internal workings of the body, and minicams are *de rigueur* at Formula One racing events. These torch-sized cameras are mounted onto the side of racing cars for dramatic, fast-moving pictures in with the action.

The most familiar use of video cameras, however, is in broadcasting, where a number of them can be used together in a studio or singly on outside locations. Until the beginning of the 1980s, recording outside the studio meant that the camera crew had to take two units, a camera and a video recorder, as well as rechargeable batteries for both. With the camcorder (a term to describe a television camera with the video recorder built in as part of the body), the whole unit is carried by one person, thereby making things more convenient and easy to use.

Television news has benefited most from new technology, as access to incidents has become easier and quicker due to the portability of the equipment. Electronic news gathering (ENG) demands pictures that can be sent via microwaves directly to the studio for transmission, and the use of video ensures that pictures are ready instantly. In the days when 16mm celluloid film was used, processing could take as much as 5 hours, so footage would often be out of date by the time it was transmitted.

Now that 'amateur' video cameras are widely available, the popularity of using Super 8mm cine (celluloid film) at home has declined. Buying and using a camcorder has become much cheaper, as mass production and the use of magnetic tape have cut costs. Video allows you to save money on processing costs, you can record over mistakes, magnetic tape is cheaper to buy, and there is no need to set up a screen every time you want to view your work. However, 16mm and 35mm film cameras still produce higher quality pictures than video.

The television camera has come a long way since its beginning, but further development is required before it can compete with the picture quality that is produced by film. Not until a television picture is comparable to projected film will it ever become a serious rival to celluloid. There are experiments taking place with high-definition television systems, but it will be some time before these become widely available.

However, the sheer ease of using video, and the savings it offers over film, has meant that film cameras are seldom used in universities and colleges, apart from in specialised film courses. To reflect this, this chapter only refers to video, although many camera techniques are equally applicable to film. For further details about film technique, you should refer to the bibliography at the end of the chapter.

Camera Set-up and Operation

The video camera is made up of two main parts: the lens and the electronics. Before using either for the first time, it is essential to be familiar with the basics.

Figure 5.2 shows a typical professional camcorder, while Figure 5.3 shows an amateur equivalent. The main difference between the two is the amount of manual control available to the user, and also the higher picture quality produced by the professional camera. A professional camera produces sharper pictures because it uses three CCDs to produce the picture electronically, as opposed to the amateur version's single CCD. Professional cameras also use large tape formats such as Betacam or U-matic SP, and feature interchangeable lenses.

Figure 5.2
A Sony professional camcorder

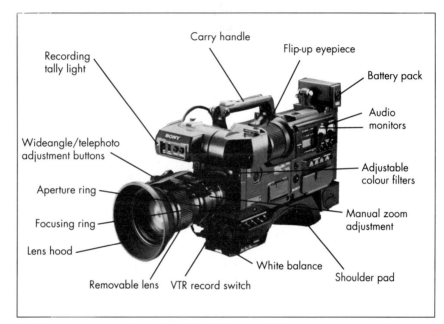

Figure 5.3
The Panasonic M40 amateur camcorder

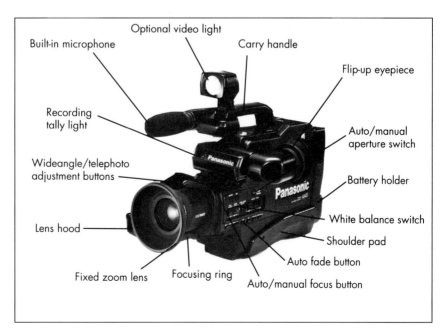

It should be noted that all amateur video cameras these days have the video recorder built into the camera body, while some professional cameras (notably U-Matic versions) have separate video tape recorders (VTRs) that are linked to the camera with a special lead. However, the controls for this type of camera remain exactly the same as for the professional camcorder.

The lens

All video camera lenses have three main adjustments: the aperture, zoom and focus (see Figures 5.2 and 5.3). Most amateur camcorders only allow the user a certain degree of manual control, with the aperture and focus normally being set automatically. Autofocus is unheard of on a professional camera, and the aperture is semi-automatic with a manual override facility.

The lens on a video camera operates in an identical way to the lens on a 35mm stills camera, so we recommend that you read the beginning of Chapter 2 for further understanding of such technicalities as focal length and depth of field.

The aperture

The correct setting of the aperture is very important, as this controls the amount of light that is let in through the lens. Wrong adjustment will result in poor quality pictures that are either too dark (underexposed) or too light (overexposed).

Normally the aperture is set automatically, and will compensate for differences in the light level as the camera is moved around. However, lighting conditions vary considerably, and the auto facility can be a nuisance. A typical example of this is when you are shooting a subject with a bright or dark background. When this occurs, the camera's automatic setting will set the aperture for the background, leaving the subject to be under-or overexposed. To overcome this, set the aperture to the manual position, and turn the iris accordingly until you have the correct exposure for your subject. Always remember to set the control back to 'Auto' after use.

Most amateur cameras have lenses built into the camera body, and lack a 'true' aperture to alter the exposure. Instead you have to use the automatic 'backlight' button, or (if the camera has it) the exposure dial. Both these methods are a poor substitute to changing the aperture manually, but they do allow you to over- or underexpose the subject as if you were using an aperture, even though the result is not as precise as manually controlling the aperture itself.

Remember: the higher the f-stop on the lens, the greater the depth of field. Depth of field decreases the higher the focal length you use. See 'The Lens' on page 35 for further details.

The zoom lens

All modern video cameras have zoom lenses to allow the focal length to be altered continuously. This means that a telephoto or wide angle shot can be achieved using just one lens. Early television cameras did not have zooms, and instead used several lenses that were rotated round and changed to alter the focal length. Today's video cameras have automatic zoom buttons to change the focal length of the lens, and these are marked 'T' for telephoto, and 'W' for wide angle.

Professional cameras have variable speed zooms that adjust depending on how much pressure is exerted on the switch. A variable speed zoom is extremely useful for carrying out smooth pull-backs from a subject, although for extreme speed in changing focal lengths (normally only used for dramatic effect) the manual zoom can be used.

Focusing

Focusing seems to create the most difficulty for inexperienced camera operators, and you should never rely on autofocus. With autofocus, the camera will often focus on the wrong subject, or will oscillate between different objects, creating annoying and amateurish shots.

The correct way to ensure perfect focus is to zoom fully into the subject (by using the telephoto setting of the lens) before pressing the record button. The focus ring should then be turned so that the picture looks pin sharp in the viewfinder. Once this has been done, you can reframe the shot (by zooming out), and the subject will remain in sharp focus.

Of course, if you need to change focus while the camera is recording, then it will not be possible to use this technique. It is a good idea to practice focusing on moving objects as much as possible before actually filming anything important. This can be done by setting the camera up by the side of a road (ensuring you and the equipment are in a safe place), and trying to keep cars moving towards you in focus for as long as possible. This is not easy, so once you have mastered this you should have no problem focusing in the future.

Preparing to use the camera

There are a number of adjustments that have to be made before using a video camera. Unlike the human eye, cameras have to be adjusted to cope with different lighting conditions (i.e. indoor lighting, sunny outdoor conditions and cloudy outdoor conditions) and this is done by altering the white balance, and (in the case of professional cameras) by changing the camera's internal filters.

As is the case for photographic film, video cameras must be set correctly for the colour temperature of the dominant source of light. With professional cameras, this will involve changing the internal filter (normally done by rotating a knob located behind a small door on the camera body) and resetting the white balance. To do this, zoom in on a white piece of paper, ensuring that it fills the frame. Once this is done, push the white balance button (normally located underneath the lens mount) until the camera viewfinder reads 'White Balance OK'. It is absolutely imperative that this is set correctly, as there is nothing worse than recording an event and finding that when it is played back the picture is unnaturally blue or orange in colour.

With amateur video cameras, most of the hard work is taken care of for you, as there is normally an automatic white balance setting, as well as two selections for outdoor and indoor filming. These *must* be adjusted every time you change location, and if there is a manual white balance facility, do use it if you can.

The shot

There are seven basic shots in television (Figure 5.4):

Shot	Abbreviation
Big close up	BCU
Close up	CU
Medium close up	MCU
Medium shot	MS
Three quarter shot	¾ shot
Medium long shot	MLS
Long shot (also known as the 'wide shot')	LS

Figure 5.4
The seven main shot angles and their abbreviations

Long/Wide shot **LS/WS**

Medium long shot **MLS**

Three-quarter shot **3/4**

Medium shot **MS**

Medium close up **MCU**

Close up **CU**

Big close up **BCU**

At first glance, you may think that each of these shots can be achieved from one camera position alone (say, a close up can only be achieved by using extreme telephoto on the zoom), but this is not the case. As in photography, using the wide angle setting on the zoom when framing a close up will result in a lot of the background being shown; while using the telephoto setting for a close up will result in a small proportion of the background being visible in the frame (see Figure 2.12 in Chapter 2). Always bear this in mind when framing your shots.

Composition

Unlike the human eye, a camera records everything impartially. It is up to the camera operator to select the important parts of the view, and compose the shot accordingly to show their importance. For example, when setting up a shot of a person, the eyeline should be in the top third of the picture, and you should allow a slight gap above the head (otherwise known as 'headroom'). 'Speaking space' (see Figure 5.5) should always be given in front of a person, unless they are talking directly to the camera. Similarly, a moving subject should have 'walking space' into which it can move.

Good composition of the picture will greatly enhance the overall quality of the final production. As a general rule, make sure you fill the frame at all times. However, don't overdo it – remember to give your subject background room to 'breathe'.

Figure 5.5
Every interviewee should be given 'talking space'

The tripod

With a video camera it is vital that you use a tripod (see Figure 5.6 overleaf), unless it is absolutely impossible to do so. Using a tripod ensures that all your footage is shake-free, and much easier to watch. Whatever you do, do not mix handheld shots with shots taken using a tripod, as the contrast between the two is extremely stark, and will make viewing uncomfortable.

Make sure that the camera is completely level when you use a tripod. Most video tripods have a spirit level mounted in the pan and tilt head. If the head cannot be adjusted (or if you have reached the limit of its movement), then shorten each leg in turn to make sure the camera is completely level. Of course, there are times when you may want to tilt the camera at an unusual angle for a particular effect.

Before shooting, check that the tripod's pan and tilt head moves smoothly and there is nothing to obstruct this movement. If you can, practise panning and tilting the camera before actually filming the shot in mind (see 'Pan and tilt head' in the Glossary on page 184).

see 'Pan and tilt head' in the Glossary on page 184

Figure 5.6
Two Vinten professional video tripods

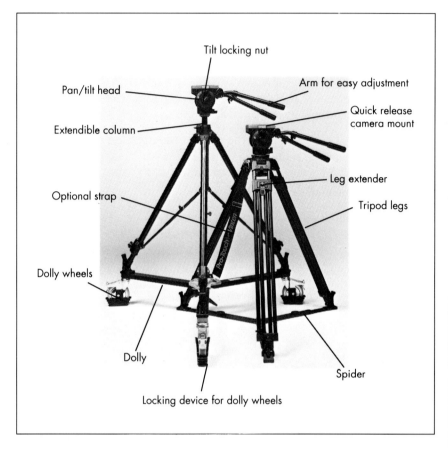

Tilt locking nut

Arm for easy adjustment

Pan/tilt head

Quick release camera mount

Extendible column

Leg extender

Optional strap

Tripod legs

Dolly wheels

Dolly

Spider

Locking device for dolly wheels

Before starting to record

If possible, place the camera at a medium distance from the subject to minimise the need for extremes of focal length. You may want to use extreme wide angle or telephoto shots for a special effect, but for most situations the zoom lens should be set in the middle of the range. If in doubt, it is better to frame a shot using a telephoto setting rather than a wide angle, because wide angle shots tend to distort things.

At all times think about the composition of the shot. Are there any unnecessary elements that distract from the main subject? Is the frame filled properly? Are there any cables lying around? Does anybody have a tree, lamp or plant coming out of the top of their head?

If you are zooming or panning, do you know where you are zooming or panning to? Will there be any distractions in the newly framed shot? Always practise the movement before pressing the record button.

It is important to let the tape record for 10sec before and after the 'action' you are recording. This allows the tape to reach its optimum running speed after being on 'standby', as well as giving you a good preroll time for editing. If you have a director as part of your camera crew it is normal for her/him to instruct the camera operator to 'turnover' when s/he wants the camera to start filming. After the 10sec preroll has elapsed, the camera operator shouts, 'Speed', to signal that s/he is ready for the action to begin.

Check that there is a tape in the recorder, that the batteries have sufficient charge for the shot, and that the white balance is set correctly for the lighting conditions you are using.

Always use well-known makes of tape (Maxell, Fuji, Scotch, Sony), as cheap tapes can cause wear and clog the video heads. If clogging does happen, the picture will be very snowy or non-existent. Head cleaning tapes are available but care should be taken when buying one. There are two main types available: one that is very abrasive and another that uses liquid to dampen the cleaning tape. We recommend using the latter. However, it is best that video heads are cleaned by someone who knows what they are doing, as a damaged video head can cost £50 or more to replace.

The portable video recorder
If you are not using a camcorder, then you will have a separate VTR, which is otherwise known as a 'portapack'. Great care must be taken when using a camera with a separate VTR, as the 'umbilical cord' between the units is not particularly long and repairs can be expensive. Make sure that you avoid banging the machine or dropping it, and if you haven't got a carrying case for it then it is sensible to get hold of one. If possible, ask someone (apart from the camera operator) to carry the VTR, as it something less for the camera operator to worry about and this will invariably improve the quality of the shots.

If shooting on a damp or cold day, a case is essential to keep the equipment dry and warm. Many VTRs have a moisture sensor, and when this is activated the machine will cut out to prevent any damage occurring. Should this happen, place the machine in a warm, dry place for a while, and the VTR will eventually reset itself.

Do not leave any video equipment in the boot of a car overnight as (apart from the risk from theft) there is the likelihood that moisture and temperature differences will stop the machine functioning when you come to use it.

Video sound
Most of the techniques for successful sound recording are outlined in Chapter 3, and it is vital that you take as much care over your video sound as over your pictures. The common mistake is to forget about sound completely, and the resulting poor quality detracts from the overall effectiveness of the video.

Most amateur video cameras have an automatic sound leveller and a built-in microphone, so there isn't much you can do to control or improve the sound quality. However, some amateur cameras have an external microphone facility using a mini-jack plug, and this can be used for certain radio microphones, tie clip mikes and other types of external microphones that allow you to get closer to your subject.

On professional machines you should always use an external microphone. This is normally a general purpose 'gun mike' that is held by the sound recordist on an extending rod called a 'fishpole'. The levels are set manually by the sound recordist using two level meters (one for each channel), and it is imperative that s/he uses a pair of headphones (or 'cans' as they are known in the trade) to monitor sound quality.

Occasionally, professional cameras have an internal microphone built into the camera body. Avoid using this if possible, as the quality will be poor; but if it is really necessary (maybe because you don't have a separate sound recordist to hold the mike), then use it with care. To set up the internal mike, move the audio switch on the camera from the 'Ext. mic' setting to 'Line'.

For further details about setting levels and audio techniques, see Chapter 3.

The Studio

The studio provides a perfect environment for all types of camera work where precise control is necessary. Up until the late 1950s, nearly all films (even the outdoor scenes) were shot in elaborately prepared studios. Today, the studio is home to most of the interior shots featured in sitcoms, films and soap operas, as well as a variety of game shows, chat shows and the news.

One of the main benefits of the studio is that all lighting can be controlled precisely, and as most studios are completely soundproof, no external noises can impair the sound quality of the programme being recorded.

Studio technique is very different to outside location work, as the programme being recorded is effectively 'edited' as it is recorded, thanks to a number of cameras (normally three or more) 'seeing' the same action from different angles. The vision mixer and producer upstairs in the control room then have to select which shot to record to tape or transmit, so all the cuts are made 'live'. As there is so much hardware to operate, studio production is a lot more labour intensive than location work, so several people are needed for it to work successfully.

The studio camera

When cameras are used together in a studio, each is connected via a cable from the studio to a camera control unit (CCU) that is situated in the engineering control room. This device allows each camera to be set up identically, eliminating any possibility of the white balance or exposure being different. As well as being linked to the CCU, all studio cameras are connected to a sync pulse generator (SPG) that ensures that all cuts between each camera are completely 'clean', without picture break-up.

In small studios, the cameras used are exactly the same as those used for outside broadcast work. Large studios (such as those used by television companies) have purpose-built studio cameras (Figure 5.7), but most of the controls remain the same.

It is essential that the operator at each camera understands fully how to use it. All instructions to the camera operators are relayed through a

Figure 5.7
A large purpose-built
studio camera in use

set of headphones from the control room, and they are normally
abbreviated so that the response is quick and accurate. Camera
operators must be able to make all zooms and camera movements
smoothly and as quickly as possible, as it may only be a matter of
seconds before their shot is needed for transmission.

The camera studio dolly

A typical studio camera will mounted on a dolly, which is basically a
tripod on wheels. The dolly allows the camera operator to move the
camera around easily, and position it to give the best picture. There are
several instructions that the director will give to indicate which way
s/he wants the camera to move.

Track in means move the dolly forward, while *track out* indicates that
the director wants the camera moved backwards. To move left or right,
the director will ask the camera operator to *crab right* or *crab left* as
appropriate. To change the height of the camera, the director will say
either *elevate* or *depress* as required. This is also known as *crane up* or
crane down. Unless you are using a very expensive dolly on an
extremely smooth studio floor, it is inadvisable to track the camera
while 'on air'. Moving a camera on a standard dolly will result in jerky
shots; but if you really want to track the camera, move as slowly as
possible.

The script

Any production should have a working script that gives both sound and
vision 'cues', and everyone involved in the production should have a
copy. The best form of script describes the shot required, as well as all **129**

Figure 5.8
A typical TV script
(courtesy of Yorkshire
Television)

dialogue and sound cues (see Figure 5.8). Most professional studio productions have each shot planned well in advance, with coloured tape on the floor to mark out different camera positions. If you manage to achieve this, the studio will virtually run itself – providing everyone keeps to the original plan and doesn't get lost!

```
STUDIO THREE                    P/N: CO91/02

                  "BAD INFLUENCE!"

PROGRAMME 2       VTR : WEDNESDAY 15TH SEPTEMBER 1993
                  T/X : THURSDAY 16TH SEPTEMBER 1993

************************************************

PRESENTERS:       ANDY CRANE          [DRESSING ROOM    2]
                  VIOLET BERLIN       [DRESSING ROOM   10]
                  ANDY WEAR           [DRESSING ROOM    1]
                  GUESTS              [DRESSING ROOM    4]
                  GUESTS              [DRESSING ROOM    5]

************************************************

PRODUCTION:

   PRODUCER......................PATRICK TITLEY
   DIRECTOR......................GRAEME POLLARD
   PRODUCTION TEAM...............DAN CLAPSON
   .............................STEVE KEEN
   .............................RICHARD MAUDE
   .............................VAL SMITH
   .............................SUSAN WALLS
   GRAPHICS......................PAUL PEPPIATE
   DESIGNER......................ROBERT SCOTT
   PRODUCTION ASSISTANT..........LESLEY KIRK
   TECHNICAL ASSISTANCE..........MATTHEW ROOK
   FLOOR MANAGER.................VAL LAWSON
   CAMERAS.......................LES FLANAGAN
   SOUND.........................PAUL VENNER
   LIGHTING DIRECTOR.............PAUL THOMPSON
   VISION CONTROL................KEN MEDDINGS
   VISION MIXER..................BRENDA WILSON
   STUDIO MANAGER................GRAHAM BAINES
   VTR...........................BRIAN ABRAM
   MAKE-UP.......................CAROL CHURCHILL
   COSTUME.......................ISOBEL BERRY
   PRODUCTION BUYER..............TBA
   PROPS.........................DAVE TUDOR
   .............................DAVE HUXHAM
   UNIT ASSISTANT................MARK HINCHLIFFE
   PRODUCTION SECRETARY..........ANNA KOST

   THIS SCRIPT IS THE PRIVATE & CONFIDENTIAL PROPERTY OF:
   YORKSHIRE TELEVISION LIMITED, LEEDS LS3 1JS.
   NO UNAUTHORISED REPRODUCTION PERMITTED
```

```
                                              - 2 -

STUDIO SCHEDULE

TUESDAY 14TH SEPTEMBER 1993:

                    RIG.....................1200-1300
                    TECH RIG................1330-2200
                    LIGHT/SET...............1300/1800

WEDNESDAY 15TH SEPTEMBER 1993:

                    COMPUTER RIG............0800/1000
                    LINE UP.................0800/0900
                    RECORD INSERTS..........0900-1230
                    LUNCH...................1230-1330
                    REHEARSE/RECORD.........1330-1800
                    DE-RIG & STRIKE.........1800/1900

PRODUCTION SCHEDULE:

                    COMPUTER RIG/REHEARSE KIDS.....0800/0900
                    PRE-RECORD NAM ROOD/REVIEWS/
                    VOICE OVERS/DIRECT FEEDS.......0900/1230
                    LUNCH..........................1230/1330
                    REHEARSE SHOW..................1330/1600
                    AUDIENCE IN....................1600/1630
                    RECORD SHOW....................1630/1800
                    GO TO THE BAR..................1800.....
```

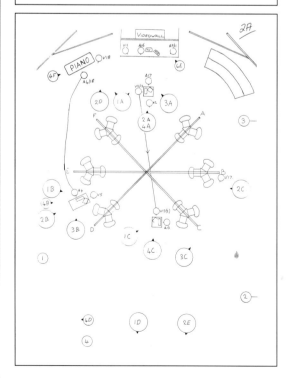

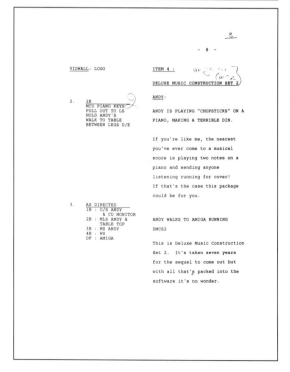

Studio set-ups

It is difficult to describe all the various options available to studio users, as it depends on how many cameras are at your disposal, the size of the studio, what you intend to do and the format of your programme. To take a chat show as an example, Figure 5.9 shows a typical three-camera set-up, and the variety of camera angles that can be used. Camera movement during shots should be avoided, so all zooms and dolly movements should be done in the time between shots, when the camera isn't being used for transmission. For example, if the producer needs a close up of a brooch on an interviewee's dress, while camera 1 does a ¾ shot of the interviewee, camera 2 (that was previously being used for a wide shot of the interviewer and interviewee) can zoom in close to the brooch; once the shot is framed, the vision mixer cuts from camera 1 to camera 2.

Figure 5.9
The typical three-camera chat show set-up

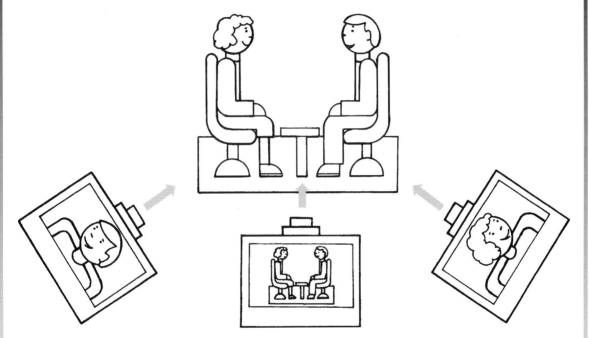

Studio lighting

Having prepared the set, the next thing to arrange is the position and direction of the lights. All television studios have a variety of lights hanging from the ceiling on movable gantries, and these must be positioned according to the subject being recorded.

The majority of studio lights use halogen bulbs to ensure that their colour temperature is consistent. There are many different types of studio light, and a selection is shown in Figure 5.10, on page 132. You must avoid the tendency to 'overlight' a set when setting up a studio, as not only does it waste electricity, but the heat created by the powerful lights can make conditions uncomfortable for the performers in front of the cameras.

To give an example of lighting, we shall look at the two most common types of studio lighting required: (i) the single person to camera and (ii) the two-person interview.

Figure 5.10
The *Sky News* television studio (courtesy of Strand Lighting)

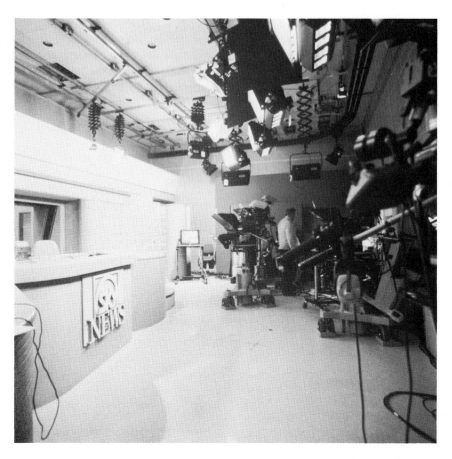

Figure 5.11
A three-point lighting rig

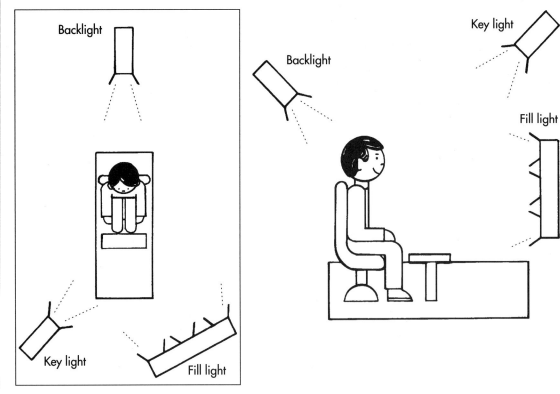

For a single person speaking to camera you should use the standard 'three point lighting' plot (Figure 5.11). As its name implies, three point lighting uses three lights to create a pleasing effect: two 'fresnel spots' (that give either a small soft-edged circle of light or a wider, less intense beam) and a 'fill light' that gives out a soft, even light to 'fill in' harsh shadows.

In three point lighting, the two fresnel spots are positioned to the front and back of the subject, and these are known as the 'key' and 'backlight'. The key is positioned in front of the subject at an angle of approximately 45°, so as to produce a nose shadow that touches the corner of the lips. On the opposite side to the key you should place the softer fill light, and this is used to light the other side of the face. If you were only to use these lights, the subject would look rather flat, so a backlight is added to give depth. The angle and height of this is quite important, as too steep an angle will illuminate the subject's head too much; while too low an angle will shine directly into the camera. Ideally, the lamp should be positioned so that the beam of light hits the back of the neck and spills onto the shoulders (see Figure 5.12). In most studios, the intensity of each lamp is controlled using a dimmer board, and you must always balance the strength of each light to give the best picture on the camera.

Figure 5.12
The effect of three-point lighting. Note the highlight and nose shadow

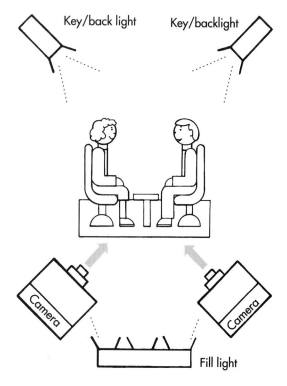

Key/back light   Key/backlight

Camera   Camera

Fill light

Figure 5.13 'right'
The upstage cross lighting technique

In the second example (the 'upstage cross lighting' technique), the same number of lights is used, although this time they occupy different positions (see Figure 5.13). Depending on which side the camera is shooting from, each fresnel spot operates as either a key or backlight, while the fill light is used to fill in any harsh shadows that may have been created.

Studio sound

There are many different types of microphone designed for studio use, and the choice of which one to use will depend very much on what you are shooting. When filming a single person talking to camera or recording interviews, the best type of microphone to use is the 'tie clip' (or 'levalier') microphone (see Figure 5.12). This microphone clips onto a tie or any other part of clothing, and will pick up the wearer's voice very clearly. However, the user must be very careful not to brush the microphone with a hand or clothes, as this will create a loud distracting noise that will drown out speech.

For studio-based drama, tie clip microphones would intrude on the 'reality' of the setting, so a boom mike (Figure 5.14) should be used. This must only be used by a skilled operator, and care must be taken to ensure that the bottom of the mike doesn't intrude into the top of the picture frame.

Figure 5.14
A boom mike on location (courtesy of Yorkshire Television)

Studio special effects

Most large studios have a variety of special effects that can be controlled from the control room, and these have a variety of uses in formal studio production. The most common devices are some kind of titling system (such as the Aston character generator), Quantel and Chromakey.

Quantel

This is a digital effects package that enables pictures to be shrunk, enlarged, rotated, inverted and, with really sophisticated versions, manipulated to create shapes like goblets, pyramids, even teapots that fly around the screen and off into the distance (think of *Top of the Pops*!). Apart from these types of effect, the most common use for Quantel is in studio-based newsreading, where a secondary picture is reduced and placed in a top corner of the screen (see Figure 5.15). Your studio technician will show how Quantel (if fitted) works in your own particular studio.

Figure 5.15
Quantel can be used to superimpose a secondary picture behind the primary studio image

Chromakey

This enables the user to superimpose a secondary video image over part of the original camera shot, providing the primary (foreground) subject is standing in front of a blue background (see Figure 5.16). Chromakey is used to superimpose a weather map behind weather forecasters, and was also the method used to make Superman 'fly'. When using this effect, it is important that the subject in the foreground is not wearing the same shade of blue as the background, otherwise her/his part of blue will be keyed as well. If you want the shot to look realistic, take care to make the foreground lighting in the studio similar to your background picture.

Figure 5.16
Although it looks as if these two men are outside, Chromakey has been used to superimpose a picture behind them in the studio

Titling

Titling allows you to insert graphics into a programme or give an interviewee a caption. To produce a title, you will need a genlocked computer or Aston character generator that is plugged into the main studio board. Using the 'downstream keyer' facility on the studio mixing desk, the title can then be superimposed over the main picture.

Always fade the title in and out slowly (a straight cut would be too harsh), and leave it on the screen long enough for you to read it three times slowly. Be careful to ensure that the title is placed over a dark part of the subject (if the letters are white), otherwise the text will merge with the picture, making it unreadable. Avoid using colours other than black or white for titling, as bright colours can look gimmicky and distract from the main image.

Autocue

Autocue is a trade name that has come to describe teleprompters used for such programmes as the news, 'Tomorrow's World' and some chat

Figure 5.17
The Autocue teleprompting device. It is recommended for all studio applications

shows. Basically, the system uses a computer to scroll the script on a television screen placed under a studio camera's lens (see Figure 5.17). A two-way mirror placed at 45° to the camera then reflects the words in front of the lens, thus allowing the presenter to read the script while looking directly into the lens. This device is well worth using if your studio has it, as it saves your presenters having to learn their words or fiddle with bits of paper.

Using the studio

Now that the first basic steps of camera operation have been covered, it is time to explore how these can be used in a studio production. Most TV studios have a minimum of three cameras, and the picture from each is displayed on separate monitors in the control room. The vision mixer (directed by the producer) selects a shot from the best positioned camera, and makes a coordinated series of cuts for the final transmission/recording. The selection of each image is made using a mixing desk (see Figure 5.18), which can, by the push of a button, switch from camera to camera, thereby making a 'cut'.

Figure 5.18
A typical mixing desk in three-camera studio

For most types of programme, a straight cut from one camera to another is all you need to use. However, most mixing desks also have 'mixes' and 'wipes' at the director's disposal. For studio-based productions, these should be used with the utmost sensitivity, as they can easily look out of place. More often than not, the use of special effects in amateur studio-based productions is overdone. Remember: just because the effects are there, it doesn't mean that you have to use them!

Using a TV studio requires a fairly large number of people, each with their own specific task to do. For a studio-based production to work successfully, each of these people must work as a team and try not to do one another's tasks. Providing everyone gets on with their own job, the production should run smoothly and the end result will be good. However, if one person disrupts the team, it can have disastrous results.

A typical line-up of people required to run a studio is:

- Director/producer
- Vision mixer
- Production assistant
- Floor manager
- Three camera operators
- Sound operator
- Miscellaneous technical operators

Figure 5.19
The different areas of a studio

These individuals are based either in the studio itself, or upstairs in the control room (see Figure 5.19). The rooms are in contact by a voice link called 'talkback'.

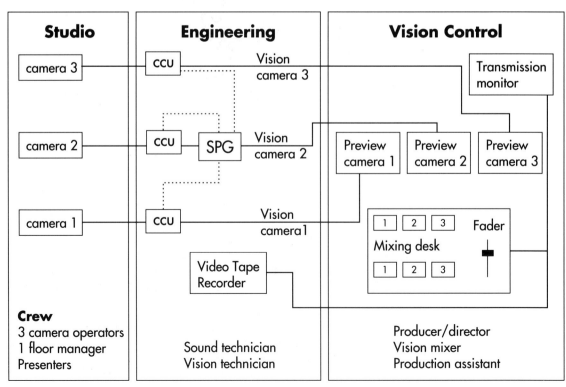

In the control room

The *director/producer* is responsible for the overall artistic quality of the production. S/he watches the three preview screens and not the script. The director should be able to remember the script well enough to know when a cut or cue is to be made. S/he then instructs the vision mixer to execute the cut and must let the camera operators know when they are to change angle. S/he is also responsible for instigating any music or lighting cues.

The *vision mixer* is responsible for making all cuts from camera to camera, and must be completely familiar with the operation of the mixing desk to carry out the necessary cuts and effects quickly.

A *production assistant* (usually the director's assistant) follows the script carefully, and announces the shot numbers to provide an early warning as to which camera/shot is required next.

The *sound operator* is responsible for all areas of sound required for the production. This includes cueing up any music or special effect CDs/tapes/records so that they appear in the right place, ensuring that all microphone levels are correct, and (most importantly) making sure that people who are off-camera are not 'wired up' for sound.

During a production, everyone concerned must be thinking ahead to the next shot if things are to run smoothly. For example, here is an extract taken from the control room:

Production assistant	Director	Vision mixer
'Shot 13; camera 3 next.'		Prepares to cut to camera 3.
'Shot 14; camera 1 next in position C.'	'Cut.'	Cuts to camera 3. Prepares to cut to camera 1.
	'Keep it steady camera 1 … A bit tighter 1 … Coming to you. Cut.'	Cuts to camera 1.
'Shot 15; camera 2 next, it's a mix. Camera 3, you're released to go to position B.'		Prepares to mix camera 2.

In the studio

The three *camera operators* are responsible for getting the shots that are required by the director. When their camera is being used for transmission/recording, it is normal for a red light to appear in their viewfinder, and above the lens for the presenter's benefit. It is absolutely imperative that the camera operator does exactly what is required of her/him, and does not attempt to experiment by zooming in or moving around without being told.

The *floor manager* is the main contact between the studio floor and the director, and s/he gives non-audible cues to the performers by using hand signals. S/he is also completely responsible for studio silence and the general running of the studio during a performance.

In the Engineering Control Room

Technical operators are responsible for the technical uniformity of the cameras, the lighting levels and any video tape (VT) recording or playback required for the production. In a broadcast studio a *technical operations manager* monitors the technical quality of the production.

The camera walk through

Once the preliminary studio preparations have been made, it is advisable to have a camera rehearsal to let everyone involved have a chance to raise any problems. Of primary importance are the camera operators, as before a rehearsal they will not know what is required of them. It is up to them to make notes on their camera cards (see Figure 5.20) for the final production, as failure to do so could result in their being in the wrong place at the wrong time.

The camera walk through allows the director to preview each shot that the cameras are offering, and make small changes if necessary. The camera walk through also gives the actors the opportunity to know which camera will be on them at each moment, thus preventing the possibility of them facing the wrong camera 'on air'.

Once everyone is in position, the floor manager has to check that everyone is in contact with one another using the talkback, and also ascertain which shot numbers are to be rehearsed. With every member of the crew listening, a typical dialogue will begin: 'We are going to rehearse shot numbers 1 to 16; this is the first three minutes of script and shooting will stop after 16. What happens during these three minutes is . . . [outline of what the performers will do]. Cameras 1 and 3 have most of the work; camera 2 has just three shots plus a caption'

All cameras should be spoken to in turn to set up their own respective shots, and any difficulties should be resolved at the rehearsal stage, rather than causing problems during the 'live' take. It is very important that the floor manager keeps the performers in front of the camera informed at all times, as they will not be wearing headsets, and will have little idea of what is going on.

With the performers in their opening positions, there should be a brief discussion with the camera operators for shot 1. As soon as what is required is understood, the floor manager can cue the performers to begin from shot 1 through to shot 16. When the rehearsal has finished, there is then an opportunity for the camera operators, sound operator and vision mixer to resolve any problems that may have occurred with the director.

The success of the camera walk through is dependent on what was required from the outset. A shooting script must have been prepared beforehand: it may be in a very rough form, but it must exist. The camera walk through will only be a waste of a lot of people's time if suitable preparation hasn't been made beforehand.

Production recording

As there is often little time allocated to a production, keeping to a strict time schedule is important. With the rehearsal completed and final technical checks made, the programme should be recorded as soon as possible.

Figure 5.20
A sample camera card. Camera operators should make notes on these for every studio production

The beginning of each production follows a similar procedure. First there is a 1min countdown before the start of the production, and from the beginning of this count the VTR starts running. This is confirmed by the technician who says: 'VT running'. It is normal for an 'ident clock' to be recorded during this preroll time, stating the production name, director, date and recording standard. At the same time, the floor manager tells the studio that the count has begun: 'One minute to go – quiet studio, please.'

At 25sec to go, a 10sec sound ident is recorded onto the video tape, and at 15sec the floor manager tells the studio to 'stand by'. The final countdown begins with 10sec to go, with the floor manager counting aloud until s/he reaches 3sec. From this point s/he uses hand signals for the remaining seconds, finally ending up cueing the first presenter with her/his hand. After that, the programme must (or at least seem to) run smoothly. Providing everything has been planned and the camera walk through was successful, the only problems you should have are ones that are completely out of your control.

Shooting on Location

Life on location is very different from the controlled atmosphere of the studio. You may not have a mains power supply, all indoor lighting must be created by using portable lights, you may have to contend with irritating background noises that can ruin your soundtrack, and you will probably only be using one camera.

In this sense, location shooting requires even more prior preparation than in the studio. You should arrive at your location knowing precisely what you want to shoot, what the lighting will be like, whether there is mains electricity or not, and you must shoot to edit. In other words, you *must* have a clear idea of what you want the programme to look like before you start filming.

Figure 5.21
Shooting on location

The treatment

In order to have a clear idea of what you want, it is absolutely imperative that you write a treatment after deciding the subject of your video. A good producer/director will find her/himself thinking in visual sequences, and the treatment helps you get all these ideas onto paper.

A treatment should give an idea of all the things that you want to include in the video. By far the best way to do this is to divide a piece of paper into two columns (one for sound and the other for vision), and write down in note form what each section of the video will comprise. You do not have to be too specific, but an idea of the interviews you require, the locations you need to visit, the sort of shots you want to include, and, above all, what your video is trying to say must be included in the treatment.

By organising your thoughts onto paper, you are then able to look once again at your idea to see if it will really work as well as you originally thought. Check and re-check your treatment to see if there really is enough material available for your idea to work, and also to see if you have left anything out. You should also allocate a time limit to each section, as there is nothing worse than a video that goes on for longer than is necessary.

Of course, the early treatment can be changed as you begin to shoot the video, although you should try and stick to it as closely as possible. Providing that your treatment has been well done, you should refer to it throughout the planning, filming and editing processes, constantly keeping yourself in check with your original ideas. You may also like to write down useful telephone numbers and contacts on your treatment, so keep it with you at all times.

The recce

The term 'recce' is an abbreviation of the word 'reconnaissance', an army term used to describe soldiers going ahead of the main body of troops to spy out the land, then reporting back so that everyone has a better idea of what to expect. In a similar way, it is advisable for video producers to visit the locations where they are intending to shoot, so that they have a better idea of what to expect, and, more importantly, so that any potential problem areas can be avoided.

When carrying out a recce, there should be several things on the producer's mind:

1 Is the location really necessary for the video? Visiting too many different locations will be time-consuming.
2 What are the light conditions like? What direction will the sun be facing when the crew are shooting?
3 Where should the camera be positioned? What sort of shots does the video need?
4 Is there mains electricity available?
5 Are there any annoying background noises that could ruin the soundtrack? For example, are there roadworks nearby?
6 Do you have permission to shoot there? More often than not, you will be thrown out of railway stations or shopping malls if you haven't previously obtained permission.

7 If you need permission to film, whom do you need to speak to?

8 Where can you park the car (if appropriate)?

9 Do you need any special equipment? For example, extra lights, gels, filters, special microphones.

You can also recce people whom you intend to interview. Talk to them before you meet them over the phone, and ask them questions that may be useful about the location or the subject. It could be that something someone says makes you change your mind completely about your original plan for the video.

Production arrangements

When shooting on location it is preferable to have at least three people to make up the crew: a camera operator/director, a sound technician and a production assistant. If necessary, you may also like to add a presenter or interviewer. Someone should be elected to be in charge of the production (normally the camera operator), and each member of the crew must be clear about objectives, timescale and their own responsibilities.

The sound technician is responsible for all sound quality. They must alter the sound levels to the optimum level, and hold the fishpole and boom mike, taking care so that it doesn't enter the shot.

The production assistant should log all shots as they are taken (using the VTR's counter as a reference). Although this is a very tedious job, it is very worthwhile, as there is nothing worse than having to scan through hours of original footage in the editing suite desperately seeking that particular shot that you vaguely remember shooting.

What do I need for location recording?

You should always take enough equipment, as it is better to have too much than too little. A typical list is shown below.

- Camera
- VTR (unnecessary if you have a camcorder)
- Tripod
- Batteries (always take as many as you can, and make sure they are fully charged *before* you leave)
- Mains adaptor/battery charger
- Lights
- Microphone
- Mains extension lead
- All the leads you need (connections to camera, monitor, microphone, mains power supply, etc.)
- Monitor (with appropriate lead linking it to camera)
- Headphones
- Several blank tapes (as many as you think you'll need plus a few extras)

If you are unsure about using any item of equipment, then learn how to use it before leaving. There is nothing worse than arriving on location and being unsure of what the various buttons do. Not only does it waste valuable shooting and battery time, but it appears extremely unprofessional to anybody involved in your production.

143

On location

Arrive on time. If people have given up their time to help with your production, it is bad manners and unprofessional to arrive late. In this respect, it is worthwhile finding out exactly how you are going to get there (normally done during the recce). If you haven't got a car, it may be difficult and time-consuming to cart all the equipment you need by train or bus.

Use a small colour monitor to view the shots as they are being taken. Not only does this allow you to check everything as it is being shot, it also double checks that the white balance is set correctly (impossible with the camera's black and white monitor). Using a monitor is important, as it allows you to check that all the shots are in focus and are of sufficient technical quality.

Don't waste time by alternating between indoor and outdoor sequences at the same location. Film all your exterior shots when you first arrive; if it happens to be raining, do the interior shots firsts, leaving the exteriors until last. However, make sure that it isn't dark when you go outside!

Don't work non-stop all day. Give your crew a break for lunch and refreshments, although large quantities of alcoholic drink should be avoided for obvious reasons!

Prepare a shooting script before you leave for the location, as this will help to make good use of time when shooting begins. If possible, plan each shot to the finest detail – your recce will help you to do this.

Things to remember while on location

1 Are the batteries fully charged?
2 Is there a video tape in the recorder? (It is a good idea to wind the tape fully forward and back before use.)
3 At each new location (whether indoors or outdoors) the white balance must be reset.
4 Zero the tape counter at the beginning of the shoot, and log the counter position at the start of each take.
5 If an external microphone is used, check that the recorder is set appropriately (normally to the 'Ext. mic' position).
6 Make sure that the strongest light source is behind the camera. If it isn't, then the subject will often appear in shadow. Wherever possible stick to the photographic convention of having the main light behind the camera.
7 Always use a tripod.
8 At the start of each recording allow at least 10sec before and after recording a sequence. Not only does this assist you when editing, it also ensures that the tape is running at the optimum speed.
9 Check the focus by zooming in close to the subject. Never try to focus in the wide shot.
10 Be positive when making movements; there is nothing worse than jerky zooms and pans.
11 Remember, the battery will only last for a limited period of time (normally only 30min). Use it wisely, especially if you only have a few batteries.

12 If you have time, check the tape at the end of the shoot to ensure that you have got all the shots you need.

13 When you have dismantled the equipment at the end of the shoot, make sure that you have everything before you leave. Be especially careful not to leave batteries or lens caps behind, as they are expensive to replace.

14 Always put the batteries on charge as soon as you return.

15 Make sure that all the used tapes are marked, and that the safety tab is removed.

16 Never leave equipment unattended in the back seat of a car, as this will be very tempting to a thief.

17 Try to avoid taking the camera out in cold weather, as the chances are that when you move it to a warmer location, the tape will not run and the lens will steam over.

Location Lighting

Unlike in the studio, where all the lighting available is artificial and tightly controlled, shooting on location using artificial lights is very tricky, as they must be balanced evenly with the natural light available. Even if an indoor location is extremely well lit, and appears not to need extra lighting, we recommend that you use portable lights to add extra contrast to your subject and to provide enough light for the camera.

For location shooting, mains-powered portable lights that sit on tripod stands are normally used (see Figure 5.22). There are two main types used for location shooting: 'redheads' (so called because of their red casing) that give out 800W of light, and 'blondes' (yellow casing), that give out 2kW. These lights can be adjusted to give a narrow (spot) or wide (flood) beam of light by turning a knob at the back, and normally come with movable flaps that enable you to control the pattern of light emitted. These flaps are called 'barn doors', and are also used to hold gels in front of the light using bulldog clips.

Figure 5.22
'Blondes' in use on location

As explained in the photography chapter, artificial (tungsten) light sources have a different colour temperature to natural daylight (3 200°K as opposed to 5 400°K). Therefore, if you illuminate a shot using redheads or blondes in conjunction with daylight, you must use coloured filters called gels over the lamps to make the colour temperature the same. To correct artificial lamps to daylight you must use a blue gel, whereas if you want to convert daylight to artificial light, you must cover all the windows with orange gel. Remember to reset the white balance and filter on your camera after you have balanced all the light sources to the same colour temperature.

Typical lighting situations

In a similar way to using lighting in the studio, you must always use the most powerful light as a key light when shooting on location. This should be placed behind (or directly next to) the camera. Other lights should then be positioned to counterbalance the shadows that occur, although do not be tempted to 'overlight' a shot and completely eliminate the shadows. Shadows give depth to the picture, and, providing they are not too harsh, will look aesthetically pleasing.

Successful lighting will draw attention to the main subject in the picture, and avoid harsh contrasts between light and shade. You can prevent this by either bouncing the light off a white reflective object (a ceiling or wall, for example), or by placing a frosted gel in front of the light. This type of gel is known as 'spun'.

Lighting for an interview

By far the most common use of lights on location will be lighting for an interview (see Figure 5.23). Be careful not to intimidate your subject by having the lights too close for comfort, and switch the lights off while you are not shooting. Always remember to carry spare bulbs when you are on location, and ensure that you have a heavy duty extension lead with a four-way socket. Never move lamps that are still hot, as bulbs are especially delicate after use.

Figure 5.23a
A typical three-point lighting set-up on location

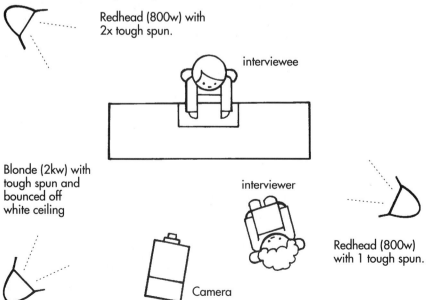

Redhead (800w) with 2x tough spun.

interviewee

Blonde (2kw) with tough spun and bounced off white ceiling

interviewer

Redhead (800w) with 1 tough spun.

Camera

Figure 5.23b

Video Techniques and Conventions on Location

Most people in Western society are exposed to television from an early age, and as a result we take film, television and video conventions for granted, rejecting programmes that disobey these 'rules' because they are 'difficult to watch'. This section hopes to introduce you to some of these conventions, and demonstrates how to use them to good effect in your own video productions.

By far the best way to learn successful video-making technique is by watching television, especially documentaries and the local and national news. As you watch, ask yourself how and why the producer uses certain shots or editing sequences to create a response from the audience. Also, think how you would have filmed the subject yourself. Would you have done anything differently?

Of course, we're not suggesting that you stick rigidly to television's conventions (most pop videos don't) but, like learning a foreign language, it is essential to grasp the basics before trying to adapt it for your own ends.

Interviews

Interviews are one of the most popular ways of getting information or views from 'experts', and they can be adapted to fit almost any genre of video. Arrange to interview your interviewee in surroundings that are familiar to them (their office or house perhaps), as this will put them at ease. Arrive on time, and set up as quickly as possible.

When recording an interview, there is no need to show the interviewer during the interview itself. Instead, concentrate on the most important person: the interviewee. Use plenty of close ups of them (generally

147

depicting head, shoulders and some chest) to avoid making the viewer feel distanced. Always position the interviewer directly next to the camera and ensure that the interviewee looks towards her/him. Never film an interview from the side, as the resulting pictures will be awkward to watch.

Try and avoid using just one zoom position, but keep the editing process in mind while you reframe. Two identically framed shots cannot be edited together without the viewer being aware of a jump cut. It is best to start the interview with a medium to wide shot (see Figure 5.24) and then, halfway through the interview, begin to zoom in close so that just the head and a small part of the shoulder are in view (Figure 5.25).

Figure 5.24
Start your interview with a wide shot . . .

Figure 5.25
. . . then move in closer

This should be done while one of the questions is being asked, and *must* be done using a slow, evenly paced zoom speed in case you wish in the future to use this footage in the final edited version. Never zoom out during an interview, as this will give the impression that you are losing interest in what the interviewee has to say, and are walking away.

At the end of the interview, record a 'two-shot' of the interviewee and the interviewer together over the interviewer's shoulder, as well as some 'noddy' shots of the interviewer nodding and smiling. These shots can be used while editing as 'cutaways' that help shorten the interview and give the impression that there was more than one camera on site.

If the interviewer makes a mistake while asking a question, carry on until the interview is finished. Once the interviewee has left, move the camera around to the other side and film the interviewer asking the same question again. This can be inserted later during the editing stage to cover up the mistake.

It is also wise to film the interviewee doing something else related to what they are talking about before starting the interview. For example, have the interviewee walk towards the camera and out of frame, or film them working at a desk. These shots can then be used later in the editing process to serve as 'wallpaper' while the commentator introduces them.

Remember to take care when interviewing people with glasses, as their lenses will often reflect the camera and lights. Also be careful not to include a clock in the frame, as when you come to edit the piece, the hands may mysteriously move forward and backward in time!

Interview Technique

Never let an interviewee read prepared notes during an interview, as the result will look ridiculous and, at best, staged. If the interviewee is nervous, help her/him to relax by explaining what you are doing, and giving an idea of the sort of questions you are likely to ask. However, try to avoid letting her/him know your questions in advance, as answers given the second time round can be stilted and lack spontaneity. No matter how nervous your interviewee is, never allow her/him to smoke on camera, as this will create grave continuity errors as the cigarette progressively burns down. Dark glasses are also a definite no-no.

Before you start the interview, make sure that you have a clear idea of the questions that you want to ask. Once you have done this, write the questions down, but do not be afraid to ask supplementary questions that arise as the interview progresses.

Avoid questions that only require short or general answers. A question like 'Are things working out as well as you had hoped?' only requires a simple answer that will, at worst, consist of a simple 'no' or 'yes'. At all times ask questions that require self-contained answers. To do this, start your questions with Who, What, When, Where, Which, Why or How, and if you have the confidence, be direct and ask the interviewee to 'Tell me how things are working out.' This forces the interviewee to elaborate, giving a much more useful answer.

Other questions to avoid include: confusing double questions ('Do you think that the government is doing a good job and did you vote for them?'), questions that are too general ('What do you think about nuclear power?'), questions that are really answers ('This hurricane – obviously a terrible surprise and personal disaster – has left you emotionally battered. How do you feel about it?'), and questions that go on for so long that the poor interviewee doesn't know where to start. Keep questions short, easy to understand and to the point.

When the interview has finished, thank your interviewee, and ask her/him to do the 'wallpaper' shots mentioned earlier. Remember to explain why these are necessary, otherwise they might just think you are messing about.

Zooms and pans

Used sparingly, zooms and pans (or a combination of both) can be very effective in a finished video. However, you must be careful not to overdo them, otherwise the video will be extremely tiring to watch. A simple way to cut down on the number of zooms or pans is to ask yourself before filming why you are using them; if you can convince yourself that they are justified, carry on.

If the zoom or pan is to be used in the programme (many camera operators leave the camera running and zoom or pan quickly to film cutaways, without any intention of using the movement), make the movement as slowly and as smoothly as possible. If your tripod has a fluid head, tighten it up to give a certain amount of resistance, to ensure that the pan or tilt is both smooth and slow. Professional video cameras offer variable speed zooms (dependent on how much pressure you exert on the zoom switch), and you should always carry out a zoom at a slow to medium speed, making sure that the zoom speed remains constant.

Practise the zoom or pan first before pressing the record button, and make sure that you know where the shot will finish. Similarly, check that the new subject in shot is correctly in focus, and that any possible focusing corrections can easily be made. There is nothing worse than a zoom to an out-of-focus close up, followed by a couple of seconds' delay while the camera operator desperately fiddles with the focusing ring.

It is advisable to hold the shot completely still for at about 10sec before carrying out the zoom or pan, and then for another 10sec once the action has finished. This will give you a choice of three shots (the wide angle shot, the zoom and the close up) in the editing suite, and offers alternatives in case the zoom or pan does not work out as well as you had hoped. Remember never to zoom in and out in one shot, as this creates a 'trombone' effect reminiscent of the worst type of home video!

The angle of view

For most types of shooting, a camera positioned on a tripod roughly at eye level using a medium focal length (half-way on the zoom setting) gives easy-to-view shots. However, for certain effects or dramatic shots, try tilting the camera a few degrees to one side, or shooting with the camera at your feet or above your head. The results will often be visually exciting and stimulate the attention of the viewer.

However, you must make sure that the your camera is stable (camera shake is the camera operator's worst enemy) and, above all, safe. It is no good coming back with the perfect shot of a car driving over the camera, if in the process the camera was ruined.

Extremes of focal length can also be coupled with unusual angles to produce eye-catching images. A wide angle lens used to frame a close-up of a subject gives the impression of importance, although you must be careful when using a wide angle lens to film a person in close up. The results can be unflattering (see Figure 2.12 on page 36).

Similarly, when filming a person it is important that the camera is parallel to their eye level, which means lowering your tripod if you are going to film children. If you film someone from above or below their eye level, not only will the resulting shots appear unflattering, they will also appear awkward to the viewer.

Shooting a sequence

When on location, you will invariably only have one camera at your disposal. This means that you will have to 'shoot to edit', otherwise you will end up with a series of completely unrelated shots that will be impossible to rearrange into a meaningful sequence.

Shooting to edit means that care must be taken at all times over such things as continuity, pace and angle of view. Figure 5.26, (below and on page 152) shows a sequence that was shot using one camera, although once edited it appears as though it was taken with several cameras in several different positions. After each take, the camera was repositioned with the editing process in mind, and each shot was cut in one after the other, making the editor's job easy.

When shooting the same subject several times at different angles, think carefully about continuity. For example, when filming a man moving from one room to another, make sure that his clothes remain the same and that he repeats his action precisely. (Was his jacket buttoned or unbuttoned? Did he open the door with his left or right hand?). Make sure also that you shoot each take from start to finish, as this makes things much easier to cut from in the editing suite. For example, when filming the man moving from room to room, the first shot shows the

Figure 5.26
Continued on page 152

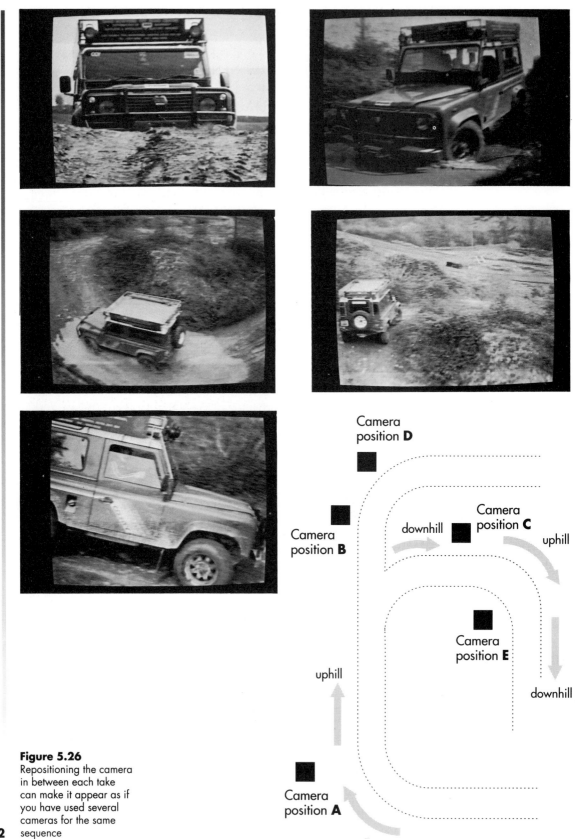

Figure 5.26
Repositioning the camera in between each take can make it appear as if you have used several cameras for the same sequence

man walking from the first room into the second, and the camera does not stop until he has left the first room and shut the door. The second shot is filmed from the second room, starts with it empty, and likewise does not finish until the action has completely stopped, and the man has sat down. Staging the sequence like this gives you plenty of options to choose from, and you can cut at precisely the point where you want the edit to take place.

The unstaged sequence

You may not, however, always be shooting something that you can repeat and repeat *ad infinitum*. In this case you must try and film the subject from as many angles as possible, taking care to ensure that what you are filming remains in the same position and is doing the same thing. If continuity is broken, the edited sequence will look very strange indeed.

Start by filming a fixed wide shot of the subject for at least 30sec; once you have done this, zoom in close to do some close ups that will provide useful material to clarify what is going on. For example, say you wanted to film a girl drawing. First the camera operator would film a wide shot, depicting both her and the drawing board to provide an 'establishing shot' of the action. After 30sec, the operator zooms in to a close up of her hand to give the viewer a clear indication of what she is drawing. This shot is then inserted to extend the sequence and prolong interest. The finished sequence is shown in Figure 5.27.

Figure 5.27
The first shot shows a wide shot (4 secs) that cuts to a close-up to explain what is going on (3 secs)

When using this technique, you *must* keep the camera still on the close up for at least 10sec before moving on. If you shoot for less than 10sec, then you will find it impossible to do inserts of sufficient length when it comes to the editing stage.

Wallpaper shots and general views

Wallpaper shots or general views (GVs for short) are shots that do not have any specific purpose for inclusion in the video, but are still relevant. They are normally used as background for a commentary that is talking about things that cannot be illustrated directly. Always remember to film plenty of wallpaper shots while on location, as they can get you out of a lot of trouble.

For example, if you were producing a video about a major company based in a large open-plan office, you should film plenty of wallpaper

153

shots of secretaries typing (from a variety of angles, including close ups of hands tapping the keys), a wide angle of the office itself, shots of people on telephones, people writing memos, people walking about, etc. These shots, although maybe not directly related to the commentary, will be useful for insertion at any point throughout the video.

Remember, though, that you must not rely too much on wallpaper shots and general views – they're no substitute for well-composed shots showing real action.

Establishing shots

The establishing shot is a wide angle view that 'establishes' exactly where the action of the video is taking place. Be it a shot of the exterior of a building that you are just about to film inside, or a wide angle view of a room, this shot places the setting for the action firmly in the viewer's mind, allowing them to set in context what is coming next.

You can also use the establishing shot to 'mislead' the viewer into thinking that your video has been shot somewhere where it hasn't. By showing a wide angle view of the city of London as an establishing shot, and then cutting to an office interior in Birmingham where you have been filming, the viewer can be misled into thinking that the office was situated in London. This technique is often used when shooting interior scenes in the studio.

The cutaway

The cutaway is another shot that will save you a lot of trouble during the editing process. As its name suggests, the cutaway is a straight cut to another related subject, and should be used to disguise a jump cut that would otherwise appear awkward to the viewer.

The most common use for the cutaway is during an interview, when the producer wants to cut out a portion of what has been said. If a straight cut were used, the interviewee's head would suddenly move, and the result would be distracting to watch. To cover this transition, the editor uses a cutaway visual (that is normally a shot illustrating what the interviewee is talking about) to bridge the gap, while the interviewee carries on talking underneath. Figure 5.45 on page 171–2 gives an example of this.

Generally speaking, you can use general views or wallpaper shots as cutaways, although you must ensure that the cutaway is relevant, otherwise the viewer will wonder why this seemingly unrelated and 'unnecessary' shot has appeared from nowhere.

Shot/reverse shot and crossing the line

When filming two (or more) people talking to each other, they must appear to be facing each other, even if the shot only shows one of them at a time. An imaginary line should be drawn between their eyes, and if this line is crossed (by facing them both in the same way) the shot will confuse the viewer. This convention is known as shot/reverse shot (see Figure 5.28) and was established during the early days of Hollywood.

Similarly, when changing camera positions to film a moving subject from a different angle, you must ensure that the subject continues to move in the same direction. Take, for example, a car moving from left to right in the frame, shot from the righthand side of the car. If you move the camera to the lefthand side and shoot the same shot again, the car will appear to be moving from the righthand side of the frame to the left, even though it is moving in the same direction in real life. Never change the direction of a moving subject without explanation, as this will not only look awkward (two conflicting movements following each other), it will also confuse the viewer.

Should you want to change the direction of a moving object, break the continuity by having the subject come towards you and out of frame. You can then start afresh and introduce the new camera position and a new direction of movement.

The problem of crossing the line becomes much more complex if you want to record a conversation between two people as they walk along. It is simply impossible to record the sequence from both sides, as one person will appear to walk from left to right, while the other will walk from right to left (see Figure 5.29). The only way to get around this is to shoot from one side only, and intercut with shots taken from the front or back.

Figure 5.28
The Hollywood convention of shot/reverse shot

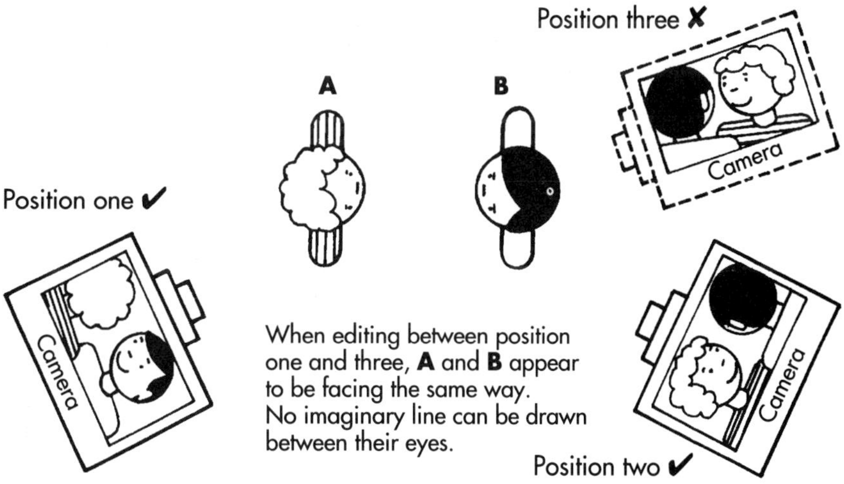

Figure 5.29
It is impossible to use the shot/reverse shot technique on actors who are moving

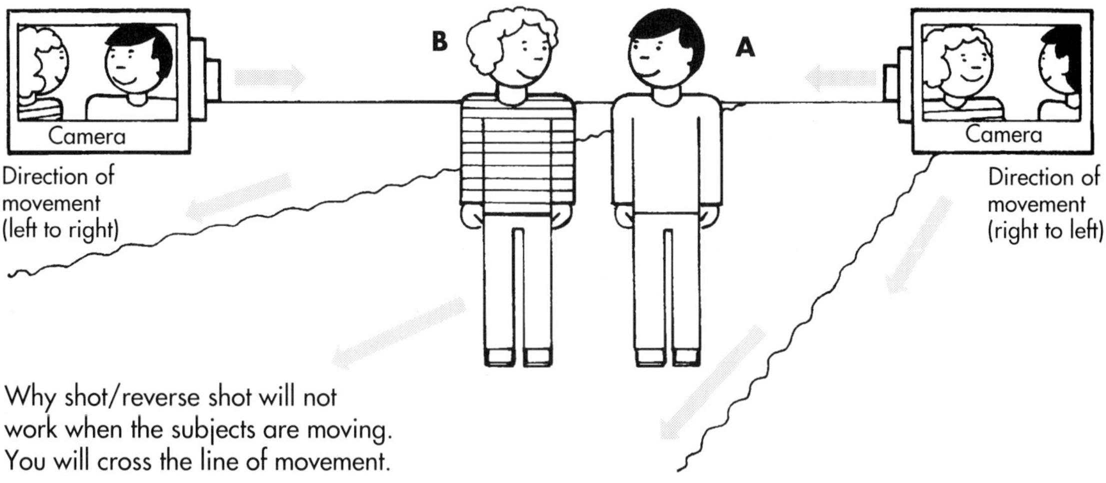

Position three ✗

Position one ✔

When editing between position one and three, **A** and **B** appear to be facing the same way. No imaginary line can be drawn between their eyes.

Position two ✔

Direction of movement (left to right)

Direction of movement (right to left)

Why shot/reverse shot will not work when the subjects are moving. You will cross the line of movement.

The tracking shot

So far we have only be talking about shots with the camera stuck securely to its tripod; the only movement has been from a pan or zoom. However, an interesting effect can be created by moving the camera itself while keeping the focal length (zoom position) static. This is known as a tracking shot.

The tracking shot serves two purposes: to keep up with moving actors as they walk along, and to increase the size of subject in the frame (like a zoom in), but keeping the angle of view constant (see Figure 5.30). The latter use of the tracking shot can be very effective if you want to create a sense of drama, and in this case you should use the widest angle setting on your camera lens.

Figure 5.30
Using a wide-angle lens and moving towards your subject from a low angle can give a dramatic effect

Professional video crews with large budgets have access to dollies that run along specially laid smooth tracks. The mysterious 'dolly grip' on film credits is so called because he pulls the dolly along the track to create a really smooth movement. However, as dollies cost at least £400 a day to hire, it is unlikely that your budget will be able to stretch to one of these. Useful alternatives include wheelchairs, prams, supermarket trolleys and a moving car, although you must be careful to hold the camera still at all times. Never attempt to do a tracking shot by walking with the camera handheld, unless you want the show the viewpoint of a character in a drama production.

Location sound

Good sound can disguise poor pictures, but bad sound can ruin even the most spectacular shots. Always shoot with the microphone switched on, even when you don't think you'll need it. There's nothing worse than trying to dub a shot using special effects tapes, as getting it right wastes time that could be spent a lot more constructively doing something else.

Remember to keep completely quiet while filming, so all instructions must be given using hand signals. If one of crew does speak while filming, it is up to the sound engineer (who should be wearing headphones to constantly monitor the sound being recorded) to stop the shot, and ask for it to be redone.

Beware of external noises. While the human brain filters out annoying background noises in everyday life, the microphone cannot. Main causes of irritating background noise include a ticking clock, a telephone that rings while you are filming, workmen outside with a pneumatic drill, traffic noise and the dreaded low-flying aircraft. If the sound engineer notices any of these while the shot is being filmed, the shot must be restaged with everything quiet. An unexplained background noise will be very distracting for your viewer.

Before leaving your location, record a 1min 'wildtrack' of sound that may come in useful for dubbing later. The wildtrack is simply a minute's 'silence', and is done by running the camera with the lens cap on, letting the microphone record the general noise of the location. This can be done at the same time as the general views.

The Rostrum Camera

Not all the pictures in a video need to move, and you will often find it necessary to insert photographs, drawings, graphics or text as part of the programme – especially if you are pushed for getting hold of the shots you need. To film photographs and other still pictures you will need to use a rostrum camera.

A basic rostrum camera sits on a movable bracket, facing downwards towards a lit platform. The artwork or photograph to be filmed is placed on the platform, and the camera uses a special macro (close-up) lens to get in really close. A professional rostrum camera will allow the mount to move through 360° so that movements and zooms can be accommodated. By zooming and panning around the still picture, not only can you pick out key elements, the movement will bring a certain amount of 'life' to what was a completely static picture.

If you do not have access to a rostrum camera, you can mount the artwork to be filmed in front of a flat board and film it using a camera mounted on a tripod. Professional ENG crews with a deadline to meet often rest artwork on top of the rear windscreen wiper of their estate car, and set up the camera on a tripod a few feet away, panning and zooming around the photograph as appropriate.

The rostrum camera can also be used in the studio to film special titles or photographs to be laid over the studio pictures using Chromakey.

Video Camera Accessories

Any item of video equipment apart from the essential video camera and VTR is known as a video accessory. Accessories such as spare batteries, tripods, external microphones and monitors you should view as 'essential' for a successful video production but there are a number of other items that, although not vital, can be useful for giving that extra finishing touch.

Your college or university will probably not have all the items listed here, but most can be hired from professional video rental agencies. But be warned, rental fees are expensive, so don't use an accessory just for the sake of it.

Batteries and the Battery Belt

The average video camera battery only lasts for about 30min, which means that you will have to change the battery several times during a day's shoot. We recommend that you always have spare batteries on charge, so that you have a fully charged battery ready when you need it. Imagine the frustration and inconvenience of having to stop filming for an hour or more while waiting for the batteries to recharge.

The battery belt (also known as a 'pag belt') consists of several battery packs connected in series, all housed in a thick belt that the camera operator wears around her/his waist. The belt should last for at least 2 hours when fully charged, although it is a bit heavy to wear while shooting. Most camera operators prefer to wrap the battery belt around the tripod legs, or sling it over the sound recordist's shoulder.

Like ordinary rechargeable batteries, it is very important that you run video batteries completely flat before recharging them. Failure to do so will result in reduced battery life and eventually kill the battery. To prevent any confusion, always mark fully charged batteries by putting red gaffer tape over the terminals.

Filters

A filter is a piece of optical glass or plastic that fits in front of the lens to create a particular effect. They have been more fully explained on page 51 of Chapter 2 and you can use the same filters for 35mm cameras for video applications. However, most video lenses are larger in diameter than their 35mm counterparts, so using smaller filters from a 35mm photography kit may be a little difficult.

Generally speaking, only graduated, polarising and colour-conversion filters are of any use for video, and these can be obtained from a variety of suppliers. Lee Filters make filters almost exclusively for video use, and the Cokin 'P' series of square filters can also be used. If you haven't got a proper square holder that is big enough to fit on your camera lens, remove the front lens hood and gaffer tape the filter into position, taking care not to get the tape in the shot. This method is not very secure, and should only be used in an emergency.

Graduated filters are useful for colouring otherwise dull skies (they were used extensively in the film *Top Gun*), but they must be used sensitively, otherwise the result will look ridiculous. When using a graduated filter, you should set the camera aperture manually (most cameras overexpose the foreground once the filter is in place), and the result should be checked in a colour monitor before filming. If you cannot check the shot before shooting, do one take with the filter in place, and another without. This gives you an 'escape route' just in case the filter shot is unusable.

Polarising filters cut out reflections on glass and water at an angle of more than 45°, and they are also capable of making blue skies almost unnaturally blue. Use them to make sunny shots look spectacular, and for shooting through glass.

Most video cameras have built-in colour correction filters to deal with different colour temperatures, but you may want to use other coloured filters to give a specific effect. Pale blue filters used at night can give the impression of moonlight, while orange filters are often used by professionals to give the impression of warmth.

Conversion Lenses

Although the standard zoom fitted to most cameras is more than adequate for most situations, there are times when an extreme wide angle or a long-reaching telephoto lens can be useful. Conversion lenses are available for both professional and amateur cameras, and they both screw onto the front of the lens. Beware of poor quality lenses, which are easily identifiable by a fall off of sharpness at the edges of the frame and vignetting. Vignetting is caused by using a lens that is unsuitable for the camera, and it results in black areas in the corner of the frame.

Portable Lights

Redheads and blondes are vital equipment for the camera operator on location, but there may be times when mains power is not available, or where high-output lights are too powerful or bulky. In this case you will need to use a lightweight portable light that is powered by its own battery pack (see Figure 5.31) or the cigarette lighter in a car.

Generally speaking, these lights give off around 125–250W of light, which is enough for most close-up situations. Like other artificial light sources, colour correcting gels must be used when mixing these lights with daylight, and some models come with their own barn doors and a flood/spot facility. Many ENG camera operators have portable lights fixed permanently to the top of their cameras, allowing them to be used at any time to give extra light to the shot.

Steadicam

This device gives the most incredibly shake-free pictures, although it can only be operated by trained personnel (see Figure 5.32). Using balanced weights and a special body harness, the camera can be moved through 360°, and is light enough for the camera operator to walk up stairs without a hint of camera shake. Steadicams are normally used for long tracking shots where a tracked dolly would be impractical, but they are very expensive to hire.

Dollies

A dolly is a movable camera platform that normally runs on temporary metal tracks to give smooth camera movement for tracking shoots (Figure 5.33, page 160). The camera operator sits on the dolly, along with the camera on a movable jib, that can be moved through 360° and up and down. The whole unit is pushed or pulled by a 'dolly grip'. Once again, dollies are expensive to hire, but they are indispensable for getting that perfect tracking shot.

Grips

A grip is a term given to any item of equipment that 'grips' the camera to an object other than a tripod. Grips enable you to hold the camera steady anywhere that a tripod cannot go, and they are particularly useful for hanging a camera off the side of a moving car. Grips can be hired from professional equipment specialists; but be warned, you may have to hire the services of a rigger if you do not know someone who is trained to install grips.

Figure 5.31
A battery-powered portable light (courtesy of Strand Lighting)

Figure 5.32
The Steadicam gives the most incredibly shake-free pictures

Figure 5.33
A dolly on location
(courtesy of Yorkshire
Television)

Cranes

As their name suggests, cranes are extending camera mounts that can
reach up to and above 35ft. They are normally used for sweeping wide
angle shots at the beginning of high-budget drama productions, and
cost several hundred pounds a day to hire. It is normal for the camera
to be remotely controlled from the ground using a special unit,
although some cranes have space for a camera operator at the end of
the jib.

Post-production

Once you've shot your video (having remembered to log the shots as
you go – it saves a lot of time later), it is then necessary to arrange all
the shots together into some semblance of order to make a programme.
This stage of the video is known as 'post-production' and editing.

As long as you have written a good treatment – and have stuck
reasonably close to it – the editing and post-production process
shouldn't really be too difficult. Problems only normally arise when
you haven't got quite enough footage, the shots that you want to use
aren't quite in focus, or when someone in your group has lost the
tapes. These problems are avoidable, but they've all actually happened
to students.

Throughout the filming process, you should have consulted your
treatment and noted any amendments that may have occurred, as well
as logging the counter number of each shot as you were filming it. This
will allow you to find your edit points easily. Failure to note the counter
numbers (or timecode) will probably mean that you have to waste
valuable time watching all your footage in fast forward, in order for you
to find the precise position of the shots you want to use.

After deciding which shots you think are usable, you are then ready to
start sculpting the programme from the raw material.

Figure 5.34
After shooting some footage with the camera, you will have to use editing machines to put it into some sort of order

Using your treatment, you should work out roughly how long each section of your video will last, and begin to start work on the commentary (if applicable). Some people prefer to write the commentary after they have completely finished editing the pictures, although we don't recommend this method. Making words fit pre-edited footage is very difficult and time-consuming. It is much better to write, or at least begin, the commentary as you edit. Providing you wrote a satisfactory treatment to start with, then writing a the commentary should not be too difficult. What you are trying to say in your video should always be in the back of your mind while you are filming and editing.

Commentary writing

Remember that the spoken commentary is only one small part of your video, and should complement and (to a certain extent) explain the reasons for your choice of visuals. Pictures are the most important part of a video, and if your commentary has been written well, it should add extra impact and can even determine what the viewer thinks about the pictures.

One temptation that you *must* avoid at all costs is to use the commentary to describe what the viewer can already see. Not only does this detract from the pictures, it is also a terrible waste of a potentially powerful opportunity to give the visuals extra meaning.

Although you must not describe what is in the picture, it is vital that the commentary fits the visuals. It is no good talking about the mating patterns of the African elephant if there is a picture of leopard on the screen. It is for this reason that we suggest your commentary should be taking shape as you edit the video, so that you have time to fit the words to the pictures. It is commonly accepted that a spoken commentary should have around three words per second – but don't forget to leave space for your narrator to take a breath!

Don't be obsessed with having commentary all the way through your video; leave space for sync. sound and some music. Remember that your viewers will need time to understand what they have been told, especially if the video contains a lot of information that is new to them. Your narrator must have a clear voice and speak slowly, as the viewers are being expected to take in a lot of information at a speed that is not of their own choosing.

When writing your commentary, avoid clichés, specialist terms, the meaningless, and don't state the obvious. If you want your video to be effective, it is far better to use simple phrases and words rather than confuse the viewers with technical jargon. While writing your commentary, try to imagine that you are speaking in sentences, not writing them; this will help you keep sentences brief and to the point. One useful device to help you do this is the dash. For example: 'The town of Brighton, which is well known for its large numbers of homeless people, has recently taken steps to alleviate the problem' becomes the much less wordy: 'Brighton – well known for its large numbers of homeless people – has recently taken steps to alleviate the problem' after adding a couple of dashes.

Try and develop a clear and concise style. You will find that you hold the viewer's attention for longer, and in doing so your video will get more information across.

Remember: when writing the final draft for the narrator, make sure the text is clearly typed with double spacing for any possible alterations. Don't use thin paper, as this tends to rustle in the background while recording the voice over to tape.

Editing

There are many different types of editing suite, ranging from a simple two-machine domestic set-up, to a highly technical three-machine professional suite, complete with digital effects mixer and character generator.

Figure 5.35
A basic two-machine 'cuts only' editing suite

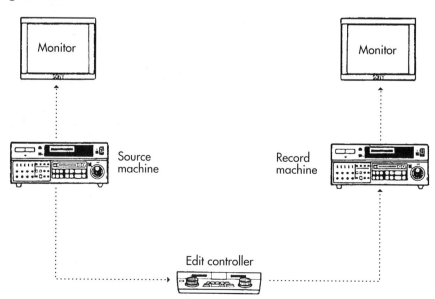

For the purposes of this book we will introduce you firstly to the fundamentals of editing using a basic two-machine edit suite (Figure 5.35), and then talk about more using more sophisticated multi-machine suites later.

Basic editing suites

Editing is the process of organising the footage you have taken on location into a meaningful series of shots and/or events. At its crudest, all you need to edit is two video recorders linked together using AV (audio/visual) leads. One machine acts as the 'source' (it plays the original footage), while the other operates as the 'edit' (or record) machine. This is used to re-record the footage in the sequence you choose. However, this type of editing (which is appropriately called 'crash editing') is very inaccurate and will give you very poor results. You should never attempt it, unless you want to experiment and don't have access to a proper suite. Using an edit controller (see Figure 5.36) synchronises all the video machines to the same running speed, and results in better and more precise results.

Figure 5.36
The Panasonic AG A770 editing controller

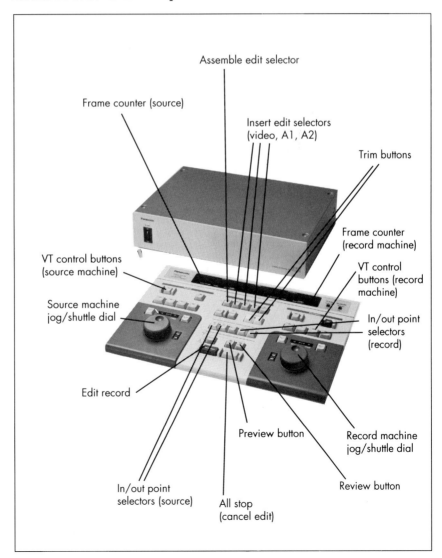

Assemble edit selector

Frame counter (source)

Insert edit selectors (video, A1, A2)

Trim buttons

Frame counter (record machine)

VT control buttons (source machine)

VT control buttons (record machine)

Source machine jog/shuttle dial

In/out point selectors (record)

Edit record

Preview button

Record machine jog/shuttle dial

In/out point selectors (source)

All stop (cancel edit)

Review button

All conventional video formats run at a frame rate of 25 frames per second. Like cartoons, each frame is a still picture which, when run at the correct speed, combines with the others to give a moving picture. The edit controller is a device that allows you to control the source machine (which may be a compatible video camera) and edit machine frame by frame, so that you can be extremely precise. The edit controller also makes the video machines perform a preroll of about 10sec, which ensures that both machines are synchronised to the same running speed before performing the edit. This prevents picture break-up.

A more sophisticated two-machine editing suite will also include a vision mixer (normally with a digital effects bank) and an audio mixer, which will be linked to a tape or CD player (Figure 5.37). The vision mixer will allow you to fade the picture to black and/or use the digital effects to strobe, solarise or reduce the image (see the later section on digital effects). With the audio mixer, you can add a separate pre-recorded commentary or music to your edited video. However, a two-machine edit suite is limiting, as you cannot mix or wipe between two different pictures – for this you need a multi-machine suite.

Figure 5.37
A two-machine editing suite linked to an audio and vision mixer

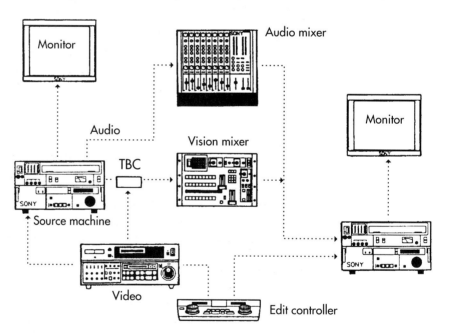

Multi-machine editing suites

These suites are the norm for professionals, and are infinitely more flexible than the standard two-machine package. With a multi-machine suite (that normally consists of two source machines and one recorder coupled to a vision/audio mixer, Figure 5.38), you are able to fade or wipe between two different images, rather than being limited to just the straight cut. Each machine is controlled individually by the edit controller, and the fade/wipe is carried out to single frame accuracy. Many of these types of editing suite are computer controlled, with a memory that stores each edit on floppy disk if required.

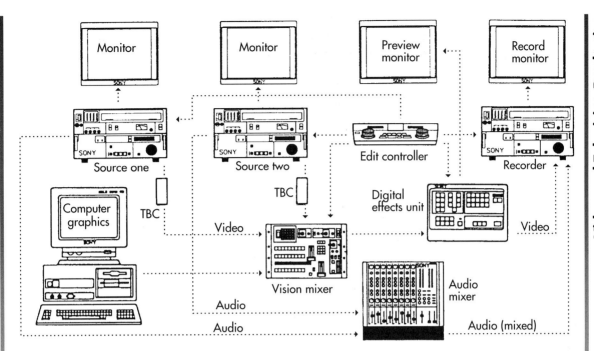

Figure 5.38
A more advanced multi-machine editing suite

The Digital Video Effects Machine

The digital video effects (DVE) machine is connected between the source machine(s) and the recorder, and is used to digitally alter the picture for special effects purposes. Most DVEs are capable of the following effects:

- *Freeze frame*: digitally freezes the picture, even though the source tape continues playing
- *Strobe*: a sequence of freeze frames, frozen at variable intervals
- *Mosaic*: turns the picture into squares, as used for protecting an interviewee's identity
- *Solarisation*: reduces the number of colours available in the picture, resulting in a basic image devoid of detail
- *Picture reduction*: the picture can be reduced, using a joystick, to any size
- *Vertical/horizontal reveal*: the picture from source 1 moves off the screen, revealing source 2's picture underneath (only available using a three-machine edit suite)
- *Vertical/horizontal push-off*: source 1's picture is pushed off the screen by source 2 (only available using a three-machine edit suite)
- *Mosaic mix*: source 1's picture turns into a mass of indistinguishable squares, to be replaced by source 2, that materialises into a proper picture (only available using a three-machine edit suite)

For other effects specific to your own machine, consult your user's manual – but once again, remember not to overdo the effects!

The Vision Mixer

This device (Figure 5.39, page 166) is found on multi-machine editing suites, and allows you to mix and/or wipe between each source machine. A mix is where source 1 dissolves into source 2 (or vice

165

versa), creating a smooth transition between each picture, while a wipe is a more direct method of cross-fade, using a direct line between each image (see Figure 5.40). Wipes can be simple or complex, but, like mixes, they must be used with sensitivity. Too many will detract from your video, resulting in something that looks like a demonstration tape for the vision mixer.

Figure 5.39
The Sony SEG-2550AP
vision mixer

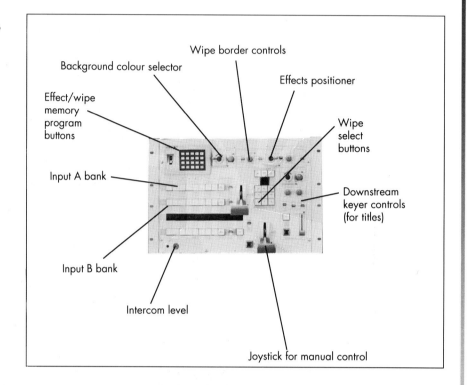

Figure 5.40
A wipe is a convenient
way of cutting from one
location to another

Figure 5.41
Titles can be generated by
computer and
superimposed using the
downstream key facility
on the mixer

Most vision mixers also have titling facilities (see Figure 5.41) that make use of the downstream keyer. This allows titles to be faded in and out, and a variety of colours are available.

Insert and assemble editing

There are two different types of editing, and to explain the differences between the two we shall use an analogy substituting the recorded pictures and sound on the tape with train carriages on a track.

In *assemble mode* (which is selected by pushing a button on the edit controller), the audio and video tracks of the master/source tape are transferred across to the record machine together, and each edit is done one after the other. In other words, the 'carriages' (pictures and sound) are built up in succession, until the 'train' (edited video) is complete. With assemble editing, the 'control track' on the video tape (that all VTRs 'read' to ensure that the tape is running at the right speed) is built up with each edit. You cannot edit without a control track on the tape.

In *insert mode*, the control track has to be laid down in advance before editing takes place, and this is done by pre-recording the tape using a conventional recorder. This procedure is known as 'blacking up'. When blacking up, it is very important you ensure that the control track lasts for as long as you intend to edit, as without a proper control track, the videos in the edit suite will simply not synchronise properly.

Insert mode allows you to transfer the sound and video tracks separately, so insert editing should be used for overlaying pictures over pre-recorded sound or vice versa. Using the 'Video', 'Audio channel one' and 'Audio channel two' buttons on your edit controller, select which track(s) you want transferred to the edit machine, and then proceed as you would for an assemble edit. Insert edits allow you to use any of the following audio/vision combinations:

■ Vision only (no sound)

- Vision and audio track 1
- Vision and audio track 2
- Audio track 1 only (no vision)
- Audio track 2 only (no vision)
- Audio tracks 1 and 2 (no vision)

Unlike assemble edits, insert edits can also be 'dropped in' over pre-edited footage. However, don't forget that anything you record over will be lost for good. Inserting a piece of footage doesn't, unfortunately, mean that all the following edits will be magically moved along to make room for it!

Performing an edit

In both types of editing, it is necessary to select the point at which the sound and/or pictures from the source machine will transfer across to the recorder. This is done by programming in 'in points', which tell the two (or more) video machines where to start the edit. To do this, you will need to position both the source and edit tapes at the start of the edit (on the source machine, this should be the start of where you want the original footage to start to transfer from, and on the recorder, it should be the point where you want this material to be placed) using the jog/shuttle dials on the edit controller for frame accuracy. After the in points have been set, hit the 'Edit start' button, and the tapes will run back approximately 10sec for the 'preroll', which allows each machine to synchronise to the same speed. Once the edit is complete, you can either press 'Edit stop' on the edit controller, or, for more accuracy, set an 'out point' at the same time as you select an in point. See Figure 5.42 for a diagramatic explanation of the above.

Figure 5.42
A diagrammatic explanation of an edit

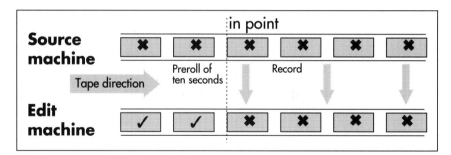

One useful feature that all edit controllers have is the 'preview' function. This allows you to view an edit without actually recording it onto tape. Always use this if you are unsure whether an edit will work technically or not; once an edit has been recorded, it is impossible to undo.

Multi-machine editing (mixes and wipes)

When using a three-machine edit suite, you have the option of mixing or wiping between each source machine. Most three-machine edit suites are controlled from the edit controller and, providing the vision mixer is also connected to this, performing mixes or wipes is very easy.

To perform a mix from source 1 to source 2 first set the in point of both source 1 and the record machine (as you would do normally), and then set an in point for source 2 at the precise frame you want that machine to start. Then, set an out point on source 1 to allow the edit controller to know when you want the transition from one machine to the other to begin. You will also have to enter in the desired duration of the mix/wipe in seconds and/or frames, before pushing the 'Edit start' button. The edit controller will then control the entire operation for you (see Figure 5.43).

Figure 5.43
A diagrammatic explanation of a mix from source to source

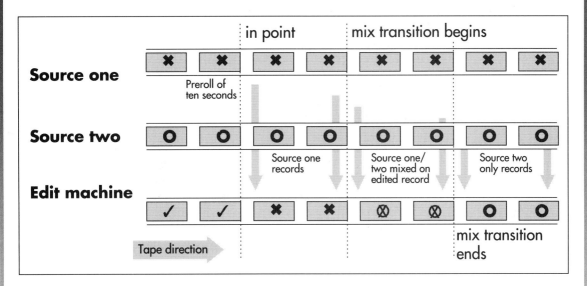

Figure 5.43
A diagrammatic explanation of a mix from source to source

Setting sound levels

Professional source and edit machines have built-in sound level indicators, complete with gain adjustment (see Figure 5.44). Providing that you set the levels correctly on the camera when you were shooting your footage, these should be left in the middle position, with the needles peaking at the 0dB rating. However, if for some reason your original sound levels are too low, then you may adjust the gain on the record machine to compensate. Be careful not to overdo it, though, as all sound levels that peak too high (over 0dB into the red band) will distort badly.

Figure 5.44
The JVC BR-S622E SVHS editing machine

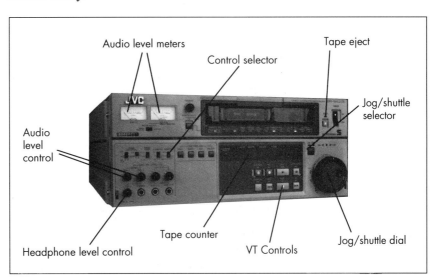

When using an audio mixer for importing and/or mixing sound from other sources (a tape player, CD, DAT machine, etc.), you should pre-set the levels on the record machine before starting to edit. This is done by playing a sample of your audio track to be dubbed (be it commentary, sound effects (SFX) or music) at its highest level, and then altering the levels on the record machine accordingly. You can then fade the audio source in or out using the audio mixer, rather than having to fiddle around with the buttons on the record machine.

See Chapter 3 for further details on using a multi-track mixer.

Editing Techniques

The key to editing is finding the precise point at which a shot starts being interesting and the precise point at which it stops being interesting.

H. Watts *On Camera*

Like shooting technique, editing technique has developed from a set of unwritten rules that were established to produce the most 'natural' and aesthetic sequences. Jump cuts, shots that last too long, awkward changes in movement and unexplained changes of scene are all good examples of bad editing technique, and must be avoided at all times. Providing you thought about how you were going to edit while you were filming, then all these editing 'no-nos' are avoidable. It is for this reason that we recommend that all camera operators who have no intention of ever sitting down at an editing suite read this section before going out and filming shots that could be next to useless for editing purposes.

Fade to Black
A video should always start with a black screen, and the opening shot should be faded in from this. If you begin a video with a straight cut from black, it will look awkward and start off badly. Similarly, fade the video out at the end, although a dramatic 'snap to black' can be used for dramatic effect. When fading in from black, you may like to experiment with fading in the audio tracks slightly before the picture starts to appear. This can create a pleasing effect, although you must be careful not to fade the sound in too early.

The Jump Cut and Compressing Time
Very early cinema shot all its footage in 'real time', resulting in long movies that showed a lot of irrelevant shots. If we used this convention nowadays, a shot of a woman getting home from work would start from the time she drove up the drive, and would only end (possibly as much as five minutes later) once she had entered the house. It is easy to see that spending five minutes on something as trivial as this would quickly bore the viewer, so tricks have been devised to get the woman into the house as quickly as possible.

An edited video has amazing power to shorten time, although you must be careful when doing this to avoid the 'jump cut'. This describes the time–reality gap that can be caused when careless editing has been done.

Suppose we wanted to shorten the sequence we talked about earlier. If we showed a shot of the woman getting out of her car, followed immediately by a shot of her inside the house, the time–reality gap has been broken – how did she suddenly get into the house?

Clearly it would be over the top to spend five minutes showing her stopping the car, undoing her seatbelt, getting out of the car, locking it, getting her briefcase from the boot, walking towards the house, unlocking the house, opening the door, and finally getting inside. Instead, you should insert a couple of brief cutaways that make the viewer think that all these things have been done, without actually showing them in real time.

If, however, you don't want to use cutaways, you can overcome the problem of the jump cut by simply having a shot without the woman in it. For example, as she gets out of the car, she should walk past the camera and out of shot, leaving just the car in frame. You can then cut to a shot of a closed door, and after around 15 frames (just over half a second), the woman should enter shot from the opposite side to the way she just left. Although there is only a brief gap between the two shots without the woman, it is enough for the viewer to imagine that she has walked the distance required to reach the door. Using this technique will make your sequences seem natural to the viewer, even though they don't actually conform to the reality of time.

Remember also to always make a mental note not to 'cross the line' while editing.

Inserting Cutaways

Cutaways are immensely useful devices that can get you out of a lot of trouble when editing. One of their primary uses is to shorten interviews, and we will use an example of this to demonstrate.

Our example is taken from a promotional video for an electronics firm. The interviewee lost track of what he was saying, and stumbled over his words. However, during editing it was decided that this was a key

Figure 5.45
This cutaway of the object being talked about covers a break where the interviewee stumbled over his words (see overleaf)

section, and we wanted to use it. But how could we cut from where he made the mistake to where he corrected himself, without drawing attention to the gap? We realised that the audio track could be cut together easily enough, but doing this would result in an awkward picture jump where he moved his head. The only solution was to insert a related cutaway that we had filmed especially for the purpose, and this disguised the jump perfectly (see Figure 5.45).

To drop in a cutaway, use the insert facility on the edit suite, but knock out the audio channels so that only the picture is transferred. Set in and out points as usual, ensuring that the cutaway is long enough to cover the picture jump – around 4sec is the right length. If in doubt, preview the edit before you record it to tape, and once you are satisfied, press 'Record'.

Shot Length

This is a very difficult area, and one that has no real set rules. Harris Watts' quote at the beginning of this section sums it up very well – the moment a shot becomes boring is the time you should remove it from the screen. A static shot of a house in the distance will look very boring if left on the screen for several seconds, although the same shot given movement with a slow zoom will hold the viewer's attention for considerably longer.

You should also take into account the overall pace of your video. If your video shows dramatic, fast-moving action, cut the shots accordingly by keeping things short. In a situation like this, it would also be a good idea to use tilted camera angles for extra impact, but these must, of course, be shot while on location. This demonstrates the importance of a thorough treatment that considers the editing process.

Cutting on Movement

Never cut a shot while it is panning or zooming. Doing so will produce awkward and unprofessional results. Always let your pans and zooms come to a halt before changing shot.

Similarly, do not cut from a moving subject to something static. A shot of a car driving along a road followed immediately by a shot of it parked by the kerb will look ridiculous. Cut to a shot of the car coming to rest, or let it go out of frame before cutting to a shot of it being parked.

Mixes

The mix can be one of the most attractive ways of changing shots, although if it is overused it will detract greatly from the overall production. A simple rule is: if you don't notice the mix while watching the video, it has worked.

Advertisements make great use of mixes, and we recommend you watch several adverts to learn successful mixing technique. Ask yourself why the mix was used. What does it add to the video? How would the same edit look without the mix? Once you can successfully answer these questions, you will know how and when to use a mix.

Remember: use mixes sparingly, and always justify them before performing the edit.

Wipes and effects

If in doubt, don't use them. When editing, it is very easy to be drawn into the trap of using every possible effect on the DVE and vision mixer. Like mixes, you should ensure that every effect and wipe that you use in your video can justify itself. For example, a wipe may be used in a promotional video to clearly mark the end of one section and the beginning of another, but to use one to cut from one related shot to another will have ridiculous results. Similarly, if you want to use a strobe effect, make sure that you don't make a straight cut from a strobed shot to a normal motion shot. It's much better to use a mix to make a smoother transition.

Slow Motion

Used in the right context, slow motion sequences can look spectacular. **173**

However, you may be constrained by your editing suite. Only video players that have a direct motion control facility can play true smooth slow motion, and you will have to use a time base corrector to ensure that there is no flickering on screen caused by poor video synchronisation.

Alternatively, you can patch in a domestic video capable of slow motion into your vision mixer, and record straight from that. However, it will not be possible to preroll or synchronise that machine, and the resulting edit may be of poor quality.

Remember that the pace of your video will be drastically reduced by slow motion, and you may like to use slow mixes to maintain this slow pace.

Dubbing the Audio Tracks

Most edit suites have two audio channels, and if you intend to add a commentary to your video, it is advisable to leave one channel (normally A2) free. The other channel can be used for sync, sound and/or music.

If you intend to write your commentary at the end of the video, be prepared to re-sync. the video so that the commentary can be heard over the 'background' noise. However, for most general shots, wild tracks can be used as background noise, thus avoiding any necessity for a labour-intensive re-sync.

Figure 5.46
A dubbing chart

If your video requires extensive dubbing (you intend to add music, SFX, sync, sound and a commentary), before starting to record, you will need to make a dubbing chart (see Figure 5.46) which should list the counter numbers at which you intend to introduce or remove audio track. This not only helps you to organise your ideas, it also provides cues for the narrator and sound technicians.

Credits

At the end of the video, it is normal to list all the people who helped to produce it. This can be done using a simple character generator or computer, plugged into the downstream keyer. It is up to you whether you scroll the credits, or have them fading in and out from black. Don't overdo the credits, though, as it will be very boring for your viewers to have to sit through a list of everybody who added the tiniest morsel to the production of your video. How many people sit and watch all of the credits at the end of a film?

Things to Remember When Editing

1 Always start and end the video by fading from/to black.
2 Avoid jump cuts – use cutaways, or have subjects move out of frame.
3 Insert cutaway shots to disguise discrepancies or change angle.
4 Keep shots as short as possible and as long as necessary.
5 Establish an editing pace to your video and stick to it.
6 Never cut on a zoom, pan or any type of movement.
7 Use mixes, wipes and effects sparingly. Justify them before adding them.
8 If you intend to add a commentary, keep one audio track free for this.
9 Keep credits short.

The future: digital non-linear computer editing

Technological progress over the past few years has resulted in computers becoming more and more integrated into the edit suite, to the extent that some non-linear edit suites now work exclusively using computer disks rather than conventional tape (Figure 5.47).

Taped footage is downloaded onto optical or magnetic disks; using the computer screen, the editor is able to select the shot required at the click of a mouse button, eradicating the need to wait while the tape shuttles into the right position. As you create the programme, the computer screen arranges all the edits in order, and because this is stored in the computer's memory, you are able to re-edit or extend sequences at any point in the programme, without affecting the material positioned afterwards. A multi-track audio-visual timeline can also be called up on the screen, to give a precise overview of all edits, sound cues and video images.

Fades, wipes and mixes can all be easily executed using the computer, and because nothing is recorded to tape until you are quite satisfied, fades and wipes can be altered time and time again, without any loss of quality. There is even a graphics package available, so that titles can be incorporated automatically. Once you are satisfied with the edited programme as it stands on the hard disk, a 'Print-to-Tape' function allows the computer to create a final master tape, with the edit machines controlled entirely by the computer.

Although this amazing software and hardware is now widely being used in broadcasting, it unfortunately may be some time before universities and colleges can afford the high purchase prices of the equipment.

Figure 5.47
The Avid Media Composer in action (courtesy of John Ward – Television Buyer)

Case Study

To demonstrate most of the points we have been trying to convey in this chapter, we shall use a simple 60sec case-study. Filmed by a student, it is a copy of a 'classic' Renault advertisement from the late 1980s and uses many of the techniques we have been talking about. See Figure 5.48 for a complete shot-by-shot breakdown.

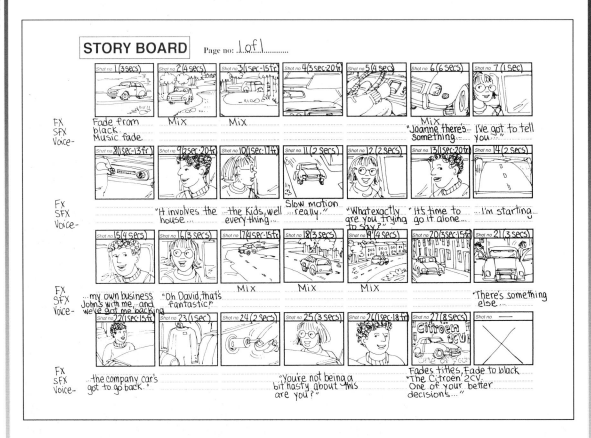

Figure 5.48
A complete shot-by-shot breakdown of the 2CV video

Before shooting, the student wrote out a complete treatment outlining what shots he wanted, based on the shots he had seen in the original advert. He then recce'd a local stately home, ensured that he had permission to shoot there, and worked out the best time of day when the lighting conditions would be right. He then organised all the props that were needed, as well as asking friends to 'star' in the video. Finally, he booked the camera (a simple one-CCD Sony Hi-8), tripod, monitor, external microphone and appropriate leads, and ensured that the batteries were fully charged.

On the day of the shoot, the treatment was invaluable for ensuring that all the shots required were quickly filmed. A monitor was used to check every shot as it was filmed, and each shot was logged on a master sheet for easy retrieval in the editing suite. With everything 'in the can' the cast and crew went off for a well-earned drink!

Before editing, the original footage was 'dumped' from the Hi-8 onto two U-Matic SP tapes, to allow mixes to be carried out. In the editing suite, the treatment and shot list ensured swift location of each shot. A few experimental shots were added because 'they worked', and the

177

occasional mix was used when deemed appropriate. The final shot used a caption generated by a computer, before the whole picture was faded back down to black.

The dub was fairly straightforward, with appropriate non-copyright music being added to track A2 after the sync. sound was at the correct level on track A1. The final punchline 'The Citroën 2CV – One of your better decisions' was recorded in the studio, and added at the end on track A1. Finally, the whole edited 'advert' was dumped from U-Matic SP to VHS for ease of viewing, taking care that the two audio tracks were converged together for the final copy.

Reference Section

This short section offers a handy reference guide to the variety of connection leads, colour conversion filters and video tape formats available.

Video and Audio Connections

It is vital that the video producer knows what the variety of video and audio connection leads are called, so that s/he can specify the type of lead required for a certain piece of equipment. All connections are of the male and female variety – you plug the male into the female. Figure 5.49 shows the variety of connections and what they are called.

Figure 5.49
A variety of audio-video connectors

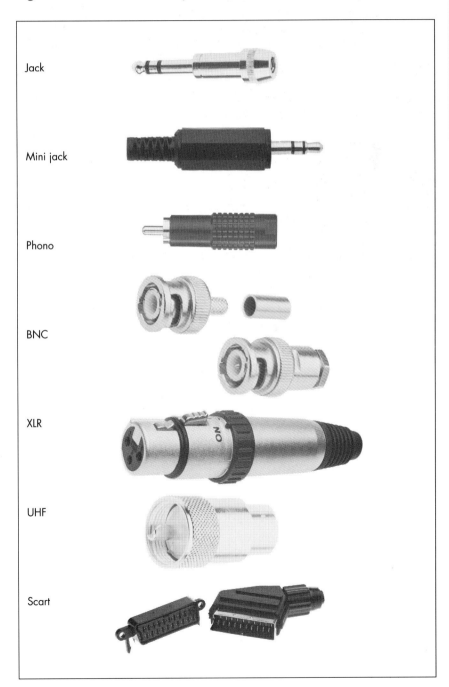

Jack

Mini jack

Phono

BNC

XLR

UHF

Scart

Gels and Colour Conversion Filters

Colour conversion filters are normally placed over portable lights, to ensure that the colour temperature emitted matches that of the dominant light source. Filters over lights are normally known as gels, and can be used to create special effects as well as for colour correction.

If your dominant light source is daylight and you are using tungsten lamps, then you will need to use a medium blue CTB gel over the light. If, however, tungsten light is your dominant light source, and you have a small window that you want to cover, use a medium strength orange CTO filter. For balancing with fluorescent lights, use a medium green gel over your tungsten lamps. This should match the lamps' colour temperature to the dominant fluorescent source, although you may need to experiment (using a monitor) with a variety of shades of green before you manage to attain the perfect match.

Diffusing gels cut down the amount of light emitted from the lamp, and the light produced is much softer. This is useful for direct indoor shooting, and the diffusers are known as 'frosts' or 'spun'. 'Tough spun' is the most effective diffuser, and frost diffusing gels are normally coloured blue to correct tungsten lamps to daylight.

Other filters can be used over lights to create certain effects. Flickering reds and oranges can be used to simulate the light emitted from a fire, while pale blues can be used to simulate moonlight. Skin tones can be enhanced by using a pale orange filter, and you can go for some really bizarre effects with dark red, green and blue lighting. For further details consult the handy guide available from Lee Filters. Their address is printed in the Resource list section at the back of this book.

Video tape formats

There is a huge variety of video tape formats available these days, and the most popular tapes for acquisition are U-Matic SP, Betacam SP, Hi-8 and SVHS. These all record high quality, sharp images, and the tapes are strong enough to withstand heavy editing. Each time original footage is recorded onto another tape it is said to have 'dropped a generation', and this will mean a loss in quality. Professional film crews only use completely blank video tapes for acquisition, although the drop in picture quality is almost insignificant if you do choose to use pre-recorded tapes in your camera.

We haven't listed every tape format available, as there are simply too many. Instead we have selected the most commonly used for college/university acquisition and editing purposes.

Full-size VHS

This is the most popular domestic video format, and you will probably end up with your final edited programme on VHS for easy viewing. VHS is not recommended as an acquisition format, as the pictures quickly lose quality each time you drop a generation. Tape lengths: 15min, 30min, 60min, 120min, 180min, 240min.

Compact VHS (VHSC)

With the introduction of small domestic camcorders, camera manufacturers needed a tape size that was compatible with VHS but much smaller. The result was the half-sized VHSC tape that can be loaded into a special adapter and played back using a normal VHS video recorder. Tape lengths: 30min, 45min.

Full-size Super VHS (SVHS)

An identical size and shape to conventional VHS, the SVHS tape (Figure 5.50a) is able to record pictures of greater clarity thanks to its more advanced tape. SVHS videos can be inserted into a conventional VHS player, although any pictures recorded in the SVHS mode will not play back. Tape lengths: 15min, 30min, 60min, 120min, 180min, 240min.

Figure 5.50a
An SVHS tape

Compact Super VHS (SVHSC)

Like full-size SVHS, this (Figure 5.50b) is basically a SVHS version of the VHSC tape. Once again, it can be placed in an adapter and played in a full-size SVHS player. Tape lengths: 30min, 45min.

Figure 5.50b
An SVHSC tape

8mm and Hi-8

These tapes (Figure 5.50c) revolutionised the domestic camcorder market, as they were very small and offered extended record times thanks to their thinness. Conventional 8mm tapes are low in quality and should only be used for home videos, although the Hi-8 format offers incredibly high quality pictures from such a compact tape. Many professionals are switching to Hi-8 with high-quality 3 CCD cameras. 8mm or Hi-8 tapes cannot be played back in a VHS machine. Tape lengths: 15min, 30min, 60min, 90min, 120min.

Figure 5.50c
A Hi-8 tape

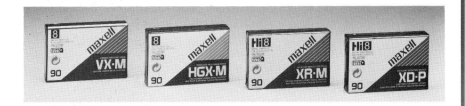

U-Matic and U-Matic SP

U-Matic was the first widely used professional tape for ENG at the end of the 1970s. It has since been superseded by the higher-quality U-Matic SP (Figure 5.50d). The tapes are fairly large, which means that you can only use the 20min version in a portable VTR. The 30min and 60min versions are designed for editing or studio use in large machines. Tape lengths: 20min, 30min, 60min.

Figure 5.50d
'far right'
A U-Matic SP tape

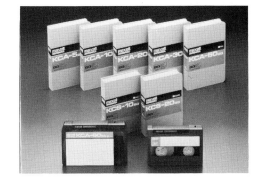

Figure 5.50e 'above'
A Betacam SP tape

Betacam, Betacam SP and Betacam SP Digital

Betacam SP is probably the most commonly used acquisition tape for professional ENG units. The tapes themselves are comparatively small, so they can be used in professional one-unit camcorders. Betacam SP Digital records picture and sound digitally, which means that there is no loss of quality every time you drop a generation (Figure 5.50e). Tape lengths: 5min, 10min, 20min, 30min, 60min, 90min, 120min.

Copyright

Most student videos have been shot for practice purposes only, and are not intended for resale or distribution. However, using someone else's music, photograph, film footage, story, etc. that is protected by copyright, without paying for the privilege, may result in copyright infringement. Make sure you are clear about copyright material before you use it. Being careless could mean that you end up with a large fine to pay.

Glossary

Listed below is a selection of video technical terms and what they mean.

A & B roll editing: Three-machine editing: two play, one record.

Aperture: Adjustable iris that controls the amount of light entering the camera through the lens. It is normally set on automatic ('A'), although on professional cameras it can be set to manual ('M') for tricky light conditions.

Audio cut: Edit on sound only.

Autocue: Computer-based prompting device. A two-way mirror in front of the camera lens reflects text for the presenter to read.

Autofocus: Focusing is automatically carried out by the camera. Best left alone, as the camera often focuses on the wrong subjects.

Backlight: Light used for three-point lighting. Placed behind the subject to produce an attractive halo effect around the head.

Barn doors: Movable flaps positioned around many types of portable and studio light. They control the angle of light emitted.

Blacking up: Recording a black picture on video tapes to create a control track.

Blonde: Portable light with a yellow casing. Emits 2kW of light.

Camcorder: Camera with the video recorder built into the camera body.

Camera card: Used to list camera instructions in studio-based productions.

Cans: Television speak for headphones.

CCD: Abbreviation of *charge coupled device*. These are image sensors that are used to 'translate' light entering the camera through the lens into electric signals, for recording onto tape.

CCU: Abbreviation of *camera control unit*. These are used to remotely control and balance studio cameras.

Chromakey: A device that allows you to superimpose a different background behind a subject filmed in the studio. The subject must be in front of a blue background for the 'keyer' to work.

Chrominance: The relative colour intensity of a television picture.

Colour correction filter: Used to balance the different colour temperatures emitted by artificial and daylight.

Colour temperature: Explains the different colours of light emitted by different sources. Daylight colour temperature is around 5 400°K, while artificial (tungsten) lights emit light that is 3 200°K.

Contrast: A gain control range between dark and light levels of the video picture.

Control room: The nerve centre of the studio. Images from the cameras are selected by the producer, and mixed by the vision mixer. Sound levels are mixed by the sound engineer.

Control track: A band on the video cassette that 'locks' the tape to the correct running speed.

Crane: Large boom arm that carries a camera for sweeping, high angle shots.

Cutaway: A shot inserted to provide a convenient break from the action. Should be used to cover jumps in continuity when editing.

Depth of field: The range of objects in focus, controlled by the *f*-stop. The lower the *f*-stop (e.g. *f*22), the greater the depth of field.

Dimmer board: Lighting control for the studio.

Dolby: Type of noise reduction system.

Dolly: Camera platform on wheels. Can be used for tracking shots, but the route used *must* be smooth.

Downstream keyer: Device on the vision mixer for superimposing secondary images (i.e. a computer-generated title) over the original image.

Dub: Replacing or supplementing the original soundtrack with another. The picture remains unchanged.

DVE: Abbreviation of *digital video effects*. Normally refers to the machine that creates these effects.

Edit controller: A unit that controls and synchronises the video machines being used for editing.

ENG: Abbreviation of *electronic news gathering*. The acquisition of video pictures for news purposes.

Establishing shot: A shot (or sequence of shots) that establishes the situation for the action.

Edit tape: The video cassette being used for rerecording the original footage in an edited order.

***f*-stop:** The numbers indicating the size of the aperture in use. *f*1.7 is wide (it lets a lot of light in), while *f*22 is small (it lets very little light in).

Fade to black: Recommended at the end of a video. The last picture fades to black using a mixer.

183

Fill light: Light that fills in any shadows.

Fishpole: Extendible microphone pole.

Focal length: Describes the position of the zoom lens. For video: 8mm is wide angle, while 120mm is telephoto.

Frost: A gel that softens the light emitted by diffusing it.

Gaffer tape: Sticky tape that is useful for almost any application. Always take gaffer tape with you when on a shoot.

Gain: Increases the sensitivity of the CCD, which is useful for nighttime or dusk filming. However, increasing the gain results in an increase of video 'noise' in the pictures – in other words, the picture will be more grainy.

Gel: Large coloured filters that should be bulldog-clipped to the barn doors of portable lights, to alter their colour temperature.

Generations: The number of times a video clip is copied or processed. This must be kept to a minimum on analogue systems, as a loss of quality accompanies each generation drop.

Genlock: A device that 'synchronises' a computer with other studio devices. This ensures that the picture doesn't break up when a cut is performed.

Grip: Any type of camera mount. Used for attaching cameras to cars, walls, etc.

GV: Abbreviation of *general view*. Normally a wide angle shot that shows a complete view of the scene.

Ident clock: Countdown clock that should placed at the beginning of any video or studio production. The last 10sec should be counted down, with the clock fading to black with 3sec to go.

Jog/shuttle dial: A movable dial on the edit controller, allowing you to precisely locate a frame on the video cassette. 'Shuttle' moves the tape forwards or backwards at a variable speed, while 'Jog' nudges the tape backwards or forwards frame by frame. Push the dial down to change between jog and shuttle.

Jump cut: A careless edit in which the image jumps inexplicably. This should be avoided at all times by the use of cutaways.

Key light: The main light used on a subject. This should normally be near the camera.

Lavalier: Another name for a tie clip microphone.

Luminance: Monochrome component of a colour television signal.

Master: First generation recording. Also applies to the final edit.

Mike/mic: Abbreviation of 'Microphone'.

Minicam: A small lipstick-sized camera used for getting shots from otherwise inaccessible places.

Mix: A smooth dissolve between one image to another. Can only be done with three-machine editing suites.

Mixing desk: The main visual control unit in the studio. It allows the vision mixer to cut/fade/wipe from camera to camera, and also normally houses Quantel and Chromakey.

Monitor: A high quality television for viewing video. Battery operated portable monitors should be used when shooting outside.

Noddy shot: A shot of an interviewer nodding that can be used for a cutaway later.

OB: Abbreviation for *outside broadcast*. Although not strictly a 'broadcast', this term is commonly used for any shoot outside the studio.

Pagbelt: A string of camera batteries housed in a waist belt. This gives very long shooting time.

Paglight: Another term for a battery operated portable light.

Pan: A sweeping motion from one side to the other, normally using a tripod. To be effective, pans should be slow.

Pan and tilt head: The camera mount on the tripod that allows movement up and down (tilt) and side to side (pan).

Portapack: A camera linked to a separate video recorder.

Post-production: Any editing or effects added after the acquisition of the video footage.

Preview: A look at an edit, without actually recording the edit to tape.

Preroll: A pre-edit run up, used to synchronise the tapes to the same speed.

Quantel: A powerful digital effects generator, that can do almost anything to the video image.

Recce: A pre-shoot visit to a location.

Redhead: Portable light with a red/orange casing. It emits 800W of light.

Reflector: A piece of white card or collapsible round piece of material (Lastolite) used to reflect light onto the subject.

Rostrum camera: Camera on a special mount, used for recording still pictures or still lifes.

Rough cut: The first assembly of edited shots in their intended script order.

Rushes: The uncut original footage before editing.

SFX: Abbreviation of *special effects*.

Skew: Vertical break-up at the top of a picture.

Slomo: Abbreviation of *slow motion*.

Source tape: The original master of unedited footage.

SPG: Abbreviation of *sync. pulse generator*.

Spider: A device for holding the legs of the tripod at an even distance.

Spun: Fairly thick material used for diffusing light emitted from a light.

Steadicam: Device used for obtaining remarkably shake-free pictures.

Storyboard: A pre-editing list of shots, special effects and sound cues. May include rough drawings of the shots.

Talkback: An voice link between the control room, studio and other relevant areas of the area.

TBC: Abbreviation of *time base corrector*. The TBC is a device that corrects time-based errors of a VTR which build up during copying. It is especially useful for dubbing particularly poor quality material.

Tally light: A red light on the front of the camera that illuminates when the camera is being used for recording.

Timecode: An accurate time counting system that is 'burnt in' to the tape. This allows you to change tapes, and still be able find the footage you require.

Tracking: VTR adjustment for optimum head alignment with the video tape. Bad tracking causes 'noise' to appear on the picture.

Treatment: A pre-shoot plan of what the video will include. A well-produced treatment is vital for any successful video production.

Trim: A device on the edit controller that lets you alter the 'in' or 'out' point already set frame by frame.

Tripod stand: A three-legged stand for holding portable lights.

Two shot: A shot of the interviewer and the interviewee, normally shot from behind the interviewer. This can be used later as a cutaway.

VT: Abbreviation of *video tape*.

VTR: Abbreviation of *video tape recorder*.

Wallpaper: General shots that can be used for cutaways or 'fillers' later.

Whip pan: Very quick pan that can be used to show a change of location.

White balance: Alters the colour balance sensitivity of the camera. It should be carried out by framing up a piece of white paper, and pushing the 'white balance' button on the camera. The white balance should be changed every time you alter your lighting set-up.

Wildtrack: A 1min recording of background noise, that can be used for dubbing later.

Wipe: A transition from one picture to another, using a direct line (or series of lines). As wipe is only possible with three-machine edit suites.

Further reading

Bermingham, A. (1990) *The Video Studio* Focal Press.

Blythe-Lord, R. (1992) *Captions and Graphics for Low Cost Video* Focal Press.

Brown, B. (1993) *Motion Picture and Video Lighting* Focal Press.

Browne, S. (1993) *Film and Video Terms and Concepts* Focal Press.

Browne, S. (1993) *Videotape Editing* Focal Press.

Jackson, K.G. and Towsend, G.B. (eds) (1993) *The TV and Video Engineer's Reference Book* Focal Press.

Millerson, G. (1991) *Lighting for Video* Focal Press.

Millerson, G. (1983) *Effective TV Production* (2nd ed.) Focal Press.

Rowlands, A. (1993) *Continuity in Film and Video* Focal Press.

Watts, H. (1984) *On Camera* BBC Books.

Wilkie, B. (1977) *Creating Special Effects for TV and Film* Focal Press.

Winston, B. and Keydel, J. (1987) *Working with Video: a comprehensive guide to the world of video production* Pelham Books.

6 Desktop Publishing, Basic Graphic Design and Multimedia

> **W**hen people read something, they don't just read the words; the way it's presented also makes a difference.
>
> (Nicholas Saunders, quoted from *Into Print*)

Introduction Over the past few years there has been nothing less than a computer desktop publishing (DTP) revolution. Since the launch of the now-archaic Sinclair ZX80 in the early 1980s, computers have become cheaper, more 'user-friendly' and, when connected to a laser or bubblejet printer, it is very easy to produce documents that look professional and are clear to read.

Newspapers and magazines use DTP and computers extensively. Newspapers like the *Daily Telegraph* have large computer networks that handle everything from the basic text input from journalists to page layout and graphic design. The 'pre-print' stages of the paper are almost exclusively carried out on computer, making it ready for downloading to the automated printing presses.

Nowadays, a laser or bubblejet printer is virtually *de rigueur* for all businesses, colleges and universities. Their high print quality is simply incomparable with the old-fashioned dot matrix or daisywheel type of printer and, providing your computer is fully compatible, the list of typefaces (or 'fonts') they can print is endless.

Compare the two documents in Figure 6.1. The first was printed on a six-year-old nine-pin dot matrix printer using a word processing program, while the other was formatted using a DTP program, and printed on an Apple bubblejet printer – there's no doubt which one is more effective. When presenting words in a written format, good presentation is undoubtedly one of the keys to successful communication.

This chapter aims to show you some of the techniques used by the professionals, but with the constraints of limited equipment. To produce documents similar to the ones in this chapter, you will need a computer with at least 4MB (megabytes) of RAM (memory to run the system), and a hard disk of 40MB of ROM (storage space) connected to either a bubblejet or laser printer (see Figure 6.2). Some other accessories (like a scanner) may be useful, but you may not have access to one of these. Check with your university or college's computer centre.

Figure 6.1
This is the same text printed on a dot matrix and then DTPs and printed on a bubblejet printer. Which one do you think is more effective?

This is a piece of sample text. It will be used to demonstrate the various functions and layouts described in this Chapter. There's little point in you actually reading it as it means absolutely nothing and will almost definitely bore you.

This is a piece of sample text. It will be used to demonstrate the various functions and layouts described in this Chapter. There's little point in you actually reading it as it means absolutely nothing and will almost definitely bore you. I'll pad this section out a bit, so that we haven't got paragraphs that are all the same length.

This is a piece of sample text. It will be used to demonstrate the various functions and layouts described in this Chapter. There's little point in you actually reading it as it means absolutely nothing and will almost definitely bore you. This is a piece of sample text. It will be used to demonstrate the various functions and layouts described in this Chapter. There's little point in you actually reading it as it means absolutely nothing and will almost definitely bore you.

This is a piece of sample text. It will be used to demonstrate the various functions and layouts described in this chapter. There's little point in you actually reading it, as it means absolutely nothing, and will almost definitely bore you.

This is a piece of sample text. It will be used to demonstrate the various functions and layouts described in this chapter. There's little point in you actually reading it, as it means absolutely nothing, and will almost definitely bore you.

This is a piece of sample text. It will be used to demonstrate the various functions and layouts described in this chapter. There's little point in you actually reading it, as it means absolutely nothing, and will almost definitely bore you.

This is a piece of sample text. It will be used to demonstrate the various functions and layouts described in this chapter. There's little point in you actually reading it, as it means absolutely nothing, and will almost definitely bore you.

This is a piece of sample text. It will be used to demonstrate the various functions and layouts described in this chapter. There's little point in you actually reading it, as it means absolutely nothing, and will almost definitely bore you.

This is a piece of sample text. It will be used to demonstrate the various functions and layouts described in this chapter. There's little point in you actually reading it, as it means absolutely nothing, and will almost definitely bore you. Its all exactly the same apart from this bit.

Figure 6.2
All you need to produce professional-looking documents: a computer linked to a bubblejet or laser printer (Photograph courtesy of Hewlett Packard)

The variety of software available is huge, and your choice should depend on what exactly you want to do with your computer. For basic word processing (i.e. no page layout and for limited graphics use), we recommend trying Microsoft Word or MacWrite II, while for DTP we have used both Aldus PageMaker and QuarkXPress. To produce posters and graphics, Aldus Freehand or MacDraw are two favourites, and there are programs available that offer word processing, spreadsheet, graphics and DTP facilities in one package. Two examples of these are ClarisWorks and Microsoft Office.

We have tried not to be too software-specific while writing this chapter, but it is inevitable that our own preferences will come across. Primarily, we intend to give you an idea of what your hardware and software is capable of, along with a few hints from the world of graphic design. Many of the programs featured are available for both IBM PC and Apple Macintosh computers, so you should find something that is relevant to your own set-up.

The Equipment

As explained earlier, you need very little equipment and software to start producing professional-looking documents. The only restriction is that a minimal amount of RAM/ROM results in incredibly slow document processing and printing, and this can become a little frustrating after a while. If you just intend to do basic word processing, there will be no problem, but if your sights are set higher (a several-page newsletter with graphics and several typefaces, for example), you may have to wait as long as several minutes for graphic/text resizing to complete, and printing an A4 page could take as long as 15 minutes!

If you have access to several computers in your college or university's computer centre, pick the one that is best suited to your needs. Using a powerful computer with a fast processing speed to produce simple letters is a waste of the computer's potential power, and you may be preventing someone else with a complex document from using it.

Monitors

The monitor is the computer's first output for the user. Macintosh and PCs installed with 'Windows' use a WYSIWYG (What You See Is What You Get) system that allows you to preview exactly what will be outputted to the printer. Text and graphics are displayed lifesize on the 100% screen setting, allowing you to make very accurate alterations before committing the document to the printer.

One drawback with this system is the small size of some computer monitors. When designing an A4 page on a screen that is 13×13 inches square, part of the document will be 'hidden' off the screen. To combat this, A4 portrait monitors (see Figure 6.3) and even A3 monitors have been produced – although their drawback is their extremely expensive purchase price (up to £2 500 for a 21in colour version). If you are limited to a small screen, make general layout alterations to a document in the 'Fit in Window' mode, which will allow you to look at the whole picture, albeit in a rather reduced form. For detailed alterations, use either the 200% or 400% enlargement scale, although this will limit you to just a small part of the document.

Figure 6.3
The A4 portrait monitor lets you see the whole page of an A4 document (Photograph courtesy of *Computer Shopper* magazine)

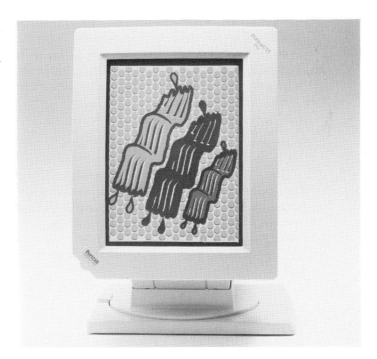

Monitors are available in both colour and black and white versions. Even if you haven't got a colour printer, working in colour is preferable, as (for example) ancillary ruler guides are much easier to distinguish from the document. The level of 'screen stress' is also reduced with a large colour monitor.

Printers

As outlined above, most modern printers give extremely good results. They normally operate on what is known as the PostScript system, which assures high quality text and graphics reproduction. PostScript revolutionised the DTP and graphics industry when it was launched, and it became the industry standard for laser printers. At the end of the 1980s, Apple launched its own alternative to PostScript, TrueType. This was largely to make typefaces completely compatible with their newly launched StyleWriter inkjet printer. PostScript and TrueType are pretty much interchangeable on Apple machines, although you will be limited to PostScript if you are using PC-based hardware.

The laser printer works in similar way to a photocopier, except that the printer 'draws' the original document using a laser focused onto the page. As a result, a laser printer produces printed text/graphics fairly quickly, although speed is directly related to the amount of memory the printer has. The standard quality for monochrome laser printers is 300 dots per inch (dpi), and computers can be linked to certain types of laser colour copiers to produce colour copies.

The inkjet or bubblejet printer was developed by Canon to produce laser-quality print, but at a much cheaper price. The text or graphics are printed onto the page using a jet of ink emitted by a delicate printer head. A typical bubblejet printer produces text/graphics at 360dpi, so quality is extremely good. Colour bubblejet printers are now available as well.

For the ultimate print quality, you will have to rely on the bromides of a phototypesetter, that offer resolution of 12 000dpi and beyond. However, their drawback is the enormous cost of both the paper and machine itself, so you will probably have to go to a DTP bureau to have your work printed out in this way. Nevertheless, if you are having your document printed using a printing press, you will have to have bromides to make up the printing press plate.

Scanners

If you want to integrate photographs or hand-drawn graphics into your document, you will have to use a scanner (Figure 6.4) to 'convert' your images onto disk so that the computer can 'read' them. A scanner is another mutation of a photocopier, and you should ensure that original artwork/photographs are completely straight before committing them to disk.

Figure 6.4
A scanner lets you import photographs and hand-drawn graphics into a computer (Photograph of the Agfa Arcus II flatbed colour scanner courtesy of Agfa)

Figure 6.5
Notice the difference in quality between a TIFF and a PICT-formatted photograph

TIFF

PICT

You can save scanned images in several formats: PICT (abbreviation of PICTure – drawing-type graphics), TIFF (Tagged Image File Format), or EPS (Encapsulated PostScript). TIFF gives the highest resolution, so it should be used for photographs and high quality artwork; while EPS and PICT have a tendency to 'bitmap' (produce bitty images – see Figure 6.5) when used with non-PostScript printers. When in doubt, use TIFF, although this format does take up more disk space.

As well as the large photocopier-type scanner, several 'handheld' models are available. These only have a limited amount of coverage, although they can produce good results if used correctly. Scanners can also be used to scan in large amounts of printed text, saving you from having to type everything in manually.

Getting Started with Your Text

Before embarking on any form of written communication, it is vital that you know precisely what message you want to convey. Regardless of whether you are producing a simple poster or a 30 page brochure, ask yourself the following questions.

1 Who is the audience?
2 What do they want?
3 What do I want to tell them?
4 How can I do this effectively?
5 What are their expectations from such a document (based on what they have previously seen)?

These questions will help you decide on the style (informal or formal, both in terms of layout and written text), the length (too long and you risk switching your audience off; too short and you may not say everything you want), and the format of your document (would an A5-sized poster have the same impact as an A3 equivalent?). Base your ideas on previously produced documents. Use them to ask yourself: would *your* readers/audience like them? Would it create the responses you want?

Once you've decided on the format of your document, you will need to start writing. Style is a very personal matter, although you wouldn't write an article for a church newsletter in the same style as an article for a teenage magazine. General pointers are: keep sentences short, use punctuation wisely (it is most effective when you don't notice it), ensure that your grammar is correct and spelling must be perfect. Fortunately, most computers offer a spellcheck facility – although you must make sure that your version is UK English, and that words like 'than' haven't been accidentally typed in as 'that'. The spellcheck, unfortunately, won't pick up such errors.

Type in your basic text using a word processor, leaving page layout to a specialised DTP package. Most DTP software can 'import' or 'place' text from all common word processing packages, although it is worth checking that your software is compatible *before* spending hours typing in text!

The Desktop Publishing Program

Desktop publishing is a term used to describe any kind of page layout that involves text and/or graphics. Just over ten years ago, producing any kind of page layout would have required the skills of a typesetter complete with a mechanical printing press. Nowadays, page layout can be easily carried out on the 'desktop', using an AppleMac (or equivalent) linked to a bubblejet or laser printer.

The primary function of a DTP program is to produce attractive documents that include text – they start where the word processor stops. As we shall discuss later in this chapter, there are many techniques to make text easy to read and, perhaps more importantly, make the reader want to read on. The DTP program offers the means to do this quickly, efficiently, and, above all, by yourself.

The toolbox

Any DTP program will allow you to position, manipulate, change and justify text to your own wishes, as well as providing tools to create boxes, shapes, lines and (if your printer has the facility) colour.

Figure 6.6
The Aldus PageMaker
toolbox (reproduced by
kind permission of Aldus
Europe)

Figure 6.6 shows the toolbox from Aldus PageMaker along with a guide to what each icon represents. Figure 6.7 shows a similar toolbox from QuarkXPress. Each 'tool' enables you to do different things, and an explanation is given below.

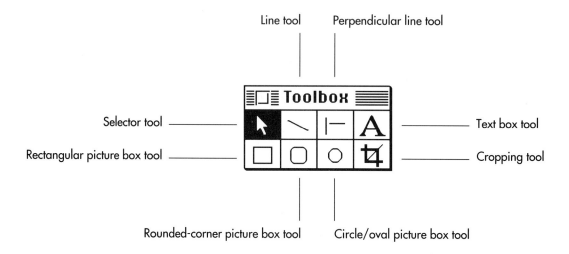

Selector tool: Enables you to 'select' a text or graphic to amend or move it around the screen. To select an item, move the cursor over the object, and click the mouse button.

Line tool: Enables you to create lines of any angle or length.

Perpendicular line tool: Enables you to create perpendicular lines.

Text box tool: Enables you to create text boxes (i.e. headlines and subheadings).

Rectangular picture box tool: Enables you to make boxes with squared off corners (depress the 'shift' key to create a perfect square).

Rounded-corner picture box tool: Enables you to make boxes with rounded corners.

Circle/oval picture box tool: Enables you to make circular/oval 'boxes' (depress the 'shift' key to create a perfect circle).

Cropping tool: On PageMaker this allows you to crop and move imported graphics. For example, to single out a head and shoulders on a group photograph.

Content tool: On QuarkXPress this tool allows to import, edit, cut, copy, paste and modify box contents (text and pictures).

Free rotation tool: On QuarkXPress this allows you to rotate any selected text or graphic box freely.

Polygon picture box tool: On QuarkXPress this allows you to create polygon 'boxes' (a polygon is any shape with three or more sides).

Orthogonal line tool: On QuarkXPress this allows you to create horizontal or vertical lines.

Linking tool: On QuarkXPress this allows you to create text chains in which stories flow from text box to text box (for example, if you want to move part of a story onto another page).

Unlinking tool: This breaks the links between text boxes.

The toolbox is your main control panel when desktop publishing, as it is vital for placing and changing graphics and text. Both programs have other ancillary palettes that can, for example, alter the colour of text or graphics, change the style of text, change the order of pages, etc. These palettes will be mentioned in later sections.

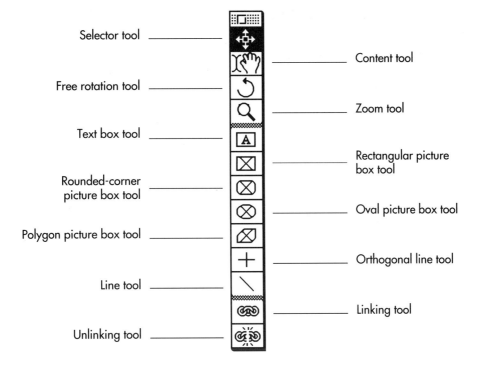

Selector tool

Free rotation tool

Text box tool

Rounded-corner
picture box tool

Polygon picture box tool

Line tool

Unlinking tool

Content tool

Zoom tool

Rectangular picture
box tool

Oval picture box tool

Orthogonal line tool

Linking tool

Figure 6.7
The QuarkXPress toolbox
(reproduced by kind
permission of QSS)

Using a desktop publishing program

As soon as the DTP program is loaded into your computer, it will ask you for details about your proposed document (see Figure 6.8). You will need to decide the size of the document (A4, A5, A3, other), whether it will be tall (portrait) or wide (landscape), how many pages it will have, and what the outside margin limits are to be. Once this has been decided, click 'OK', and the blank pages will be laid out before you. You are now ready to get creative!

Rather than go into a detailed explanation of what each DTP program can do, we shall introduce the various functions as the need arises through this chapter. Technical terms and the applications they

Figure 6.8
PageMaker's document
set-up window
(reproduced by kind
permission of Aldus
Europe)

Page setup

OK

Page: A4

Cancel

Page dimensions: 210 by 297 mm

Numbers...

Orientation: ☒ Tall ○ Wide

Start page #: 1 # of pages: 1

Options: ☑ Double-sided ☑ Facing pages
☐ Restart page numbering

Margin in mm: Inside 25 Outside 20
Top 20 Bottom 20

describe (such as *kerning*) will also be described, and the case studies on page 215 will talk through the process required to produce a typical desktop-published document.

The Graphics Program

Whereas the DTP program is imperative for documents that include a lot of text, you may also want to produce your own graphics and logos. For this, the DTP package is rather limiting, and we recommend using a good graphics program like Aldus Freehand, MacDraw, MacPaint, or the graphics package in ClarisWorks. You may also find it easier to produce posters in graphics packages, as these often don't have a lot of body text, but include bold titles that may require text effects like shadowing and stretching (see the 'Good graphic design' section). These are often more easily carried out on graphics programs.

The toolbox

Like programs designed for DTP applications, every graphics program will have a toolbox allowing you to place, manipulate and change text and graphics. The graphics program's toolbox (Figure 6.9) is normally more comprehensive than the DTP version, so it allows you to be much more creative. Below is a definition of the toolbox icons.

Figure 6.9
The Aldus FreeHand toolbox (reproduced by kind permission of Aldus Europe)

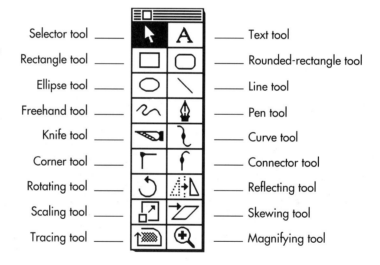

Selector tool — Text tool
Rectangle tool — Rounded-rectangle tool
Ellipse tool — Line tool
Freehand tool — Pen tool
Knife tool — Curve tool
Corner tool — Connector tool
Rotating tool — Reflecting tool
Scaling tool — Skewing tool
Tracing tool — Magnifying tool

Selector tool: Enables you to 'select' a text or graphic to amend or move it around the screen. To select an item, move the cursor over the object, and click the mouse button.

Text tool: Enables you to create text boxes.

Rectangle tool: Enables you to make boxes with squared off corners. Pressing the 'shift' key will create a perfect square.

Rounded-rectangle tool: Enables you to make boxes with rounded corners.

Ellipse tool: Enables you to make circular/oval 'boxes'. Pressing the 'shift' key will create a perfect circle.

Line tool: Produces a line from one point to another as you drag the cursor across the screen. Depress 'shift' to constrain the line to vertical, horizontal or 45°.

Freehand tool: This draws a line as you move the mouse around the screen, with the mouse button depressed.

Pen tool: This tool uses points to create lines, although if you hold the mouse button down after creating a point, it will create a curve according to your mouse movement.

Knife tool: This allows you 'cut' and remove sections of lines, by clicking on their 'joining points'

Curve tool: After you have clicked a couple of points onto the screen, this tool will join the two points together with a curved line. The curve can be altered by two 'handles' on either side of the line.

Corner tool: This needs you to click several points onto the screen, allowing the tool to create a line/shape by connecting them together. By holding the shift key down, the lines will be confined to vertical, horizontal and 45°.

Connector tool: This allows you to connect a curve to a straight line smoothly.

Rotating tool: This allows you to rotate any selected text or graphic box freely.

Reflecting tool: This reflects any selected text or graphic box like a mirror. It's particularly useful when you want two halves to be symmetrical.

Skewing tool: This puts a selected text or graphic on a slant.

Tracing tool: This enables you to 'trace' over any imported graphic or photograph, creating a near-perfect outline of it for you to manipulate.

Magnifying tool: This will enlarge the selected area on the screen, enabling you to carry out detailed modifications.

Lines and fills

Having created a shape using any of the drawing tools, you can 'fill' it with a pattern, colour or monochrome shade of your choice (see Figure 6.10). You can choose a graduated fill and create a three-dimensional sphere effect by choosing the angle of the fill. This is done in the 'Fill and line' window, that is selected from the 'Attributes' menu.

Figure 6.10
A selection of fills from Aldus FreeHand

Similarly, you can alter the 'weight' and size of a line in the same box. For guide lines needed for cutting printed documents (or for placing photographs), use the 'hairline' selection. You can also select to have arrowheads at one or both ends of a line.

Rectangle. Graduated fill at 45°

Rectangle. Radial fill

Rectangle. Patterned fill

Circle. Graduated fill at 230°

Using a Graphics Program

A graphics package like Freehand is only really limited by your imagination, artistic ability and patience! Creating a complex drawing will take several hours, and you may have to make many adjustments before you are happy with the final result. A graphics program is also perfectly suited to producing posters (see case study 2), and Freehand has many text effects that can look good if used wisely (see the section 'Good Graphic Design').

Good Graphic Design

Text and what you can do with it

> The problem with students, is that they use too many fonts and effects.
>
> (Nick Williams of Matt Black DTP, Brighton)

There will rarely be a time when you don't need to use text in a document. Text can be displayed in a variety of styles, and there can be no doubt that formatting and presenting text wisely will greatly add to the impact of your document. The DTP or graphics program is an immensely powerful tool for displaying text, and it is important that you understand fully how to use text to the best effect.

You must decide very early on which typeface will best convey the 'message' you are trying to put across. Text written in a 'quirky' typeface such as Brush Script would clearly not be appropriate for a serious thesis, for example. After deciding which typeface to use, ask yourself what size it should be in your document, and whether you want to add any effects to it or not. Bold, italic, underline, small caps, strikethrough, shadow and outline are all effects that are available on most DTP and graphics programs, and other effects such as rescaling, zoom text or free rotation are available on some others.

Remember though, that too many fonts and effects may detract from your document, making it difficult to read. Bear in mind that the primary task of a document is to communicate something to someone else. You fail if the audience screws it up and throws it in the bin.

The Font or Typeface

Every batch of printed text you read will be composed of a specific typeface or font. For example, this book uses Plantin for the main body of text, while the headings and subheadings are Gill Sans. Each typeface has its own particular name and use, and there are thousands that you can choose from (see Figure 6.11). Of these many typefaces, each is divided into two main groups: sans serif and serif. Serif fonts have embellishing cross strokes at the beginning and end of each letter (see Figure 6.12, page 198), while sans serif fonts do without, making them appear more modern and less fussy. When selecting which font to use in a document, it is worth bearing in mind the different 'mood' that each typeface can convey, although it should be noted that serif and sans serif fonts can be mixed together for good effect. The logo for the newspaper the *Guardian* is a good example of this, and the theory behind this piece of graphic design was to convey the feeling that the paper combined old with new. The serif font was supposed to represent traditional values, while the sans serif font showed that the paper wasn't behind the times either. Whether this works as a piece of graphic communication or not is up to you, but there can be no doubt that the logo does look good.

Figure 6.11
A range of typefaces

Avant Garde. 14 point.

Bookman. 14 point.

Dom Casual. 14 point.

Rockwell. 14 point.

Caslon Open Face. 16 point.

Courier. 14 point.

(Zapf Dingbats. 12 point.) ✹❂□❀ ✦✸■✳❂❀▼▲✎∾✔□❑❀■

Kuenstler Script. 14 point.

Italia Book. 14 point.

Optima. 14 point.

Helvetica Condensed bold. 14 point.

Helvetica rounded bold. 14 point.

Hobo. 14 point.

Lubalin Graph. 14 point.

Madrone. 10 point.

Arcadia. 20 point.

New Century Schoolbook. 14 point.

Times. 14 point.

Zapf Chancery. 14 point.

Gill Sans. 14 point.

Bernhard Modern. 14 point.

Figure 6.12
The difference between serif and sans serif typefaces

Helvetica. A typical sans serif font.

Avant Garde. Another typical sans serif font.

Gill Sans. Yet another sans serif face.

Times Roman. A typical serif font.

New Century Schoolbook. Another typical serif face.

Zapf Chancery. Yet another serif font.

Bearing this in mind, fonts should always be selected wisely according to your document's purpose. Don't forget that clear communication should be the main *raison d'être* for your document, so choosing the right font for your intended audience is almost as important as deciding upon the right written style. Base your choices on the following questions:

1 Does your document contain a lot of text and few illustrations? If so, you want to make your typeface as clear as possible.
2 Is your document intended to inform, persuade, entertain, or all three?
3 Is your document funny, serious, or somewhere in between?
4 Does your audience have any particular expectations from your document?
5 And, most importantly: ask yourself whether your audience really wants to see every different font and type effect that your computer is capable of . . .

Compare the text in Figure 6.13. Although the text remains exactly the same, notice how its effectiveness (and 'readability') changes with each different font. If you really aren't sure which font to use, make several copies of the same document using a shortlist of different fonts. See which one gives the best 'feel' to your text, and use that one.

The young girl looked up at the castle. It always looked so terrifying at night, with its Gothic towers shadowed against the moonlight. Suddenly she heard a noise, an evil shriek that pierced the quiet night air.

"Who's there?" She cried, hoping that it was just her imagination.

"No-one to worry about deary," came the reply. "Just the evil dead coming to get you."

Her legs turning to jelly, she tried to run back to the shelter of the village. But she found that she couldn't move; she was routed to the spot, frozen with fear.

It was then that the monster struck…

The young girl looked up at the castle. It always looked so terrifying at night, with its Gothic towers shadowed against the moonlight. Suddenly she heard a noise, an evil shriek that pierced the quiet night air.

"Who's there?" She cried, hoping that it was just her imagination.

"No-one to worry about deary," came the reply. "Just the evil dead coming to get you."

Her legs turning to jelly, she tried to run back to the shelter of the village. But she found that she couldn't move; she was routed to the spot, frozen with fear.

It was then that the monster struck…

The young girl looked up at the castle. It always looked so terrifying at night, with its Gothic towers shadowed against the moonlight. Suddenly she heard a noise, an evil shriek that pierced the quiet night air.

"Who's there?" She cried, hoping that it was just her imagination.

"No-one to worry about deary," came the reply. "Just the evil dead coming to get you."

Her legs turning to jelly, she tried to run back to the shelter of the village. But she found that she couldn't move; she was routed to the spot, frozen with fear.

It was then that the monster struck…

The young girl looked up at the castle. It always looked so terrifying at night, with its Gothic towers shadowed against the moonlight. Suddenly she heard a noise, an evil shriek that pierced the quiet night air.

"Who's there?" She cried, hoping that it was just her imagination.

"No-one to worry about deary," came the reply. "Just the evil dead coming to get you."

Her legs turning to jelly, she tried to run back to the shelter of the village. But she found that she couldn't move; she was routed to the spot, frozen with fear.

It was then that the monster struck…

The young girl looked up at the castle. It always looked so terrifying at night, with its Gothic towers shadowed against the moonlight. Suddenly she heard a noise, an evil shriek that pierced the quiet night air.

"Who's there?" She cried, hoping that it was just her imagination.

"No-one to worry about deary," came the reply. "Just the evil dead coming to get you."

Her legs turning to jelly, she tried to run back to the shelter of the village. But she found that she couldn't move; she was routed to the spot, frozen with fear.

It was then that the monster struck…

Figure 6.13
Notice how the 'feel' of
the same story alters when
using different typefaces

Font Sizing

Every font can be scaled up and down in size, using the 'point' or 'pica' system. Each point measures 0.01384 inch, while one pica equals 12 points, which is equal to 0.01666 inch. The point size of type is measured from the top of the 'ascender' to the bottom of the 'descender' (see Figure 6.14), while the x-height is the distance from the mean line to the baseline. The x-height may vary between fonts of the same point size, which explains the apparent difference in size between fonts of the 'same' point number in Figure 6.11.

Figure 6.14
Typeface jargon

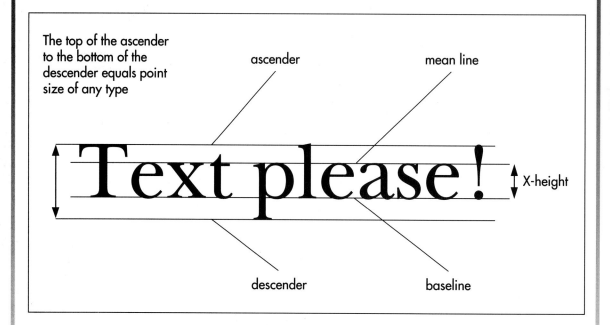

Interesting effects can be made from resizing typefaces disproportionately, but we shall discuss this later.

Leading

Once you have typed in several sentences of your text, the words will be lined up in rows as the page begins to fill up. The space between each line of text is known as 'leading' (pronounced 'ledding' after the old-fashioned method of placing lead strips between lines of type), and, like the typeface itself, this is also measured in points. Most DTP programs have automatic leading settings, although you can manually control them if you wish. Manual leading may be useful if you can't quite fit everything into the space allocated, or if you want to have extra wide leading for a particular effect (see the section on document layout, below).

When setting the leading manually, most programs measure leading as the point size of the text, plus the leading required. So a piece of 14 point text with 6 points of leading would be entered as 20 points when set manually, and a typesetter would call this 14 on 20.

Kerning

'Kerning' is the term allocated to letter and word spacing, i.e. the distance between each letter and word. Once again, this setting is normally automatic, although you may need to override it in some instances, particularly when using 'kern pairs'.

Kern pairs are letters that appear too far apart when using normal letter spacing, and examples include: To, Tr, Ta, Tu, Tw, Te, Ty, Wa, WA, We, Wo, Yo, Ya and yo. Most DTP programs have automatic kerning to take care of these problematic pairs, although you may want to decrease or increase the distance from the automatic setting. To do this, select the text section you want to change, and alter it using the program's manual kerning window. Beware of 'over-kerning' letters, as words like 'burn' may print out as 'bum' if over-kerned!

'Track kerning' is where you alter the distance between both the letters and the words in a block of text, using the DTP program's track adjustment. PageMaker, for example, has six track settings: no track, very loose, loose, normal, tight and very tight; and these can be applied to reduce the space a paragraph or headline takes up. This is particularly useful when you have limited amounts of space available, or are trying to squeeze a long headline into a narrow column. Figure 6.15 shows the different track modes applied to the same 24 point headline.

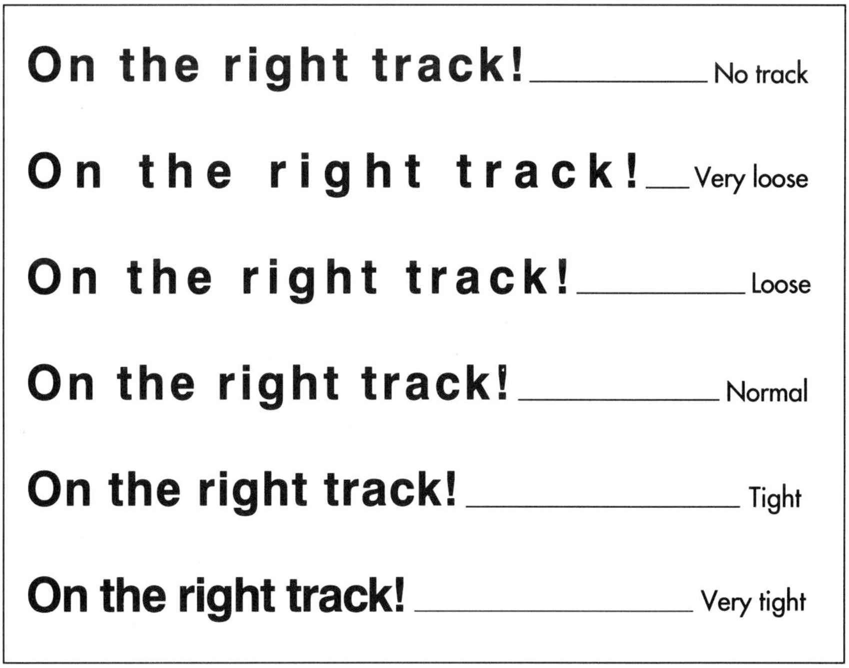

Figure 6.15
The effect of using different tracking on the same headline

On the right track!	No track
On the right track!	Very loose
On the right track!	Loose
On the right track!	Normal
On the right track!	Tight
On the right track!	Very tight

Placing Text

Every DTP and graphics program uses 'text boxes' to place text (see Figure 6.16, page 202). These are very convenient for shaping or resizing text, as all you have to do is place the cursor over one of the text 'handles' (as in Figure 6.16), and 'drag' the box out to create your new shape. However, you must make sure that your resized text box is big enough to accommodate all the text, otherwise bits of it will be left out. If this happens, and you haven't got any more space to place the text, try altering the track or point size (see above) to reduce the amount of space the text takes up.

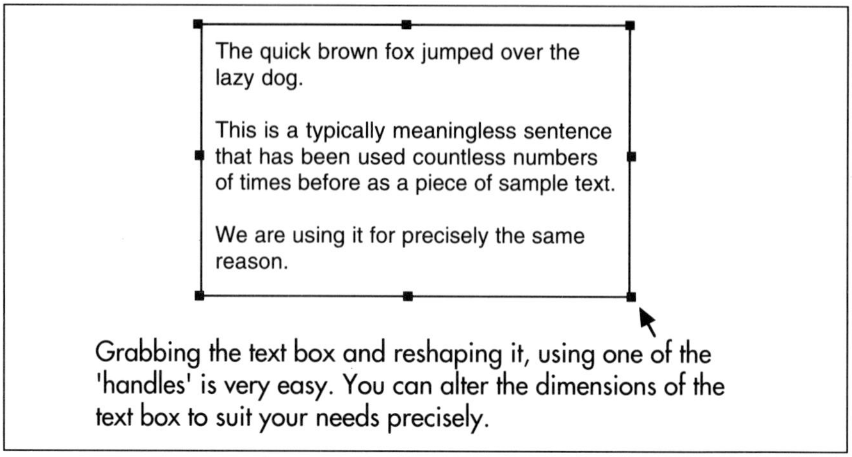

Figure 6.16
A typical text box

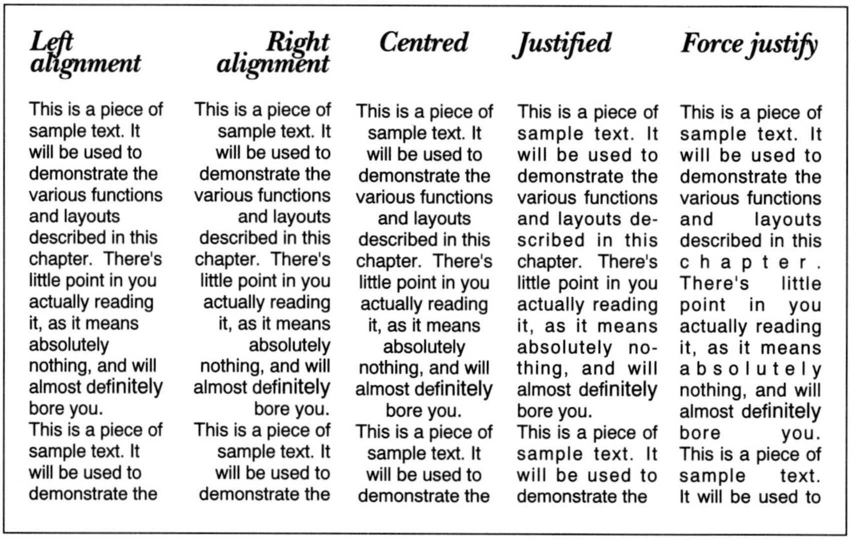

The quick brown fox jumped over the lazy dog.

This is a typically meaningless sentence that has been used countless numbers of times before as a piece of sample text.

We are using it for precisely the same reason.

Grabbing the text box and reshaping it, using one of the 'handles' is very easy. You can alter the dimensions of the text box to suit your needs precisely.

Figure 6.17
The various alignments available on most DTP programs

Left alignment	*Right alignment*	*Centred*	*Justified*	*Force justify*
This is a piece of sample text. It will be used to demonstrate the various functions and layouts described in this chapter. There's little point in you actually reading it, as it means absolutely nothing, and will almost definitely bore you. This is a piece of sample text. It will be used to demonstrate the	This is a piece of sample text. It will be used to demonstrate the various functions and layouts described in this chapter. There's little point in you actually reading it, as it means absolutely nothing, and will almost definitely bore you. This is a piece of sample text. It will be used to demonstrate the	This is a piece of sample text. It will be used to demonstrate the various functions and layouts described in this chapter. There's little point in you actually reading it, as it means absolutely nothing, and will almost definitely bore you. This is a piece of sample text. It will be used to demonstrate the	This is a piece of sample text. It will be used to demonstrate the various functions and layouts de-scribed in this chapter. There's little point in you actually reading it, as it means absolutely no-thing, and will almost definitely bore you. This is a piece of sample text. It will be used to demonstrate the	This is a piece of sample text. It will be used to demonstrate the various functions and layouts described in this c h a p t e r . There's little point in you actually reading it, as it means a b s o l u t e l y nothing, and will almost definitely bore you. This is a piece of sample text. It will be used to

When creating a text block, you will also have to decide on the text alignment. Most DTP programs offer five options: left, right, centred, justified and force-justified (see Figure 6.17). As you can see from the diagram, the most attractive of these alignments is the 'justify' mode, which should be used with auto-hyphenation to avoid peculiar word spacing. Auto-hyphenation hyphenates words (by placing a hyphen (-) at a convenient break) that are too long to fit comfortably on the line. The position of the hyphen is based on the program's own dictionary, although you can manually decide where to place it if it appears in an awkward place. Don't forget also that you can adjust the track of the paragraph as well, to ensure that all the words fit in to your allotted space.

Text Effects
There is practically no limit to what you can do to text, providing that your software is capable of it. Both PageMaker and QuarkXPress offer a multitude of different text effects (see Figure 6.18), while Aldus Freehand has even more, especially for the dedicated effects fanatic (see Figure 6.19).

No effect applied	~~Strike through applied~~
Bold applied	Outline applied
Italic applied	Shadow applied
Bold italic applied	SMALL CAPS APPLIED
Underline applied	9 point superscript applied
Word underline applied	9 point subscript applied
Double underline applied	

Figure 6.18
Standard text effects

An example of fill and stroke.

An example of heavy text.

(A sample of bold for comparison).

An example of inline effect.

An example of outlined text.

An example of shadow text.

An example of zoom text.

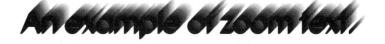

Figure 6.19
Some of the text effects available from Aldus FreeHand

However, as always, we must stress that it is very important not to overdo the effects, otherwise you risk making your document difficult to read, or at the very least, messy. Some effects, like strikethrough or zoom text, have very little practical use, although bold and italic are useful.

Never use underline or bold text in the middle of a sentence to emphasise something, as these effects are best used for subheadings or titles. If you want to place emphasis on a certain word in the middle of sentence, use italics for best effect. Similarly, superscript or subscript are useful only for chemical equations or footnotes; try to avoid using them as part of a sentence, as text that drops below the conventional leading will just look silly alongside conventional text.

Altering the Appearance of a Font

As mentioned above, most DTP and graphics programs will allow you to resize text disproportionately according to whim. This is an incredibly useful device, as not only does it allow you to shape text to your own needs, it can also make fonts appear very different from their original form (see Figure 6.20). Experiment with text until you end up with a result that pleases you – although always bear in mind the 'tone' of your document. It's no good ending up with a resized font that gives the impression of fun if your document is supposed to be appealing to a formal audience.

Figure 6.20
Note how a typeface alters its 'feel' when you resize it disproportionately

12 point Helvetica. Bold setting.

Helvetica. Height increased.

Helvetica. Width increased.

12 point Bookman. Bold setting.

Bookman. Height increased.

Bookman. Width increased.

Programs like Aldus Freehand will also allow you to do other things to fonts. Using the 'alignment' tool, you can merge text onto any type of wavy path (or a circle), allowing you to dispense with formal straight lines in the document (see Figure 6.21). However, once again, this type of effect should be used sparingly – too much use and it will become a rather ugly cliché.

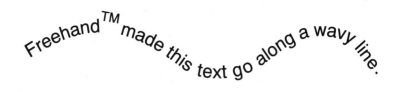

Figure 6.21
There is practically no limit to what you can do with text

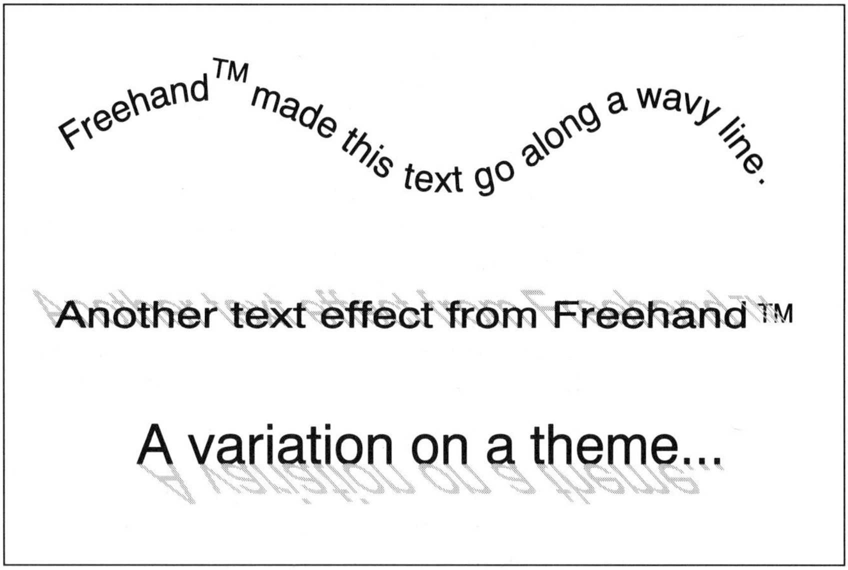

Freehand ™ made this text go along a wavy line.

Another text effect from Freehand ™

A variation on a theme...

Adding Emphasis to Text

As well as reshaping and adding effects to text, there are a number of other graphic devices to add emphasis to a headline or title. The most popular (and effective) of these is to enclose your text in a box, which can either be paper-coloured (normally white) or black (see Fig. 6.22). Although this is a well-used cliché, it remains effective, especially if you resize the font inside the box as well. Remember, if you are using a black box, to ensure that your text is paper-coloured, and use the 'Send to front' feature to ensure that it shows up on the black background. You will also have to make sure that the paper-coloured font is set to bold or 'heavy', as it may not show up very clearly otherwise.

Figure 6.22
Placing text in a box gives it extra emphasis

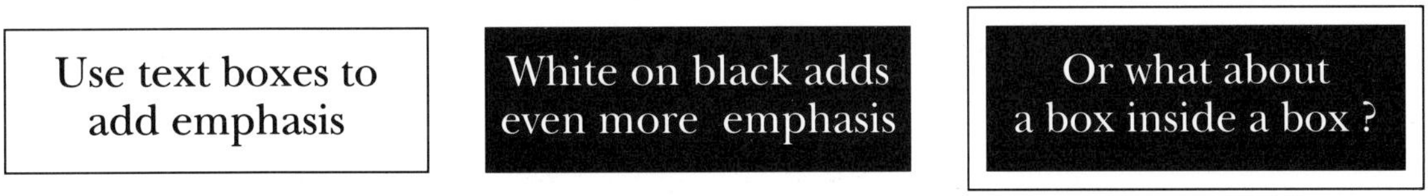

Use text boxes to
add emphasis

White on black adds
even more emphasis

Or what about
a box inside a box ?

A variation on the text box theme is to add a shadow behind the text box to add extra emphasis (see Figure 6.23). This is normally black, and you will need to use the 'Send to front' and 'Send to back' commands to end up with the effect you want.

Figure 6.23
Adding a shadow behind text in a box gives it even more emphasis

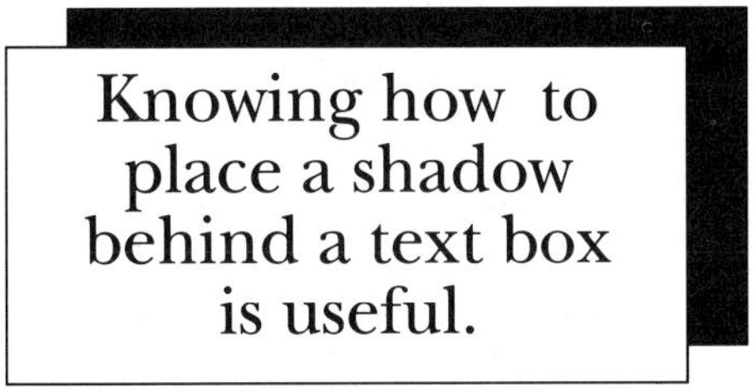

Knowing how to
place a shadow
behind a text box
is useful.

Figure 6.24
Although it looks clever, there are very few instances where this three-dimensional effect can be practically used

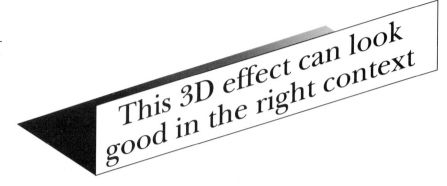

If you are feeling really adventurous (and the effect is appropriate in your document), you can make the text box appear three-dimensional by using the 'Skew' and 'Shading' commands (Figure 6.24).

Special Typefaces and Symbols

When typing in text in foreign languages, you may often want to add accents, cedillas or umlauts to your letters. AppleMacs use the 'Option' or 'Option/Shift' keys to place these in your text, and most typefaces have other symbols that are similarly useful using the option command. Figure 6.25 shows the complete range of extra symbols available via the 'Option' and 'Option/Shift' keys, and you may like to use this as a handy reference guide.

There are also special typefaces for the Russian, Arabic, Greek, Hebrew and Chinese alphabets. However, you would probably need to use a special keyboard for these, although it is possible to use a standard QWERTY-type keyboard. Similarly, special typefaces exist for scientific, musical and mathematical applications, and there is even a typeface available to illustrate Underground signs. Called Bundesbahn Pi, it is produced by Adobe.

One of the most useful non-alphanumeric fonts for DTP is Zapf Dingbats (see Figure 6.26, page 208). This font has many useful 'Pi' characters, including ticks, crosses, boxes, numbers in circles, etc. For example, when designing a questionnaire, you may like to use Zapf Dingbats to illustrate boxes on multiple choice questions. See Figures 6.37 and 6.38 for some other practical uses.

Text Techniques and Good Habits to Get Into

Good and consistent presentation of text is vital for successful communication, and this section will discuss some of the accepted 'rules' of DTP.

The dash: When using a dash (–) as a punctuation mark, make sure that you use a dash and not a hyphen. On the AppleMac, the dash can be obtained by pressing 'Option-'. Most people mistakenly use the hyphen as a dash, but the dash is longer ('–' as opposed to '-').

Punctuation rules: It is a good idea to give your text 'room to breath'.After full stops,leave a gap of two spaces before starting the next sentence,and always leave a space after using a comma.If you don't,your sentences will look very crowded,like this paragraph.

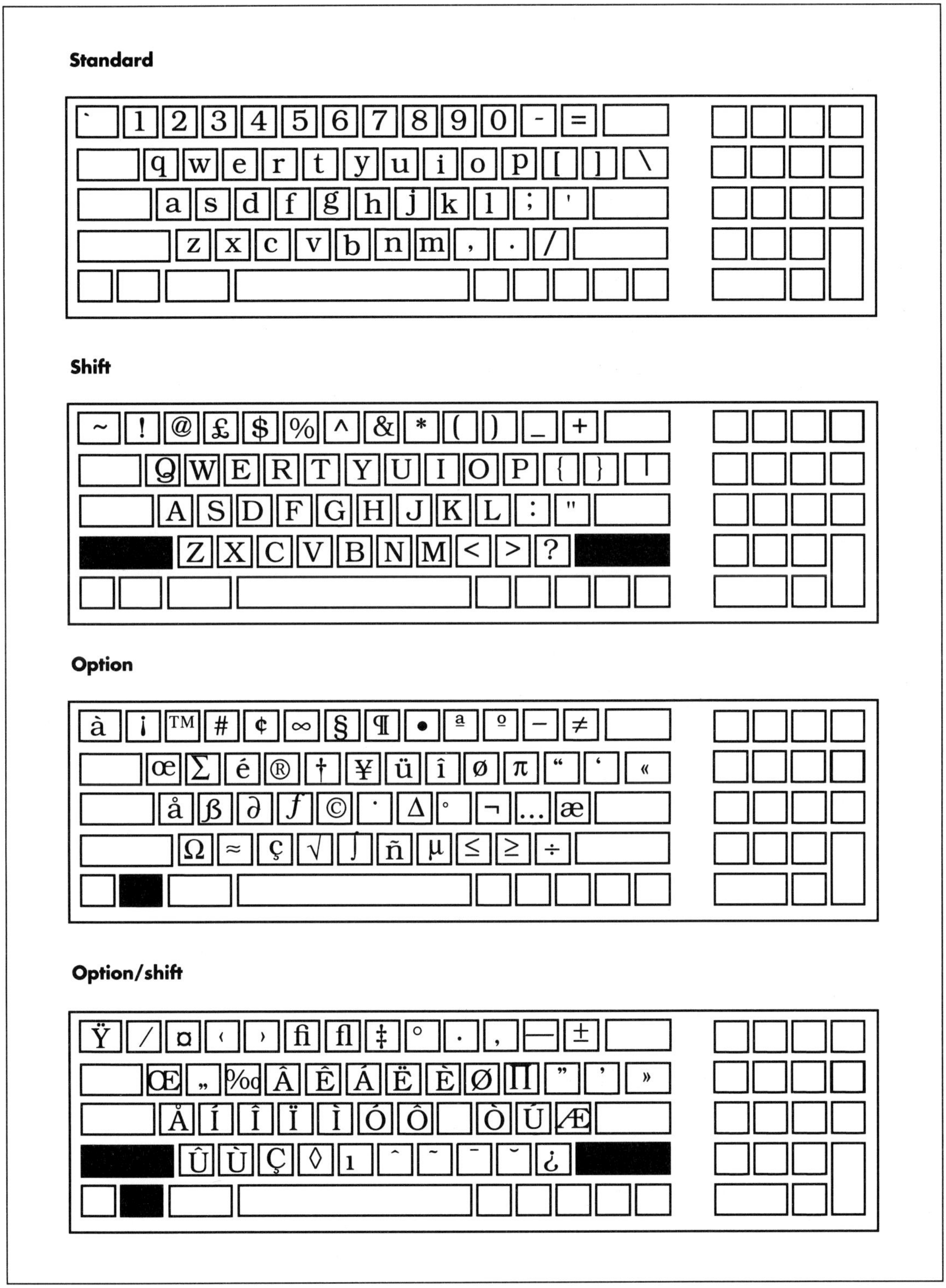

Standard

Shift

Option

Option/shift

Figure 6.25
The AppleMac characters
accessible using the
'option' and 'shift'
commands

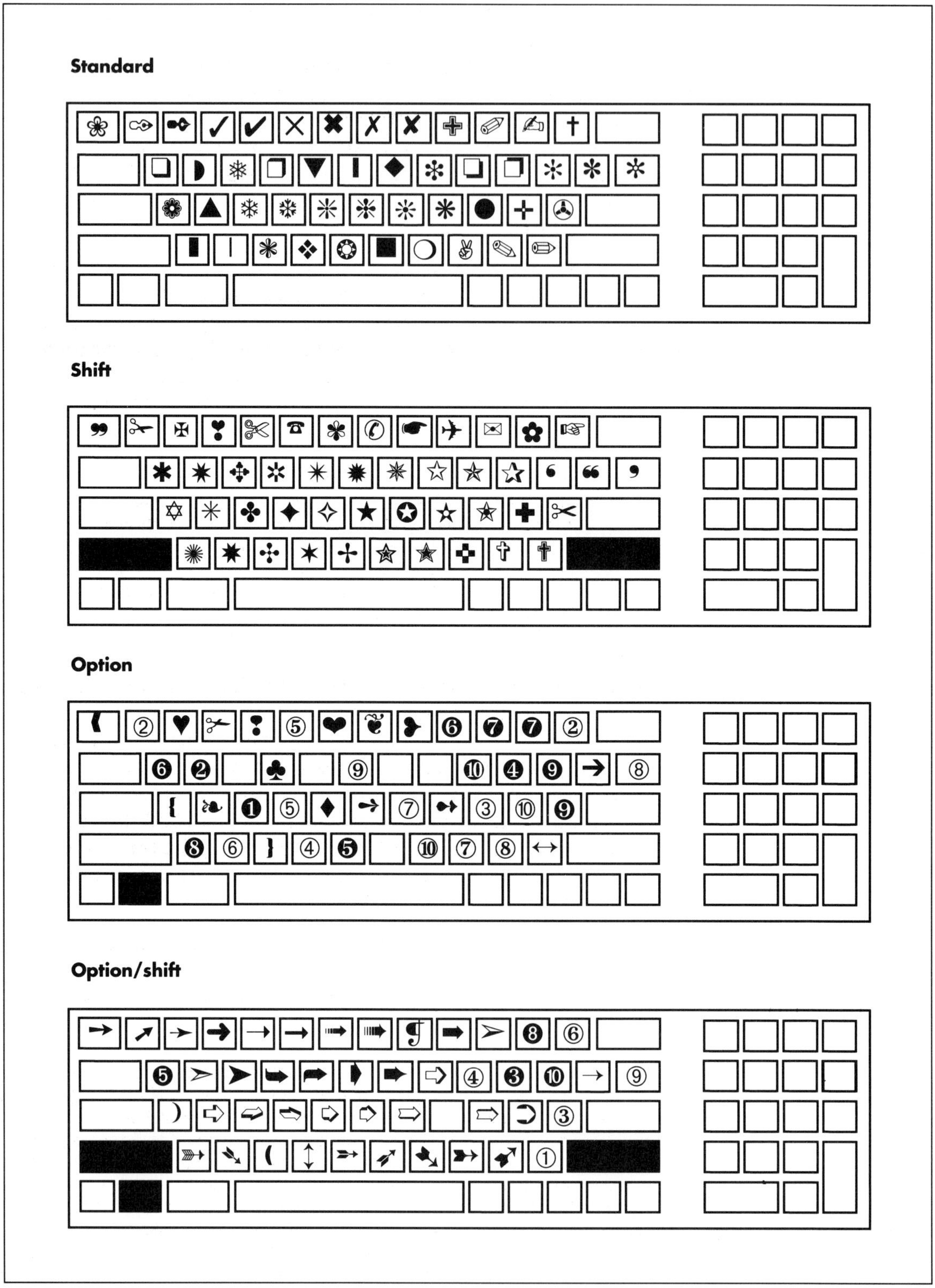

Standard

Shift

Option

Option/shift

Figure 6.26
Zapf Dingbats Pi
characters have a range
of uses

When starting a new paragraph, you can either indent by using the 'Tab' command, or leave the first letter 'flush' to the side of the margin. If you do decide to start each sentence flush, remember to leave a line gap before the beginning of each sentence. A common exception to this is when you are laying out text in columns in a newspaper format. It is conventional not to leave a line gap between each paragraph, but to signal the start of a new paragraph by indenting the first word. Look at some magazines and newspaper formats for different textual treatments.

Drop caps: It is a good idea to get into the habit of starting each 'story' in a newsletter with a 'drop cap', or oversized capital letter (see Figure 6.27). This provides a clear start to the story, and attracts the reader's eye to it. However, do not use very large drop caps for each story. Instead, decide which is your most important story, and allocate the largest drop cap to this. Other stories should have drop caps that are not as large.

Figure 6.27
The 'drop cap' gives a clear start to a piece of text

This is a piece of sample text. It will be used to demonstrate the various functions and layouts described in this chapter. There's little point in you actually reading it, as it means absolutely nothing, and will almost definitely bore you. This is a piece of sample text. It will be used to demonstrate the various functions and layouts described in this chapter.

Creating running heads: A running head is text that is printed at the top of every page of a publication. It normally consists of the title and/or the chapter heading. After deciding on the title of your running head, use a contrasting font (possibly in bold) so that it stands out from the text. Nevertheless, it is important that the running head isn't too bold, as it may detract from the document itself. To get around this, use a small point size and space the letters out by altering the track (see Figure 6.28). You may also like to draw a discreet line beneath the running head to separate it further.

Figure 6.28
Running heads should be used on all newsletters

A SAMPLE RUNNING HEAD

This is a piece of sample text. It will be used to demonstrate the various functions and layouts described in this chapter. There's little point in you actually reading it, as it means absolutely nothing and will almost definitely bore you. This is a piece of sample text. It will be used to demonstrate the various functions and layouts described in this chapter. There's little point in you actually reading it, as it means absolutely nothing and will almost definitely bore you. This is a piece of sample text. It will be used to demonstrate the various functions and layouts described in this chapter. There's little point in you actually reading it, as it means absolutely nothing and will almost definitely bore you. This is a piece of sample text. It will be used to demonstrate the various functions and layouts described in this chapter.

Document layout

Document layout is the bringing together of all your text, headlines, subheadings and graphics in the most aesthetic way. Once again, you will have to consider the expectations of your target audience and the aims of the document before doing this, although one of the most important pieces of advice is, give your text, graphics and headlines room to breath.

Figure 6.29 is the pages in this book. Notice how the graphic designers at Hodder and Stoughton have used space, different weights of type, different sizes of type and graphics to make the pages attractive to look at, functional, and above all, easy to read.

Try and examine some magazines, books, newspapers, posters, and even forms, to see how graphic designers have used page layout techniques to produce the best results. Magazines like *Arena*, *GQ*, *Car*, *Smash Hits*, *Vogue* and *Elle* are especially worth looking at for some ideas. If a technique you see in a magazine or newspaper works, why not try to copy it for your own publication?

Headlines and Text

It is inevitable that you will be limited by the quantity of text and headlines you have to work with, but Figure 6.30 gives some ideas for headline and text combinations. One of the best things about using a computer for page layout is that you can alter your page layout as your ideas develop. Previously, graphic designers had to experiment using drawings; but nowadays everything can be changed by a few clicks of a mouse button.

Notice how the headline takes up more or less importance in the different layouts. Decide on how much prominence you want to give to your headline, and this will inevitably change the layout of your text. Also think about text leading, manipulating the headline using the stretch commands, the distance between each column of type, the track setting for the text and headline, and the size of the main body text. Around 9–10 points is right for newsletters, although posters will probably demand a larger size for easy reading.

Figure 6.30
Think carefully about the relationship between text and a headline

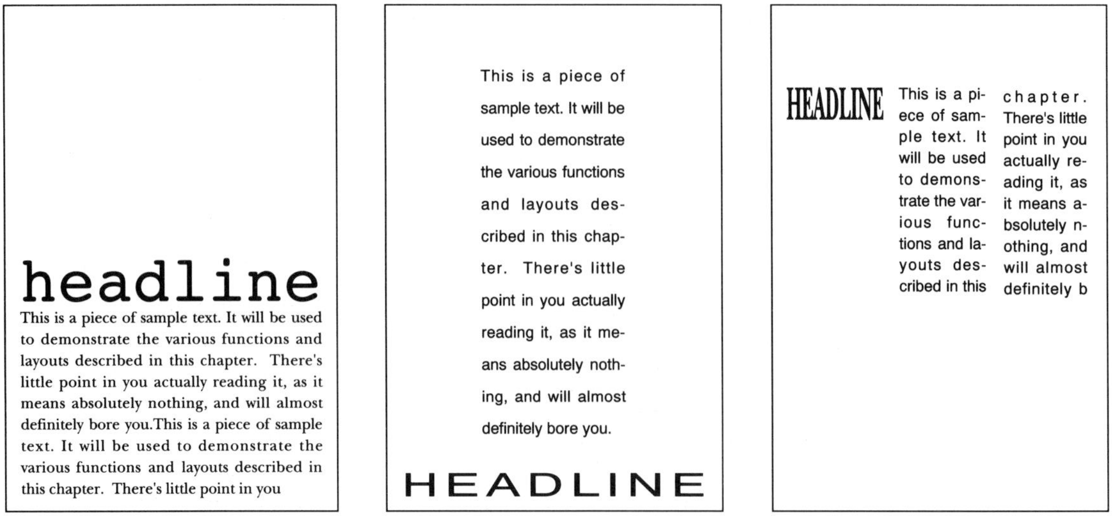

headline
This is a piece of sample text. It will be used to demonstrate the various functions and layouts described in this chapter. There's little point in you actually reading it, as it means absolutely nothing, and will almost definitely bore you.This is a piece of sample text. It will be used to demonstrate the various functions and layouts described in this chapter. There's little point in you

This is a piece of sample text. It will be used to demonstrate the various functions and layouts described in this chapter. There's little point in you actually reading it, as it means absolutely nothing, and will almost definitely bore you.

HEADLINE

HEADLINE This is a piece of sample text. It will be used to demonstrate the various functions and layouts described in this chapter. There's little point in you actually reading it, as it means absolutely nothing, and will almost definitely b

Titles

In many respects, what your title says (both in terms of its layout and content) is the most important part of your document. The reader will look at the title, and either throw the document in the bin or read on. The title is the essential hook that will entice the reader to read what you want to say, so it should be concise, easy to read and demand attention. As always, the means by which you do this will depend very much on the intended audience of your document. However, you can't go far wrong by using the tried and tested 'title in a box' approach as outlined in 'Text and What You Can Do with It', above.

Similarly, try rotating text at unusual angles, or placing it so that it runs up the 'spine' of your document. Use tracking and letter spacing to provide extra emphasis, and try to use a contrasting (but not OTT) typeface to add extra impact.

Using Columns to Place Text

If you look at most newspapers and magazines, you will notice that their stories are arranged in columns, rather than the conventional 'left margin to right margin' approach offered by most word processors. This is because more text can be fitted into a confined space, and also because it allows you to concentrate on separate text 'areas' on a page, ensuring that different stories don't get confused with one another.

All DTP programs have an automatic column-positioning facility. This allows you place text boxes alongside one another in the manner described above. It is normal for the text to be written on a word processing package, and then imported into the DTP program via the 'Place' facility (which, incidentally, also allows you to import graphics). When placing text, you can select the 'Autoflow' option to allow the text to flow freely from one column to another, or you can position it a column at a time (with the 'Autoflow' command switched off), giving you more control. You will probably have to alter the type specifications once the text is imported, as it will be imported in the typeface, style and justification in which it was originally typed in on the word processor.

Remember to position separating lines between each story, to show the reader where each story ends and begins. You may also like to add extra emphasis by placing the body text in a box, although this effect will loose impact if used more than once or twice in a document.

Graphics

Graphics and/or photographs are a very important part of document layout. They allow you to draw the reader's attention to a section of text, they can be used to illustrate points and issues raised, and, perhaps most importantly, they break up the monotony of mountains of text!

You can design your own graphics using a program like Aldus Freehand, MacPaint, or DeskDraw, although by far the best source of graphics is from a professional 'clip art' agency (see the Resource section at the back of this book). Clip art is drawn by professional artists, and is available on floppy disk ready for placing in your documents. Clip art is normally covered by copyright, although once you have purchased the disk, you are free to use it where you like.

The range of subjects covered by clip art is extensive to say the least. Examples include: patterns (every possible pattern you could imagine), illustrated drop capitals (large capitals in every style from medieval to modern), arts and entertainment (audio microphone to gramophone), business (mobile phone to piggybank), communications (compact disk to ticker tape machine), energy and environment (chain saw to 'Recyclable' symbol), world flags, food and nutrition (everything you could possibly eat), health (Red Cross to stethoscope), leisure (aerobics to champagne), world maps, sports (basketball to weight lifting), and travel (aeroplane to palm trees).

The format of each piece of clip art will vary from TIFF to EPS (see 'The Equipment', page 188), and typical examples of each (that were printed on a budget Apple StyleWriter) can be found in Figures 6.31 and 6.32.

Figure 6.31
A sample of TIFF clip art (reproduced by kind permission of Dynamic Graphics)

Figure 6.32
A sample of EPS clip art (reproduced by kind permission of Dynamic Graphics)

It is also possible to use Pi typefaces like Bundesbahn Pi or Zapf Dingbats (see Figure 6.26) as 'infographics' that add visual emphasis to text in any publication, and to use the 'bullet' character (option '8' on the Macintosh) when setting out a list (see Figure 6.33).

Figure 6.33
Always use bullets when making a list

> You should use bullets when making a list, as it:
> - adds impact
> - avoids messy punctuation
> - puts a break in mountains of text
> - is effective
>
> Do you see what we mean?

Photographs

Scanned photographs seldom look impressive when printed out on a laser or bubblejet printer, and they also use up a lot of memory while you are laying out your document. It is much better to display and print an empty box (to the precise dimensions of your photo), leaving you to stick on the original photograph when it comes to photocopying the document.

However, if you intend to alter the size of your photograph in the document, then (unless you are able to produce an exact sized copy) you will have no choice but to print the photo using a printer. To obtain the optimum resolution, make sure that your photograph was scanned in at the same dpi rating as your printer (normally 300dpi for laser printers).

It is advisable to place the photograph in a box to give it extra emphasis; if your photo has a caption, place this at the bottom inside the box.

Integrating Text and Graphics/photographs

With your graphic or photograph in place, you must decide upon its relationship and position to the text that accompanies it. The conventional way to position graphics/photographs is above the body text, but below the headline. This works for most large graphics/photographs, but when using graphics without borders and smaller photographs, you may like to place the graphic or photograph within the text itself (see Figure 6.34, page 214).

This is very easy to do with most DTP programs, and Figure 6.35, page 214, shows the 'Text wrap' box from Aldus PageMaker. Simply select how you want the text to wrap itself around the graphic, and enter in the 'stand-off' position in millimetres. You may need to experiment with this to obtain the best result but, used sensibly, integrating graphics into text will normally be effective.

Figure 6.34
Graphics can be easily
integrated into text

USING TEXT WRAP WITH GRAPHICS

This a piece of sample text. It will be used to demonstrate various functions and layouts described in this chapter. There's little point in actually reading it as it means absolutely nothing, and will almost definitely bore you.
This a piece of sample text. It will be used to demonstrate various functions

and layouts described in this chapter. There's little point in actually reading it as it means absolutely

nothing, and will almost definitely bore you.
This a piece of sample text. It

will be used to demonstrate various functions and layouts described in this chapter. There's little point in actually reading it as it means absolutely nothing, and will almost definitely bore you.
This a piece of sample text. It will be used to demonstrate various functions and layouts described in this chapter. There's

Figure 6.35
The 'text wrap' window
from Aldus PageMaker
(reproduced by kind
permission of Aldus
Europe)

Selects how the
text should wrap
around the picture

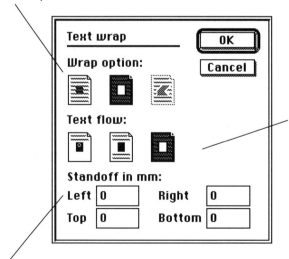

This governs how
the text will wrap
around the picture

Distance between
the border of the
graphic and the text

Case Studies

1. A simple graphic

You may need to produce an eye-catching graphic for use on a society letterhead, a newsletter or a poster, and graphics packages like Aldus Freehand are well suited for doing this.

Our first case study is a logo that was designed to be used on letterheads, newsletters and posters produced by the University of Sussex Photographic Society (see Figure 6.36). Previously, the society had just used a typewritten logo that didn't really do justice to the quality of photography produced by the society's 100 or so members.

Figure 6.36
A simple but effective logo for the University of Sussex Photographic Society

Before embarking on designing a graphic, it is worth having a 'brainstorm' session with a blank piece of paper and a pen, outlining what exactly the logo is to be used for. In this case, because the logo was to be used for a letterhead, it was decided that the design should be 'subtle' (otherwise it might detract from the content of the letter), and because the logo was likely to be used on sheets that would be photocopied, we were limited to using just black and white.

First thoughts were to integrate a photograph into the design, but because of the inevitable quality loss through photocopying, this idea was rejected fairly early on. Nevertheless, it was decided that the logo should incorporate something to do with photography, so that the viewer could tell at a glance which society the logo belonged to. In the end, a graphic depicting 35mm film was found in a clip art library, and we decided to integrate this in some way.

The name 'Photographic Society' was also shortened to the more practical 'Photo Soc.', as designs incorporating the whole name looked oversized and clumsy. It was also decided that the two words should be in contrasting typefaces, to add extra impact to the logo. The words 'University of Sussex' were also added to give a 'home' to the society.

With these elements on the computer screen, it was time to experiment with the different ways they could be presented. Initial designs had the 35mm film strip running underneath the words 'Photo Soc.', but this was rejected as being too messy. By rotating the film strip around, and integrating it with a black box, a tidier link was established.

The words 'Photo Soc.' were coloured white and placed in the box, allowing us the chance to experiment with different typefaces. Both words had to be clear to read, but we wanted something that would represent the 'feel' of the society. In the end, the 1930s-style typeface Marquee Engraved was chosen for the word 'Photo', as somehow (maybe through association with Dada and Surrealist photographers) it has a 'photographic/arty' feel. This was enlarged and given extra emphasis by placing a large white underline underneath. The word 'Soc.' was deemed relatively unimportant, so was reduced and rotated through 180° to be placed alongside the filmstrip.

Finally, the words 'University of Sussex' were placed flush along the top of the box, and the text was stretched to fit. The graphic was then saved as an 'EPS' (Encapsulated PostScript) file, for easy importation into any document the Photo Soc. wanted to produce.

2. A poster

With the arrival of Student Union sabbatical elections, every candidate wanted a poster and flyer that would set out their aims and objectives and get them known. We were asked to produce posters for three

Figure 6.37
A practical use of a DTP program to produce a poster for student elections

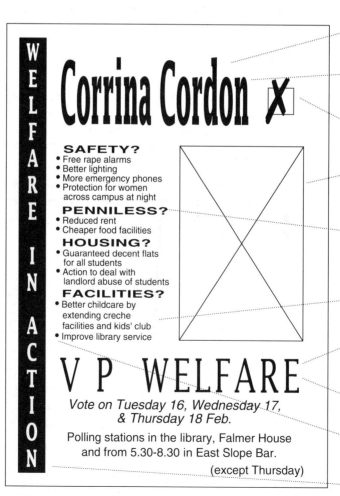

candidates who were standing as a team. Each poster had to state the candidate's name, the position they were standing for, the voting dates, where the voting could take place, and an idea of the candidate's 'manifesto'. The posters were also intended to be used as flyers, so the message would have to be clear.

It was obvious that mountains of text would be inappropriate, as no one was likely to spend time reading it. The poster would have to be punchy and clear, with all the really important information (the candidate's name and the position they were standing for) really standing out.

Figure 6.37 shows one of the posters produced, with a list of all the design techniques used to make the poster as effective as possible. When looking at the poster, ask yourself if you would have done it the same way. If not, how would you have changed it, and why? Would you vote for this person on the strength of the poster?

3. A newsletter

A newsletter is a small version of a magazine that is designed for a select audience, normally to inform, educate and entertain. Typically, newsletters are A3 size, folded in half to make four A4 portrait pages. You may want to make your newsletter smaller (A5) or bigger than this, but remember that you may be constrained by photocopying or duplication costs.

Figure 6.38 shows three pages of a newsletter produced by students at the University of Sussex. It was produced on a Macintosh LC using Aldus PageMaker, and printed on an Apple StyleWriter bubblejet printer. The print run of 1 000 copies was typeset and printed by the University's print unit, using the original printouts from the StyleWriter.

Figure 6.38
Three pages from a student newsletter produced at the University of Sussex

Note how many of the techniques we have talked about in this chapter have been used to produce a newsletter that is easy to read. Figure 6.38 displays some of the techniques used, and you may like to use this as a basis for your own newsletter.

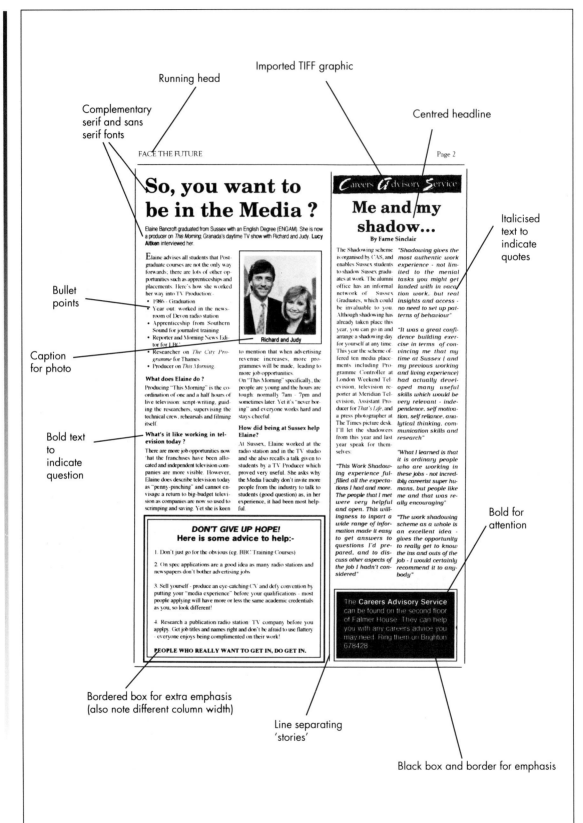

Running head

Imported TIFF graphic

Complementary
serif and sans
serif fonts

Centred headline

Bullet
points

Caption
for photo

Bold text
to
indicate
question

Italicised
text to
indicate
quotes

Bold for
attention

Bordered box for extra emphasis
(also note different column width)

Line separating
'stories'

Black box and border for emphasis

FACE THE FUTURE

Page 2

So, you want to be in the Media ?

Elaine Bancroft graduated from Sussex with an English Degree (ENGAM). She is now a producer on *This Morning*, Granada's daytime TV show with Richard and Judy. **Lucy Aitken** interviewed her.

Elaine advises all students that Postgraduate courses are not the only way forwards; there are lots of other opportunities such as apprenticeships and placements. Here's how she worked her way into TV Production:

- 1986 - Graduation
- Year out: worked in the newsroom of Devon radio station
- Apprenticeship from Southern Sound for journalist training
- Reporter and Morning News Editor for LBC
- Researcher on *The City Programme* for Thames
- Producer on *This Morning*.

What does Elaine do ?

Producing "This Morning" is the coordination of one and a half hours of live television: script-writing, guiding the researchers, supervising the technical crew, rehearsals and filming itself.

What's it like working in television today ?

There are more job opportunities now that the franchises have been allocated and independent television companies are more visible. However, Elaine does describe television today as "penny-pinching" and cannot envisage a return to big-budget television as companies are now so used to scrimping and saving. Yet she is keen to mention that when advertising revenue increases, more programmes will be made, leading to more job opportunities.

On "This Morning" specifically, the people are young and the hours are tough: normally 7am - 7pm and sometimes later. Yet it's "never boring" and everyone works hard and stays cheerful.

How did being at Sussex help Elaine?

At Sussex, Elaine worked at the radio station and in the TV studio and she also recalls a talk given to students by a TV Producer which proved very useful. She asks why the Media Faculty don't invite more people from the industry to talk to students (good question) as, in her experience, it had been most helpful.

Richard and Judy

DON'T GIVE UP HOPE!
Here is some advice to help:-

1. Don't just go for the obvious (eg. BBC Training Courses)

2. On spec applications are a good idea as many radio stations and newspapers don't bother advertising jobs

3. Sell yourself - produce an eye-catching CV and defy convention by putting your "media experience" before your qualifications - most people applying will have more or less the same academic credentials as you, so look different!

4. Research a publication/radio station/TV company before you applpy. Get job titles and names right and don't be afraid to use flattery - everyone enjoys being complimented on their work!

PEOPLE WHO REALLY WANT TO GET IN, DO GET IN.

Careers Advisory Service

Me and my shadow...

By Farne Sinclair

The Shadowing scheme is organised by CAS, and enables Sussex students to shadow Sussex graduates at work. The alumni office has an informal network of Sussex Graduates, which could be invaluable to you. Although shadowing has already taken place this year, you can go in and arrange a shadowing day for yourself at any time. This year the scheme offered ten media placements including Programme Controller at London Weekend Television, television reporter at Meridian Television, Assistant Producer for *That's Life*, and a press photographer at The Times picture desk. I'll let the shadowers from this year and last year speak for themselves:

"This Work Shadowing experience fulfilled all the expectations I had and more. The people that I met were very helpful and open. This willingness to inpart a wide range of information made it easy to get answers to questions I'd prepared, and to discuss other aspects of the job I hadn't considered"

"Shadowing gives the most authentic work experience - not limited to the menial tasks you might get landed with in a vacation work, but real insights and access - no need to set up patterns of behaviour"

"It was a great confidence building exercise in terms of convincing me that my time at Sussex (and my previous working and living experience) had actually developed many useful skills which would be very relevant - independence, self motivation, self reliance, analytical thinking, communication skills and research"

"What I learned is that it is ordinary people who are working in these jobs - not incredibly careerist super humans, but people like me and that was really encouraging"

"The work shadowing scheme as a whole is an excellent idea - gives the opportunity to really get to know the ins and outs of the job - I would certainly recommend it to anybody"

The **Careers Advisory Service** can be found on the second floor of Falmer House. They can help you with any careers advice you may need. Ring them on Brighton 678428

Running head

Reduced track and character width

Imported TIFF graphic

Different column widths and fonts to separate 'introduction' and 'story'

Contrasting serif and sans serif fonts

Box denoting 'information panel'

Border to enclose photo

Drop cap

Bold and italicised text to separate from 'story'

Page borders

THE PAGE 3 GRAD!

Julia Somerville, Sussex Graduate, bares all:

Interview by Helen Aitken and Sara Dyer.

sympathetic boss I managed it. Two years later I applied for the BBC''s Journalism Scheme and was accepted, I was in radio for about eleven years before I transferred to television in 1984 when I joined the *Nine O'Clock News*. In 1987 I joined ITN, initially to present its lunchtime programme, before joining the *News at Ten* three years ago.

Is it difficult being a woman in the media ?

I am conscious that I have tried throughout my career, to be treated as an equal. I don't want to be treated as better or worse. In the past there has been a tendency to characterise news-reading partnerships on screen as being experienced and dewy-eyed, dolly side-kick and it is stereotyping such as this that I have striven to avoid. I think that the world of television has grown up a bit and that it is now really for seasoned women as opposed to bright-eyed eager young girls. In fact, I harbour ambition to be the first grizzled female on telly and some unkind people might say I've already realised that ambition !

And the future?

I know I'm in the sort of job where one of these days a man in a grey suit is suddenly going to decide he doesn't like the look of me anymore and will remove me from the screen, and I just live with that knowledge. It doesn't really phase me one way or another.

Julia Somerville graduated from Sussex University in 1969. She Studied English in EngAm

When did you first have aspirations to go into broadcasting ?

Well it was really journalism. When I was here we used to have a student newspaper called *Wine Press* and I used to contribute to that. When I left here I had two possible goals in mind, one, believe it or not, was to be an advertising copy writer and I'm so glad I didn't do that, but that

was probably my number one desire. In the end I went into journalism and I joined IPC Magazines as a temporary sub-editor on *Homes and Gardens*. After then joining the PR section of *Woman's Own* I took the biggest career leap I ever made and returned to Brighton as editor of a computer group's house magazine. I rather bluffed my way into the job with absolutely no knowledge of how to do it but knowing I had a month to produce an eight page newspaper. Miraculously and with the help of a very

One long festival ?

"It's not sweet, but there are some sweet moments". Lucy Aitken talks to Dan Simmons who worked for Festival last year:

What were you doing at Festival?
I was reviewing films with my brother. We handed in four reports and mixed them live in one take. The editors often made changes which we didn't always like, but any con-

tributor must understand that the editors have the final word.
How would you describe Festival Radio?
The remit is idiosyncratic and quirky, a sort of Capital Radio with attitude.

How were volunteers, like yourself, treated at Festival?
Festival Radio needs volunteers and sometimes they overlook their valuable contributions. In voluntary work, as soon as you feel you're being taken for granted, you don't feel it's worth it. All it takes is good management to recognise enthusiasm.

Sometimes I found Festival Radio was badly organised and it got on my nerves, but it didn't detract from the learning experience. However, some of our contributions were very well received and I think you have to study the circumstances in which Festival Radio is working: it's this dormant creature for eleven months of the

year and then suddenly it wakes up. If they were on air permanently, such problems wouldn't exist

What did you gain most from your time at Festival Radio?
I learnt a lot about telling a story to match the station's output which I think is one of the most important lessons to

be learned.
How did experience at CROW help you?
The environment that CROW offers is the key thing: you're a working news team, as if it's the real thing. It's CROW workshops that students are need most if they have a sincere enthusiasm for radio.

What's the set-up at Festival Radio and what does it offer students? **Lucy Aitken** spoke to Daniel Nathan, Programme Director.

Most of Festival Radio's 150 volunteer workforce are students. Students involved gain experience on Festival Radio through Community Radio Open Workshops (CROW). In CROW's publicity, it states that *"CROW, in association with Festival Radio, is providing radio training...Students also gain valuable hands-on experience by working on "The CROW Show" - a community issues programme broadcast on Festival Radio."*

Daniel Nathan reiterated this commitment to students when he voiced his disappointment that plans to repeat the "successful" EHE-funded scheme for Sussex Media Studies students who take Radio as an option did not actually materialise. This year, students attend a series of workshops in the Media Services Unit whereas last year, CROW workshops and Festival Radio work constituted the practical element. As the feedback from last year's students was "generally positive", Nathan made it quite clear that his enthusiasm to use Festival Radio as a means of helping students gain experience in Radio is ever-present.

If you're interested in working for Festival Radio, the best way forwards is a CROW workshop. These are for anyone in the community, and the course lasts a weekend. It costs about £16 for students.
For more details, contact Theresa Colbeck on (0273) 621856.

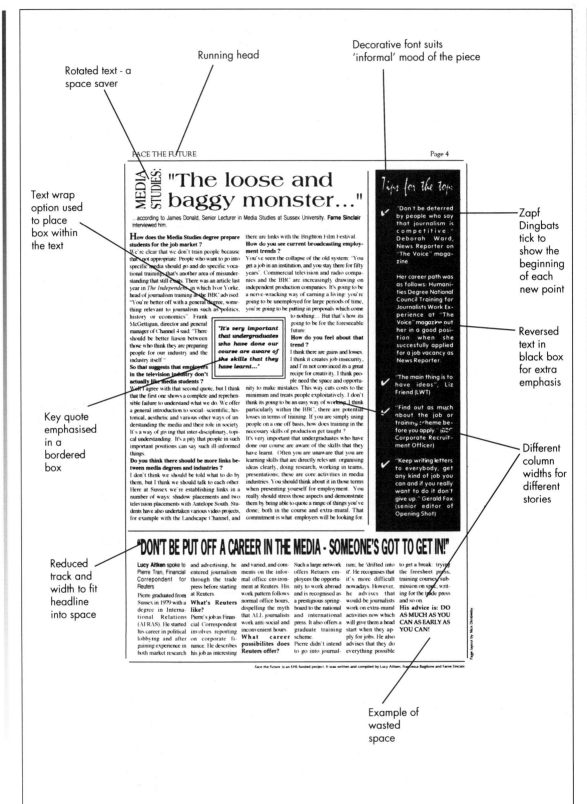

Practical Media

Rotated text - a space saver

Running head

Decorative font suits 'informal' mood of the piece

Text wrap option used to place box within the text

Zapf Dingbats tick to show the beginning of each new point

Key quote emphasised in a bordered box

Reversed text in black box for extra emphasis

Different column widths for different stories

Reduced track and width to fit headline into space

Example of wasted space

220

Summary When producing a document on a DTP system, you should constantly ask yourself if the techniques you are using really work. A computer is only capable of doing what you tell it, so you should be prepared to start questioning things, like line spacing or the choice of typeface, that you may have taken for granted on documents produced by the professionals.

Look at brochures, magazines and newspapers, and start to ask yourself why the designer used that particular typeface, why the headline was placed at a slant, why the leading was increased or decreased etc. Although DTP has made it much easier for 'amateur' designers to produce their own documents, using a program like PageMaker does not necessarily guarantee good results. If in doubt, look to the professionals for advice or inspiration.

CD ROM and Multimedia Applications

As well as being used for DTP and graphics applications, the computer is also increasingly being used in the world of 'multimedia'. Multimedia uses a computer to combine and control graphics, sound, video and animation for a variety of purposes – principally: interactive learning, visualisation and design, computer editing, and for business presentations.

Figure 6.39
Director 4, created by Macromedia, is a powerful tool for multimedia production

The computer lies at the heart of the system, but the user inputs still photographs, video sequences, sound and graphics from other sources

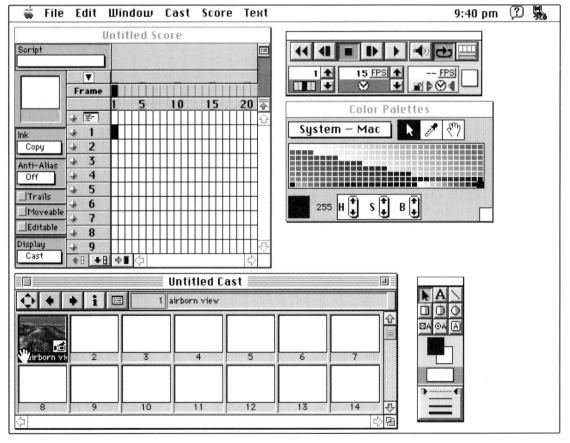

(see Figure 6.39, previous page), to create a complete audio-visual package. This can be then combined with graphics or text created on the computer itself.

Depending on the software you are using, you can use effects from video (mixes, wipes, overlays, etc.) to present this information, and certain applications allow you to 'rotoscope' graphics and photo or video images off the screen. Once a video sequence has been transferred to the computer's memory, the computer uses its inbuilt 'video cards' to run the video pictures in sequence – without even running the tape!

CD ROM and compact disk interactive (CDi)

CD ROM is 'multimedia' at its most basic. The CD ROM player plugs into the back of your computer and reads CD ROM disks, which are similar to conventional audio CDs. Each CD ROM is capable of storing 550MB of information (roughly equivalent to 700 floppy disks), so it is an incredible resource of information, all instantly accessible on your computer.

CD ROMs are already widely used in schools, colleges and universities, as they provide an excellent way to learn. CD ROMs are available on virtually any topic (from the complete works of Shakespeare to 340 000 reports on animal breeding and nutrition), and by moving the mouse around the screen and selecting 'topic' boxes, you have access to that information instantly.

A CD ROM can include photographs, text, sounds and graphics, and using the computer's animation facility, video clips can even be stored and viewed on the computer screen.

Philips has also launched CDi (Compact Disk Interactive), which bypasses the computer and plugs directly into your television and audio systems. A CDi disk can hold up to 650MB of information, which roughly equates to any of the following: over 250 000 typed pages of A4 text, 7 000 full colour photographs, 72min of moving video pictures, or 2h of hi-fi sound.

The CDi machine will also play existing CD audio disks, and can access into photo CDs produced by Kodak, making it a truly versatile multimedia machine. The Philips CDi player is controlled by a modified infra-red remote control unit, which includes a console that has similar controls to a mouse.

Multimedia

Multimedia describes the combining of several different media (normally a video player, audio player, CD ROM drive, external speakers and a television/projector) to create an audio-visual presentation that is interactive. This represents a shift from passive to active viewing, opening up new avenues in the fields of entertainment and education. The computer lies at the heart of the system, allowing the user to control each item of hardware to make a coherent presentation.

Using the various software, full colour backgrounds can be selected and incorporated with still or moving video images. The images have to be 'grabbed' using a genlocked video camera or computer scanner, and these are saved to disk for accessing later.

Once the whole presentation has been completed, it can be ordered into a sequence using a system of flowcharts (see Figure 6.40), and when the presentation is required, it is 'launched' by clicking the mouse, and the computer runs everything automatically. For larger groups, a teleprojector can be used, and it is normal to use large 'plug in' speakers instead of the computer's small inbuilt version.

Figure 6.40
A flow chart showing the 'bones' of a multimedia presentation

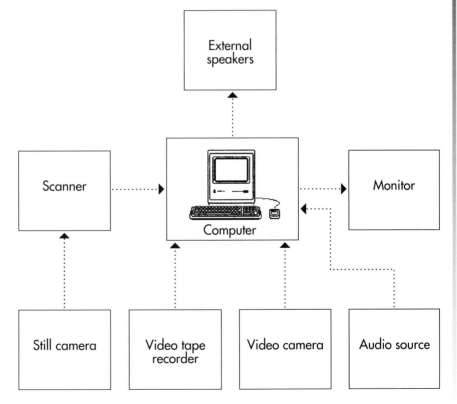

Glossary

Listed below is a selection of technical terms and what they mean.

Ascender: The part of a text character that sits above the top of the x-height.

Bit-map graphics: Graphics that have a bitty appearance. This is normally caused by trying to print them on a non-compatible printer.

Bleed: Where the edge of the text or photograph/graphic falls off the edge of the page, i.e. there is no page border or margin.

Body type: Type measured between 6 and 14 points, used to set the main body of text.

Bold: Type that has a heavy weight for extra emphasis.

Bromide: Photographic paper used for very high quality printouts. Bromide prints are normally 12 000dpi or more.

Bullets: Small dots that are particularly useful for adding emphasis to lists.

CD ROM: A compatible CD player that plugs into the back of the computer. Computer CDs can carry large amounts of information for the computer to 'read'.

CRC: Abbreviation of *camera ready copy*. This is the final version of the layout ready for printing.

Column: A vertical text block.

Crop: Selecting or removing an unwanted section of an illustration or photograph.

Descender: The part of a text character that sits below the baseline.

Display type: Type that is larger than 14 point. It is normally used for headlines and subheads.

DTP: Abbreviation of *desktop publishing*.

dpi: Abbreviation of *dots per inch*. This measures the resolution of an image/printout.

Drop cap: A large capital that gives extra emphasis to the beginning of a story. It is normally two or three lines deep.

Em: A text measurement used in DTP. An em is equal in height and width to the point size of the font you are using.

En: A text measurement used in DTP. An en is half the width of an em.

EPS: Abbreviation of *Encapsulated PostScript*. This is a file format for saving graphics to be printed on a PostScript printer.

Font: The entire set of characters in a typeface.

Footer: A section of text/graphics that appears at the bottom of every page in a document.

Genlock: A device that links a computer to a video input/output. It synchronises the video and computer to prevent any picture break-up.

Grab: The freezing and storing of a video image using a computer.

Graphic: An illustration that is not a photograph.

Greeked text: Nonsense text used for page layout before placing the 'real' text.

Guides: Lines that help you arrange or align elements on a DTP or graphics program. These are 'invisible' to the printer.

Gutter: The space between columns of text.

Hard copy: Text printed on paper or bromides, as opposed to on the screen.

Header: A section of text/graphics that appears at the top of every page in a document.

Hyphenation: The breaking up of single words onto two lines by using a hyphen ('-'). This is useful for fitting more words on a page.

Italic: Text that is placed on a slant, to add extra emphasis.

Justification: When text is placed flush to the left and right margins of a column.

Kern: Moving characters closer together to give a tighter appearance.

Kern pairs: Pairs of letters (such as 'Wa') that need to be kerned to prevent unsightly gaps between the two letters.

Landscape: A wide page format, where the width is longer than the height.

Leading: Measured in points, this governs the space between lines of text.

Margin: The outer confines of a page.

Masthead: The main title of a newsletter.

Multimedia: Using a computer to display video sequences, sounds, photographs, text and still photographs for presentation purposes. Multimedia applications are normally interactive.

Orphan: First or last lines of a story, cut off from the rest of the piece by a page break.

Pagination: Page numbers.

Pica: A measurement used in DTP. One pica equals 12 points, or 0.01666in.

PICT: Abbreviation of *PICTure* – a file format for saving graphics.

Point: A measurement used in DTP (especially for text). One point equals 0.01384in.

Portrait: A tall page format, where the height is longer than the width.

Proofs: A first rough printout, primarily for modification and checking for errors.

Runarounds: Text that sits flush around a graphic or photograph.

Sans serif: Fonts that lack embellishing cross strokes.

Scanner: A device for converting photographs and graphics to disk for the computer to read.

Screen dump: A printout taken directly from the screen.

Serif: The embellishing cross strokes at the edges of characters in a serif font.

Story: A complete section of text.

Subscript: Characters that drop below the baseline.

Superscript: Characters that rise above the x-height.

Template: A predesigned layout of guides, into which graphics and text can be pasted.

Thumbnails: A reduced printout of a page that is particularly useful for checking the overall layout.

TIFF: Abbreviation of *tagged image file format*. A high quality file format for saving graphics and photographs.

Track kerning: Where a whole line of text characters is uniformly spaced closer or further apart from normal.

Trim marks: Hairline marks that are produced on a final printout to specify where cutting or folding is to take place.

Typeface: A character style.

Widow: A single word left alone on a line.

WYSIWYG: Abbreviation of *what you see is what you get*. Computers show the document on the screen exactly how it will appear from the printer.

X-height: The height of a lowercase 'x' in a font.

Further reading

Burns, D., Venit, S. and Hansen, R. (1991) *The Electronic Publisher* Prentice-Hall.

Collier, D. (1989) *Desktop Design and Typography* Addison-Wesley.

Finch, P. (1987) *How to Publish Yourself* Allison and Busby.

Fowler and Gower (eds) (1965) *Dictionary of Modern English Usage* (2nd ed.) Oxford University Press.

Gill, B. (1981) *Forget All the Rules You Ever Learnt about Graphic Design (Including the Ones in This Book)* Watson-Guptill.

Harvey, G. and Gearing, S. (1993) *Mastering PageMaker on the Macintosh* Sybex Books.

Hewson, D. (1989) *Introducing Desktop Publishing* Spa Books.

Jones, G. (1987) *The Desktop Publishing Companion* Sigma Press.

Lieberman, J.B. (1978) *Type and Typefaces* The Myriad Press.

Miles, J. (1987) *Design for Desktop Publishing* Spa Books.

Parker, R.C. (1990) *Looking Good in Print* Ventana Press.

Quilliam, S. and Grove-Stephenson, I. (1990) *Into Print* BBC Books.

Saunders, N. (1993) *Publish!* Available from Neal's Yard DTP Studio, 2 Neal's Yard, London, WC2 9DP. (Send three first class stamps.)

Shushan, R. and Wright, D. (1991) *Desktop Publishing by Design* Microsoft Press.

Swann, A. (1987) *Basic Design and Layout* Phaidon.

White, J.V. (1993) *Graphic Design for the Electronic Age* Watson-Guptill.

Zeitlyn, J. (1987) *Effective Publicity and Design* Interchange.

Activities

These are some general ideas for you to try in producing information in a range of audio-visual media. You can of course devise your own tasks by deciding on your purposes, your content, your intended audience, your desired effects and your chosen media appropriate to the identified needs.

1. Create an Exhibition for a Tourist Attraction

Identify a tourist attraction with which you are familiar. It could be in town or country, a museum or craft centre, or whatever you want.

You are required to design and produce display stands with photos and text, a collection of slides with sound tape that can be shown in a small projection room, or a video showing activities at the centre. For example, if your centre is in a country park you could film a day or a year in the life of a conservationist.

Select your media and write a treatment and plan of action to present to the management board of the centre, clearly indicating what you would present and how you would present it.

2. Education Pack for Year 11 Students about Local Radio

You are being commissioned by a local radio station to produce a learning pack for use with secondary school students to encourage them to listen to local radio. Prepare an outline of what you would produce, showing the content and your treatment of it. Your outline must consist of sample storyboard, some sample script and picture ideas as well as notes for an oral presentation to the senior managers at the station.

The radio station public relations officer has suggested that you include material such as: tapes of selected extracts, a week's schedule of programmes, interviews with station staff, possible slides, photos or video of the station at work and in and out of the studios, and a case study of an advertising campaign broadcast on the station. But she leaves you to suggest other alternative content and media.

As part of this outline you must also prepare an outline budget and timescale for production. It has been suggested that the budget should not exceed £3 000 and it must be completed within 30 days.

3. Fire Service Show

Your previous work for the fire service has led them to commission you to produce an exhibition and materials that can be taken to county shows and local fetes and trade fairs.

They suggest your materials could include display panels with photos, drawings and text, possibly a video tape and/or slides and commentary. There can also be merchandising items to give away or sell to adults and children. As well as showing the work of the fire service, they also want to include safety information about how to prevent or deal with fires.

You have been asked to produce ideas for six display boards, to produce an outline for a video, and to suggest possible leaflets that can be given away and items that could be sold in aid of the fire service.

Resources

Magazines and Journals

There are many more magazines available than the few listed here: we suggest you browse in any large newsagents. Those listed below are not always available in newsagents and include professional and trade information.

Ariel, weekly staff magazine of the BBC, Room 5360, BBC White City, 201 Wood Lane, London W12 7TS

Audio Visual Communications for business, a monthly trade journal for the audio-visual industry

EMAP Business Publishing Limited
Audit House
Field End Road
Eastcote
Middlesex
HA4 9LY

Broadcast, weekly; see also *International Broadcasting* 'on broadcasting technology' and *Screen International* 'trade paper for cinema film makers'

7 Swallow Place
London
W1R 7AA

Campaign, monthly news magazine for the advertising industry

22 Lancaster Gate
London W2 3LY

Creative Review, monthly on advertising and design, including film, TV and photography

50 Poland Street
London W1E 6JZ

Journal of Educational TV, three times a year, on the use of TV and related media in education

King's Manor
Exhibition Square
York
YO1 2EP

Sight and Sound, monthly film magazine of the BFI

21 Stephen Street
London
W1P 1PL

Hardware and Software Manufacturers/ suppliers

This list is by no means exhaustive, but it should serve as a handy reference guide for those who want to get started in their own media productions.

Chapter 1

Publications and Marketing
BBC Television Training
BBC Elstree Centre
Clarendon Road
Borehamwood
Herts WD6 1JF

Chapter 2

Film manufacturers

Agfa Gevaert Ltd
27 Great West Road
Brentford
Middlesex
TW8 9AX

Fuji Photo Film (UK) Limited
Fuji Film House
125 Finchley Road
London
NW3 6JH

Ilford Photographic
14–22 Tottenham Street
London
W1P 0AH

Kodak Limited
Swallowdale Lane
Hemel Hempstead
Hertfordshire
HP2 7EY

Hardware suppliers

Bronica UK Limited
Priors Industrial Estate
Windsor Road
Maidenhead
Berkshire

Canon UK Limited
Camera Division
Units 4 & 5 Brent Trading Centre
North Circular Road
Neasdon
London
NW10 0JF

Climpex Limited
Hammers Lane
Mill Hill
London
NW7 4DY
(stands & clamps)

Durst (UK) Limited
Felstead Road
Longmead Industrial Estate
Epsom
Surrey
KT19 9AR
(enlargers)

Kaiser UK Limited
CCS Centre
Vale Lane
Bedminster
Bristol
BS3 5RU
(enlargers)

Nikon UK
380 Richmond Road
Kingston
Surrey
KT2 5PR

Pentax UK Limited
Pentax House
South Hill Avenue
South Harrow
Middlesex
HA2 0LT

Miscellaneous

Billingham Limited
Little Cottage Street
Brierley Hill
West Midlands
DY5 1RG

Courtenay Photonics Limited
280 Oxlow Lane
Dagenham
Essex
RM10 8LL

Jessop of Leicester Limited
98 Scudamore Road
Leicester

Keith Johnson and Pelling
Promandis House
19/21 Conway Street
London
W1P 5HL

Kenro Photographic Products
The Oppenheimer Centre
Greenbridge Road
Swindon
Wiltshire
SN3 3LH

Kentmere Limited
Stavely
Kendal
Cumbria
CA8 9PB

Lastolite Limited
8 Vulcan Court
Hermitage Industrial Estate
Coalville
Leicestershire
LE6 3FL

Leeds Photo Visual Limited
20–26 The Brunswick Centre
London
WC1N 1AE
(equipment hire)

Photon Beard Limited
18 The Brunswick Centre
Marchmont Street
London
WC1N 1AE

Chapter 3

Music Suppliers
KPM Music
127 Charing Cross Road
London
WC2H OEA

Sound Stage Production Music,
'Kerchesters'
Waterhouse Lane
Kingswood
Surrey
KT20 6HT

Hardware Suppliers
Canford Audio
Crowther Road
Washington
Tyne & Wear
NE38 OBW

Raper & Wayman
Unit 3
Crusader Industrial Estate
167 Hermitage Road
London
N4 1LZ

Sony UK Limited
Pipers Way
Thatcham
Newbury
Berkshire
RG13 4LZ

Chapter 4

Slide/tape Systems
Imatronic Limited
5 Fir Tree Lane
Little Baddon
Chelmsford
Essex
CM3 4SS

Chapter 5

Miscellaneous
Aston Electronic Designs Limited
123–127 Deepcut Bridge Road
Deepcut
Camberley
Surrey
GU16 6SO

Autocue Limited
Autocue House
265 Merton Road
London
SW18 5JS

Quantel
31 Turnpike Road
Newbury
Berkshire
RG13 2NE

Video Equipment Hire
Grip House
5–11 Taunton Road
Metropolitan Centre
Greenford
Middlesex
UB6 8UQ

Filter Manufacturers
Lee Filters Limited
Walworth Industrial Estate
Andover
Hampshire
SP10 5AN

Hardware Suppliers
JVC Professional Products Limited
Alperton House
Bridgewater Road
Wembley
Middlesex
HA0 1EG

Panasonic Broadcast Europe
107–109 Whitby Road
Slough
Berkshire
SL1 3DR

Sony Broadcast and
Professional UK,
The Heights
Brooklands
Weybridge
Surrey
KT13 0XW

Strand Lighting
Grantway
off Syon Lane
Isleworth
Middlesex
TW7 5QD

Vinten Broadcast Limited
Western Way
Bury St Edmonds
IP33 3TB

Chapter 6

Software Manufacturers/suppliers

Aldus (Europe) Limited
Craigcrook Castle
Craigcrook Road
Edinburgh
EH4 3UH

Microsoft
Excel House
49 De Montfort Road
Reading
RG1 8LP

QSS Limited
Kilbarry House
Dublin Hill
Cork
Ireland
(QuarkXPress)

Hardware Manufacturers/suppliers

Apple Computer Limited
Eastman Way
Hemel Hempstead
Hertfordshire
HP2 7QH

IBM
IBM South Bank
76 Upper Ground
London
SE1 9PZ

Research Machines
Mill Street
Oxford
OX2 0BW

Clip Art Suppliers

Dynamic Graphics Limited
Media House
Eastways Industrial Estate
Witham
Essex
CM8 3YJ

MacSoft
Bridge House
Unit One
Wellington
Somerset
TA21 0AA

Miscellaneous

Computers Unlimited
2 The Business Centre
Colindeep Lane
London
NW9 6DU

Letraset UK Limited
195–203 Waterloo Road
London
SE1 8XJ

Techex Limited
Techex House
Vanwall Road
Maidenhead
SL6 4UB

Index